W9-ARE-616

ILLINOIS CENTRAL COLLEGE
PN1998.A3G785
STACKS
The films of D. W. Griffith /

A12900 274754

WITHDRAWN

WITHDRAWN

54412

PN   Wagenknecht, Edward
1998   Charles, 1900-
.A3
G785   The films of D. W.
              Griffith

DATE			

© THE BAKER & TAYLOR CO

THE FILMS OF
D.W. GRIFFITH

BOOKS ON RELATED THEMES

By Anthony Slide

Early American Cinema
The Griffith Actresses

By Edward Wagenknecht

The Movies in the Age of Innocence
Merely Players
Seven Daughters of the Theater
As Far As Yesterday

THE FILMS OF D.W. GRIFFITH

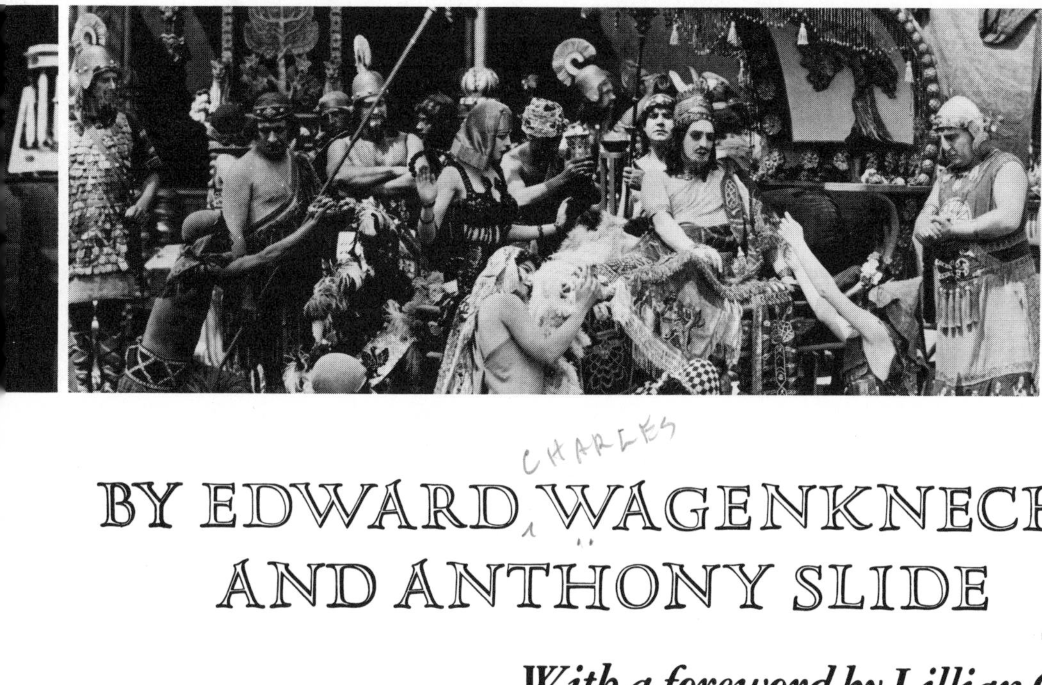

BY EDWARD WAGENKNECHT
AND ANTHONY SLIDE

With a foreword by Lillian Gish

CROWN PUBLISHERS, INC. New York

I.C.C LIBRARY

54412

PN
1998
.A2
G 785

The quotation from James Agee which is used as epigraph
is from *Agee on Film*, vol. 1, by James Agee, © 1948 and 1958
by the James Agee Trust, and is reprinted by permission of Grosset
& Dunlap, Inc.

© 1975 by Edward Wagenknecht and Anthony Slide

All rights reserved. No part of this book may be reproduced
or utilized in any form or by any means, electronic or mechanical,
including photocopying, recording, or by any information storage
and retrieval system, without permission in writing from the publisher.
Inquiries should be addressed to Crown Publishers, Inc.,
419 Park Avenue South, New York, N.Y. 10016.
Printed in the United States of America
Published simultaneously in Canada by General Publishing Company Limited

Designed by Shari de Miskey and Laurie Zuckerman

Library of Congress Cataloging in Publication Data

Wagenknecht, Edward Charles, 1900-
    The films of D. W. Griffith.

    Bibliography: p.
    Includes index.

    1. Griffith, David Wark, 1875-1948.   I.   Slide,
Anthony, joint author.   II.   Title.
PN1998.A3G785   791.43'0233'0924   75-19196
ISBN 0-517-52326-4

For
MARY PICKFORD, BLANCHE SWEET, *and*
LILLIAN GISH
and remembering
DOROTHY GISH, MAE MARSH, *and*
CLARINE SEYMOUR

He achieved what no other known man has ever achieved. To watch his work is like being witness to the beginning of melody, or the first conscious use of the lever or the wheel; the emergence, coordination, and first eloquence of language; the birth of an art; and to realize that this is all the work of one man.

JAMES AGEE

CONTENTS

PREFATORY NOTE

For generous cooperation in the making of this book, grateful acknowledgment is made to Killiam Shows, successors to the Estate of D. W. Griffith. Many stills have been drawn from the collections of the Academy of Motion Picture Arts and Sciences (now encompassing the Paul Ballard Collection), the Museum of Modern Art Film Library, George Eastman House, and the Wisconsin Center for Theatre Research. Eileen Bowser and Charles Silver have been kind at MOMA, George Pratt at George Eastman House, and Susan Dalton at the Wisconsin Center. We have also been helped by William K. Everson, John Stone, Robert R. Gitt, and the staff of the Motion Picture Section of the Library of Congress. To Robert Cushman at the Academy our debt is very large. The scenes from Mary Pickford Biographs in the first section are from his own collection and are used with his permission; in addition to this, he has made the prints from which a very large number of our other reproductions have been made.

Except for the contributions signed by other hands, the entire book has been written by the two writers named on the title page. Mr. Slide is responsible for all the credits and Mr. Wagenknecht has written the captions and the story summaries. The latter has seen all the feature films treated in this book except *The Battle of the Sexes* (1914) and *The Escape*, but it has not been possible for him to re-view all of them recently; in some cases, therefore, he has been obliged to incur indebtedness to story summaries published in contemporary trade journals, programs, etc.

All the critical commentaries except the contributed pieces are signed either "A. S." or "E. W.," and each writer is solely responsible for the evaluations formulated. Each has read and commented upon the work of the other, but all final decisions have been made by the writer himself.

FOREWORD

The Films of D. W. Griffith tells of the unfolding and discovery of a new art form. The power of film has affected our century and will affect many centuries to come. We are the first to leave a living record of our people, life-style, and certainly our history.

By the time I joined D. W. Griffith's company he was telling his young people not to demean their work by calling film "flickers." He told us, "You are taking the first baby steps in something predicted in the Bible and called the universal language. When silent film reaches perfection, it could, combined with music, speak to the world without the use of words. Wars come about because people cannot clarify their issues. In future the difficulties could be filmed for all to see and understand, and even bring about the millennium." No wonder Griffith's vision enriched so many lives.

Some of his ideas for his stories and characters came from Shakespeare, Dickens, George Eliot, Laura Jean Libbey, the Brontës, Bret Harte, the Bible, and the daily newspaper. His interests and studies included music and the great works of that world.

Today millions are spent on films telling stories that are sometimes no better than some of Griffith's that cost a few hundred dollars. Of course every Griffith film had the advantage of rehearsals, his major pictures for long and tedious weeks. A play or a symphony is never put before an audience unrehearsed. With film, rehearsals tell how strong or weak your story structure is before it is exposed to that most accurate critic—the camera. Its mystical eye quickly distinguishes the true from the false. You must not get caught acting a character; you must be the character. And timing and tempo, the very essence of every film, is evident. And by "film" I mean both big and little screen. Without this foundation how could *The Birth of a Nation* have been made in nine weeks for $60,000 and *Broken Blossoms* in eighteen days and nights for $91,000?

Griffith's genius is clearly put before you in this book that ought to be at the right hand of everyone seriously interested in the history and future of film.

Lillian Gish

D.W. Griffith

I

THE BIOGRAPH PERIOD

The first film directed by D. W. Griffith, *The Adventures of Dollie,* was released by Biograph on July 14, 1908. By the time he left the company in September 1913, he had directed about 450 films.[1] One of these is a four-reel feature, *Judith of Bethulia* (which is treated separately in this volume). Eleven, by my count, are two-reelers.[2] Most of the rest are one-reelers, though some, toward the beginning, were shorter.

A kind Providence seems to have hovered over Griffith's Biograph films. Only a handful have not survived in any form.[3] This record cannot be matched by any other early producer.

This does not mean, however, that the student of Griffith is now free to screen his entire output. Though more subjects are being readied all the time, this is unfortunately still far from being the case. A seriatim consideration of all Griffith's early films would therefore be impossible even if space limitations did not forbid it, and no doubt this consideration has played a part in creating the absurd situation which until now has left the most important figure in screen history without a systematic pictorial record of his films in book form while *Films of . . .* books devoted to a variety of figures some of whom have little or no claim to either historical or aesthetic significance have been sprouting all over the place. With the aid of contemporary reviews and the recently published Bulletins, it is now possible to achieve a fairly comprehensive account of the content, point of view, and values of the Biographs as a whole, though considered critical evaluation of the product must still be confined to those films which the chronicler has himself seen or on which he has careful reports from viewers whom he is able to trust.

The most striking obvious characteristic of the Biographs is their contemporaneousness; the vast majority of the films deal with Griffith's own land and time. His interest in standard literature being what it was, the number of adaptations he made from classics and near classics is surprisingly small. To be sure, one must allow here for the taste of his employers being considerably less cultivated than his own, though this must have been offset by the ever-pressing need to find two or three fresh stories every week and the fact that both the classics and contemporary literature represented ever-available opportunities for pilfering. Yet, except for *The Taming of the Shrew,* made during his first year, he never filmed a Shakespeare play, though *Heart Beats of Long Ago* must, in some measure, have been indebted to *Romeo and Juliet.* In view of his special devotion to Dickens, whose relationship to him has been carefully studied by Sergei Eisenstein,[4] it is even more surprising that he should have filmed only *The Cricket on the Hearth.* In *Brutality,* however, a man is reformed through discerning a resemblance between himself and Bill Sikes in a stage production of *Oliver Twist,* and of course the influence of *A Tale of Two Cities* can be seen clearly in *Orphans of the Storm* in feature days.

George Eliot is the only other Victorian novelist he touched; *A Fair Exchange* was a "free adaptation" of

[1] I am following Eileen Bowser's ascriptions in her *Biograph Bulletins, 1908-1912.* It is possible that future study may somewhat modify the figures given here. See Gordon Hendricks, *Beginnings of the Biograph: The Story of the Invention of the Mutuscope and the Biograph and Their Supplying Camera* (New York: The Beginnings of the American Film, 1964). Together with two other books by Mr. Hendricks—*The Edison Motion Picture Myth* and *The Kinetoscope*—this has now been reprinted in an omnibus volume published by Arno Press.

[2] *His Trust* and *His Trust Fulfilled, Enoch Arden, A Temporary Truce, A Pueblo Legend, The Little Tease, The Yaqui Cur, The Mothering Heart, The Reformers, The Massacre, The Battle at Elderbush Gulch, Brute Force. His Trust* and *His Trust Fulfilled* were, by Biograph fiat, released as separate films with separate titles. A caption at the beginning of *His Trust Fulfilled* summarized the action in *His Trust.*

[3] Mrs. Bowser lists *How She Triumphed, The White Rose of the Wilds, A Tale of the Wilderness, Billy's Stratagem, Heredity, Oil and Water,* Fate,* A Misunderstood Boy,* The Yaqui Cur, Two Men of the Desert, Brute Force,* but prints of the three marked with an asterisk have now been found.

[4] See "Dickens, Griffith, and the Film Today," in Eisenstein's *Film Form* (Harcourt, Brace, 1949).

Silas Marner. The titles *The Suicide Club* and *A Lodging for the Night* probably came from Stevenson, but the stories are quite different. *To Save Her Soul* was indebted to a late and far from classic Victorian, Hall Caine, in *The Christian.*

Among the poets, Tennyson and Browning each gave Griffith two films: Tennyson *Enoch Arden* and *The Golden Supper* and Browning both the famous *Pippa Passes* and *A Blot on the 'Scutcheon. Enoch Arden* would seem to have been something of an obsession. The 1911 two-reeler had been preceded by a one-reel 1908 modernized version, *After Many Years,* and in 1915 Griffith, during his Reliance–Majestic period, "supervised" a beautiful four-reel *Enoch Arden,* with Lillian Gish, Alfred Paget, and Wallace Reid, which was directed by Christy Cabanne and released through Mutual. Finally, one of the very last Biographs, *Two Men of the Desert,* presented a modified *Enoch Arden* situation in a Western American setting. Charles Kingsley provided inspiration for *The Unchanging Sea* and *The Sands of Dee* and Thomas Hood for *The Song of the Shirt.*

The most important adaptation from a Continental source was the almost foolhardy attempt to do Tolstoy's *Resurrection* (with a very austere ending) in one reel in 1909. *The Necklace* was an unacknowledged modern adaptation of the story by de Maupassant. The play generally called *Ingomar* is also of Continental origin, but Griffith must have taken his version, *The Barbarian Ingomar,* from Maria Lovell's translation, which had figured importantly in the stage careers of both Mary Anderson and Julia Marlowe. The 1908 production *The Devil* was probably triggered by the Molnár play, then enjoying great success in America with George Arliss. The world of opera, which he loved, Griffith touched directly only once: *A Fool's Revenge* gives the story of *Rigoletto.* But *The Heart of O Yama* may well have been suggested by *Madame Butterfly,* either the opera or the Belasco play, though the torture scene brings it closer to another Puccini opus, *Tosca,* and *The Violin Maker of Cremona* strongly suggests that Griffith, or somebody, had been hearing *Die Meistersinger.*

Ramona, a celebrated film in its time, was the principal adaptation of an American novel; Biograph paid $100 for the rights and made scrupulous acknowledgment to the author, Helen Hunt Jackson, and to her publishers, Little, Brown, no doubt by their stipulation. *Leather Stocking* was "freely adapted from the tales of James Fenimore Cooper," and *A Mohawk's Way* was announced as a "subject of the James Fenimore Cooper Type." *The Death Disc,* on the other hand, was "cribbed" from Mark Twain, and there were two unacknowledged borrowings from O. Henry: *The Sacrifice* comes from "The Gift of the Magi" and *Trying to Get Arrested* from "The Cop and the Anthem." Nor was any notice given that *A Corner in Wheat* was taken directly from Frank Norris's story of the same title and his novel *The Octopus* (which seems also to have influenced *The Usurer*). Both *For Love of Gold* and *Money Mad* had the basic situation that has been used again and again in literature since Chaucer's "The Pardoner's Tale" (its most famous modern screen embodiment was in *The Treasure of Sierra Madre*), but Griffith probably got the idea from Jack London's story "Just Meat." As for contemporary American drama, the betrayal of the wounded fugitive in *The Fight for Freedom* by the dropping of his blood from the loft where he is hidden is obviously borrowed from Belasco's *The Girl of the Golden West;* the title of *In Old Kentucky* must have been intended to recall that of Charles Dazey's play; and Theodore Kremer's *The Fatal Wedding* may well have influenced both *At the Altar* and *The Medicine Bottle. What Drink Did,* too, surely echoes the old chestnut *Ten Nights in a Bar-Room.*

It is interesting that in spite of his devotion to Poe (cf. *The Avenging Conscience*), Griffith never filmed a Poe story as such. *Edgar Allen* [sic] *Poe,* a nonhistorical account of the writing of "The Raven" and of Virginia Poe's death, was designed as a centenary tribute. The climax of *The Sealed Room* (which is partly repeated in *When Kings Were the Law*) has pretty obviously been suggested by Poe's story, "The Cask of Amontillado."

Griffith's contemporaneousness does not mean that he imprisoned himself in his own time, however. As one might expect from the future director of *The Birth of a Nation,* the Civil War provides the favorite historical background. The first Civil War picture was *The Guerrilla* (November 13, 1908), the last *The Informer* (November 21, 1912); in between came *In Old Kentucky, The Honor of the Family, In the Border States, The House with Closed Shutters, The Fugitive, His Trust* and *His Trust Fulfilled, Swords and Hearts,* and *The Battle.*

The future director of *America* concerned himself with the American Revolution, never a favorite subject with moviemakers, only once—in *"1776" or, The Hessian Renegades.* Twice he invaded Puritan New England—in *The Better Way* and *Rose O' Salem-Town.* Of *Billy's Stratagem,* one of the lost films, I know only that it deals with "early days on the frontier." [5] Early California

---

[5] This is by no means the only film whose period and locale are only vaguely indicated. Some of these ambiguities might well be cleared up if we could see the films themselves, but early filmmakers were rarely accurate about period costuming. *Rose O' Salem-Town* has Massachusetts *burning* witches, and the colonial legal processes are absurdly caricatured. In *The Sealed Room,* Arthur Johnson, as the king, is preceded by trumpeters wherever he goes!

figures in *In Old California, The Gold Seekers,* and *In the Days of '49,* while *The Road to the Heart* and *The Eavesdropper* deal with rancheros, obviously in the Southwest or in Mexico.

One of the European films, *The Slave,* has a Roman setting. Three are medieval—*Love Finds a Way, The Cloister's Touch,* and *The Call to Arms. Heart Beats of Long Ago* harks back to fourteenth-century Italy. There is at least one entry from prerevolutionary France—*The Golden Louis*—while the Revolution itself is treated in *Nursing a Viper* and *The Oath and the Man.* Ireland, probably in the eighteenth century, furnishes Mary Pickford's background in *Wilful Peggy,* and the Franco-Prussian War contributes *The Russian Spy. The Roué's Heart, The Winning Coat, The Cardinal's Conspiracy, The Sealed Room, The Duke's Plan, Taming a Husband,* and *The Punishment* are all "costume" plays, but I cannot pin down the period. *When Kings Were the Law* takes place in "Romanda" and *Love Among the Roses* is frankly set in Never-Never Land. The scene of Mary Pickford's *Lena and the Geese* seems to be Holland, but it comes closer to the fairy tale world of *Die Königskinder,* in which Geraldine Farrar had had live geese on the stage of the Metropolitan Opera House, than to any actual country, and such films as *The Brahma Diamond, The French Duel, The Mountaineer's Honor, Madame Rex, The Revenue Man and the Girl, Love in the Hills, A Feud in the Kentucky Hills, In the Aisles of the Wild,* and *Gold and Glitter* all seem more remote in place, from the point of view of most contemporary nickelodeon patrons, than they are in time.

A similar remoteness, for most of Griffith's customers, attached to his "Westerns," none of which were quite that in the Broncho Billy–William S. Hart–John Wayne sense. Some of these, like *Broken Ways,* are definitely assigned to the "early" West; in other cases, it is difficult to say just how close to our own time we are supposed to come. Disregarding for the moment the Indian pictures, not all of which were set in the West, the farce *Getting Even,* presented on a split reel, on September 13, 1909, was Griffith's first "Western"; between it and *The Battle at Elderbush Gulch,* I count more than fifteen, with such famous films as *The Last Drop of Water, The Female of the Species, Friends,* and *The Massacre* among them. There is no reason to suppose that Griffith had any special interest in his "Westerns" or thought of them as a class apart, but both *The Massacre* and *Elderbush* are among his finest achievements.

Biograph produced many farces, generally on "split reels" (i.e. two subjects to a reel); indeed what is generally called "Keystone comedy" began as Biograph comedy. Farces never greatly interested Griffith however, and only

Blanche Sweet in *The Lonedale Operator*

Mary Pickford in *The Mender of Nets*

The Informer. Henry B. Walthall and Mary Pickford

A Beast at Bay. Mary Pickford and Mae Marsh

during his first years did he direct them personally. In the famous "ad" that he published in the *New York Dramatic Mirror* on December 3, 1913, he claimed that "for two years from the Summer of 1908" he had "personally directed all Biograph motion pictures. Thereafter as general director he superintended all Biograph productions and directed the more *important* features until Oct. 1, 1913." This does not seem entirely accurate however. According to Billy Bitzer, Frank Powell's *All on Account of the Milk* (January 13, 1910) was the first Biograph during the Griffith period not directed by D. W. himself.[6] It was Powell who first inherited the farces after Griffith had given them up; later "Keystone" Mack Sennett himself took charge of them.

No tally of Griffith's farces can command universal acceptance, for farcical elements necessarily appeared in many films that are not farces in the Keystone sense, but my figure, for whatever it may be worth, is 152. The first, *Deceived Slumming Party* (July 31, 1908), seems to show a Méliès influence unique in Griffith's work. Here the Bowery puts on a show for credulous visitors, and a woman falls into a sausage machine only to resume her former shape when the machine is reversed. The most popular of the early ones was *The Curtain Pole*, which appears to have been as wild as anything that Sennett, who appeared in it, ever achieved in kind, and which outsold all other Biograph subjects issued up to its time.

[6] Eileen Bowser denies Griffith *The Black Viper* and *The Tavern-Keeper's Daughter* because production records show that, though released after *The Adventures of Dollie*, they were shot earlier. See her *Biograph Bulletins*, p. viii.

The only one of the very first farces I have seen is *A Calamitous Elopement*, which is peep show material, interesting only because it shows the exterior of the Biograph studio on Fourteenth Street, with Griffith himself as a policeman, nor can I say much more for the only "Jones" subject that has come my way, *The Joneses Have Amateur Theatricals*, which gives the impression of having been completely improvised. There were, by my count (they do not all have "Jones" in the title), ten "Jones" pictures, beginning with *Mr. Jones at the Ball* (December 25, 1908) and ending with *Mrs. Jones's Lover; or "I Want My Hat"* (August 19, 1909). They featured John Compson and that fine actress Florence Lawrence, who must have been quite wasted in them, and were among the very early "series" pictures. One of them was *Her First Biscuits* (June 17, 1909), which is called the first picture in which Mary Pickford acted, though it was not released until after *The Violin Maker of Cremona*. Other attempts at "series" pictures were not greatly developed. *They Would Elope*, with Mary Pickford and Billy Quirk, had two sequels—*His Wife's Visitor* and *The Test*—but *His Wife's Visitor* is not altogether a farce. In 1910 the same pair appeared in *Muggsy's First Sweetheart* and *Muggsy Becomes a Hero*, and in 1911 there were some farces about one Priscilla (Florence Barker), but these were not directed by Griffith. *The Gibson Goddess* was and may well have seemed a little daring in its time, for here the stately Marion Leonard, oppressed by a multitude of admirers at the seashore, delivers herself by stuffing the stockings of her bathing costume so as to make it appear that she has ungainly legs.

Domestic life and domestic problems make up the

4

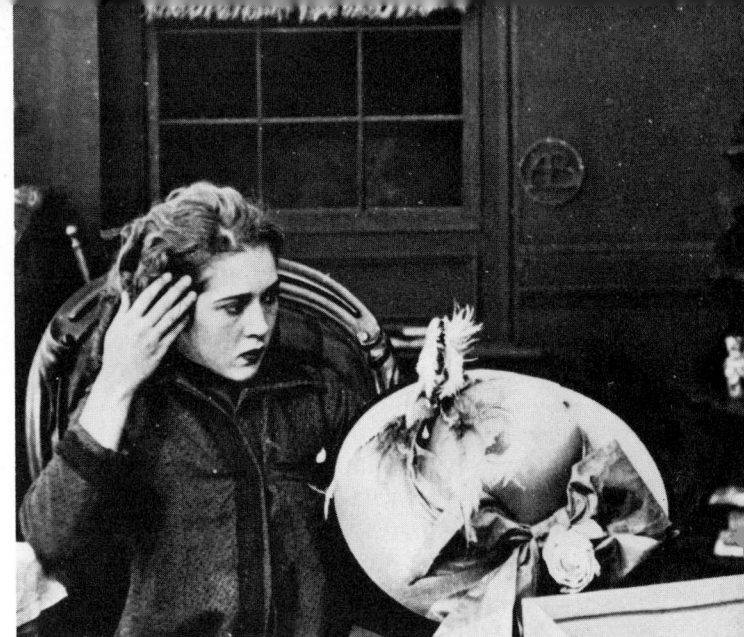

Friends. Henry B. Walthall and Mary Pickford

Mary Pickford in *The New York Hat*

subject matter of the largest group of Biographs, though melodramatic incidents and attempted crimes often intrude. If Griffith was not very successful in his own domestic arrangements, there can be no question about his appreciation as an artist for domestic felicity and fidelity, and nothing could be much more beautiful than the acting of Harry Carey in the opening scenes of a quite uncelebrated film called *Olaf—An Atom*, where the boy's mother dies and he sets out in the world alone.

Romantic love is omnipresent, but the treatment of sex is carefully guarded. *A Baby's Shoe* and *The Rocky Road* skirt the incest theme (brother and sister in the first, and father and daughter in the second), but in both cases the true relationship is unsuspected, and when it is revealed, everybody behaves properly. There is transvestism in *The Woman from Mellon's* and *The Duke's Plan*, but this was common in the early twentieth-century theater and did not generally carry unpleasant sexual overtones. Griffith heroines in general tend to regard even a stolen kiss as an insult, though in both *Fate's Turning* and *The God Within* we are invited to sympathize with a woman who has borne an illegitimate child, and in *The Little Tease* Mae Marsh gets two whole reels to get herself betrayed, come to her senses, and return to her forgiving father.

Marital infidelity occurs, with the husband generally the offender, though the dancer whom the proper Bostonian weds in *Oil and Water* turns out to be his moral inferior and unable to rise to his level or accept his way of life. Wifely infidelity, contemplated or achieved, is important in *A Flash of Light, In the Days of '49, The Voice of the Child,* and *Near to Earth.* There are women

who neglect their children also, and *A Plain Song* concerns a daughter's temptation to desert her helpless parents. Griffith may seem to be anticipating the Cecil B. DeMille of the twenties when in *Out of the Shadow* he blames a wife for driving her husband astray by indulging in excessive grief after their child's death or suggesting, in *His Lesson*, that a man who neglects his wife deserves to lose her, but these pictures are unusual. The extreme of quixotic puritanism would seem to have been attained in *On the Reef*, where a girl who had been forced into marriage with a man she did not love falls in love with another, but both high-mindedly stifle their passion, and even after the husband dies, the widow refuses to marry her lover!

Modern viewers sometimes read questionable implications into *Friends*, which, though not notably successful as to story, was one of the best showcases for the Pickford personality that Griffith ever achieved. Here the girl lives alone and receives her friends in a room over the barroom of the Golden Creek Inn. The statements in the Biograph Bulletin that she is the daughter "of the late proprietor" of the inn, that her father had been the "great friend and adviser" of the miners, and that the girl is their "pet" and has "always commanded their greatest respect" may have been framed to ward off such interpretations, but if so, they seem to have been successful with contemporaries, and, what is more to the point, the girl is never treated like anything but a lady in the film itself. All in all, the most likely guess is that we simply have here one of the many unbelievable situations (realistically considered) with which early films abound. *Fate's Interception*, another 1912 Pickford film, with Mary as a Mexican Indian girl, is a very different matter however, and something of a freak in the Griffith-Biograph oeuvre. Here is a *Madame Butterfly* situation without a mock marriage. After the girl has been deserted by her American lover, she sends a Mexican admirer to kill him; by one of the ironical twists in which the Biographs abound, the Mexican is accidentally killed instead, after which the girl resumes her relations with the American! "Who shall blame?" asks a subtitle. I should think there must have been many takers. Other freakish films are *The Test of Friendship*, in which a young man carries the testing of his sweetheart to maniacal extremes and destroys all sympathy for himself, and *A Summer Idyll*, where "the sight and aroma" of the cigarette butt which his discarded "bohemian" sweetheart encloses in a letter is enough to win a man away from the charming country girl with whom he had supposed himself in love!

Sex, marriage, and domesticity mean children as well as lovers. Griffith's very first picture, *The Adventures of Dollie*, revolved about a child, and the number of films in which children play an important role is comparatively large; I count nearly fifty of them. This does not mean that all these films are child centered (*I Did It, Mamma* seems to be the earliest in which practically the whole action is carried on by children), but even when adult problems are under consideration, children often play a determinative role, as by serving as an agent of reconciliation (*The Diamond Star, The Crooked Road, The Trail of Books*), awakening the better nature of an adult (*The Zulu's Heart, The Female of the Species*), helping an erring soul to see himself with new eyes (*As in a Looking Glass*), etc. Add to this the large number of films in which the action revolves around young adults, and it is hard to resist the conclusion that Griffith either had a special affinity for youth or supposed his audiences to possess it. He once told an interviewer that he had often seen men stop on the street to pet a dog but that the animal chosen was nearly always a puppy.

The children in the Biographs were more often girls than boys—Adele de Garde, with her wonderful eyes, who came close to stealing *A Drunkard's Reformation* from Arthur Johnson, Gladys Egan, and others. In later years Jack Pickford sometimes played the boys, but the most remarkable of the Biograph children was probably Edna Foster, who seems always to have appeared as a boy. I spot her first in *A Country Cupid* (July 24, 1911), and thereafter I count seven or eight more films: *The Ruling Passion, The Old Confectioner's Mistake, The Adventures of Billy, As in a Looking Glass, A Terrible Discovery, The Baby and the Stork, Billy's Stratagem,* and possibly *The Voice of the Child*. My initial identification of her I owe to Billy Bitzer's annotations on the Biograph

Bulletins reproduced in Eileen Bowser's book. According to an article in the trade journal *Motography* (XII, July 4, 1914, pp. 3–4), Edna was born in 1900, the daughter of a Chicago exhibitor, and both she and her sister Flora, who was two years older, had then been with Biograph for five years, where they seem especially to have admired Blanche Sweet and Harry Carey. Since they are also spoken of as having played with Reliance (the Classic Film Exchange of Los Angeles still has prints of *Prince Charming*) and Thanhouser (Flora was their juvenile David Copperfield), and since Edna says that she played "the little crippled girl in *The Escape*," this may not be entirely accurate, but it is obvious that we do not have the full record of their activities. If I may judge by her work in *A Country Cupid* and *The Adventures of Billy*, both of which have been reissued by Blackhawk, Edna at least was a very talented girl with a very winning personality, and her disappearance from later screen history is as puzzling as it is regrettable.

The moral problems in Griffith's films were by no means confined to considerations of sex. To be sure, we must always remember that truly enlightened morality is independent and creative, and it is the great moral limitation of popular art that it is always inclined to accept established standards at face value. Thus popular art tends, for example, to accept war as an institution (including the citizen's obligation to fight for his country) and thus to reject the criminal because he falls below the current social standard on the subject of killing, but at the same time to reject the conscientious objector because he rises above it. Though Griffith was the son of a Confederate officer, he was far from being a militarist. Both *The Birth of a Nation* and *Intolerance* gave considerable comfort to pacifists, and even *Hearts of the World*, which was a World War I propaganda film, opens by questioning whether war ever settles anything. Yet Griffith did make war propaganda films, and in such an art form as the motion picture, it would be pretty difficult to avoid bidding for audience plaudits when the cavalry rides to the rescue. A good example of the conventional attitude toward war is *The Battle*, in which Blanche Sweet taunts Charles West unmercifully when he flees in a funk from the fighting and rewards him with her love when he not only returns to his post but courageously carries out a dangerous mission. In *Swords and Hearts* and *The Informer*, even women are involved in the killing. The most remarkable entry on the other side of the ledger is the late two-reeler, *The Yaqui Cur*, in which an Indian becomes a conscientious objector through his devotion to "the Love Man," Jesus. Cast out by his tribe because he refuses to fight, he rejoices at last to die for another. What a pity that *The Yaqui Cur* is one of the lost films! No wonder so little has been heard of it; it must have been far ahead of its time.

Films have also generally accepted private fisticuffs as an ultimate arbiter, assuming that, however peacefully he may be inclined, the "good guy" must, in a sufficiently serious emergency, always hold himself ready to knock out the "bad guy." Griffith's Biographs are by no means untouched by this assumption. In *Dan the Dandy*, a young man who has become effeminatized during his years at college (thus reflecting a possible prejudice on the part of the nickelodeon's predominantly noncollege audience) must learn how to behave like a man after his return home. But the most interesting, because the most thoughtful, films in this general area are four that probe the difference between true and false courage: *Was He a Coward?*, *Bobby the Coward*, *A Beast at Bay*, and *The Spirit Awakened*.

> Rightly to be great
> Is not to stir without great argument,
> But greatly to find quarrel in a straw
> When honour's at the stake.

If the heroes of these films do not quite follow Hamlet's advice to "find quarrel in a straw," they do decline, even at the risk of calumny and misunderstanding, to be involved in meaningless brawls, only to rise to a real issue when it presents itself. Interestingly enough, the girls involved are not always able to make such distinctions clearly until they have been pointed out to them.

Less conventional in their outlook are a number of films in which private vengeance seems to be sanctioned and we are asked to accept the killing of an evil character, or, at least, in which vengeance is not specifically condemned. Such are *The Ingrate*, *The Reckoning*, *A Burglar's Mistake*, *"1776" or, The Hessian Renegades*, *Nursing a Viper*, *The Call to Arms*, *A Mohawk's Way*, *Broken Ways*, and, in a way, *Near to Earth*. *The Reckoning* seems the most outrageous, for here a husband shoots down both his wife and her admirer after the lady has entertained the man at lunch! In *A Burglar's Mistake* a blackmailer is killed in cold blood when his victim finds him robbing his house and hence considers it safe to kill him, and in *Nursing a Viper* another evil character is deliberately released to a French Revolutionary mob. In *Near to Earth*, a young man half accidentally kills the seducer who is running off with his brother's wife, and sends the lady home! In *"1776,"* private vengeance is organized through the recruitment of neighbors. This ties up with the war theme, for the Hessians are the enemies of the avenger's country, or of what he hopes will soon be

that, but his primary concern is to punish them for killing his son. In *Broken Ways*, the sheriff has a legal right to kill the worthless, inconveniently returned husband of the woman he loves, for the man has come stained with a fresh crime, but the slaying can hardly be called wholly professional or disinterested. In *The Punishment*, on the other hand, the villain gets his deserts through an accident which we are presumably intended to take as an "act of God," while in *The Root of Evil*, retribution comes, without intent, through a child. In *The Usurer*, too, it is chance, or accident, not human design, through which the notorious exploiter meets his richly deserved fate. In such cases we get a chance, morally speaking, to eat our cake and have it too. Griffith's love of irony and his playing on curious coincidences inevitably comes to the fore in dealing with many situations of this kind. Thus, in *Fate*, a hooligan accidentally blows up his friend instead of the grandchildren of his enemy, and in *The Coming of Angelo*, Guido is himself destroyed by the blast he had intended for his rival.

On the other hand, it must not be overlooked that there are films in which the desire for vengeance is overcome by love or compassion, and these seem more characteristic of the spirit of Griffith's work. Examples may be found in *The Mended Lute*, *The Oath and the Man*, *The Revenue Man and the Girl*, *The Fugitive*, *His Mother's Scarf*, *The Goddess of the Sagebrush*, *The Female of the Species*, and *A Cry for Help*. In *The Mended Lute* it is an Indian who is moved to compassion by the fortitude of the rival who lies wholly within his power. The situation in *The Fugitive* is particularly touching, for here a Confederate mother shelters and saves the Union soldier who has killed her son.

Not all the struggles between good and evil in the Biographs deal with this particular temptation, however. Sometimes money is the issue. The noble old retainer in *His Trust Fulfilled* is tempted to steal to send the girl who has no resource except himself to school, and the miser in *The Miser's Heart* knows that a child will die unless he turns his treasure over to the burglars. There is a particularly fine and imaginative touch in *An Arcadian Maid*, where Mary Pickford, having stolen from her employer at the behest of an unscrupulous and deceitful wooer, shows her sense of guilt by setting aside the rosary she now considers herself unworthy to wear, resuming it later when she has come to her senses and made restitution.

In *The Way of Man* and *The Light That Came* a disfigured girl has to choose whether to be selfish or unselfish in love. In the first, the girl knows that her lover will be faithful but she also knows that he loves her cousin; she solves the problem by the melodramatic ex-

Scenes from *The Battle*, with Blanche Sweet and Charles West, released November 6, 1911, and of great interest as illustrating Griffith's masterly use of Civil War material four years before *Birth of a Nation*.

Above:
Scenes from *The Last Drop of Water* with Blanche Sweet, Charles West, and Joseph Graybill, released July 27, 1911.

Right:
Scene from *Three Friends*, released January 2, 1913, showing Henry B. Walthall and Blanche Sweet as the unhappy couple, reduced to poverty.

Below:
Scene from *The Golden Supper*, adapted from Tennyson's poem and released December 12, 1910, showing Charles West and Dorothy West, an interesting example of an early Biograph "costume" film.

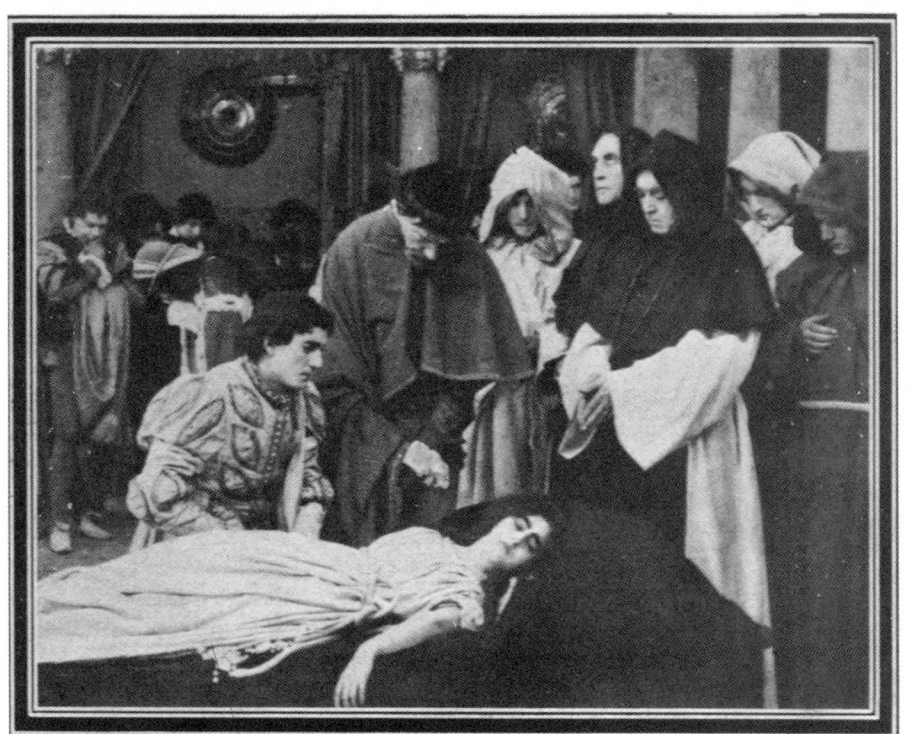

pedient of feigning suicide and devoting herself to good works. The girl in *The Light That Came* is luckier. Her betrothed is blind. When she learns that an operation might restore his sight, she gives up her earnings to pay for it, though fearing, groundlessly as it develops, that he may not want her, having seen her as she is.

In *For a Wife's Honor* a man consents to rest under suspicion of burglary rather than save himself by putting his friend's innocent wife in a compromising position. The policeman hero of *His Duty* faces a difficult decision when he learns that his brother is a thief, and Ben Tilton, in *A Tale of the Wilderness*, finds his brother leading an Indian attack against the stockade that shelters the girl Ben loves. The sheriff in *The Modern Prodigal* is supposed to turn in the escaped convict who has saved his son from drowning, and rather subtle ambiguities for one-reelers appear in two Blanche Sweet pictures, *The Lesser Evil* and *A Change of Spirit*, in which "the soul of goodness in things evil" manifests itself in a smuggler captain and a thief. The extreme dilemma, however, is in *The Country Doctor*, a glorification of the Hippocratic oath, whose hero must leave his own critically sick child unattended to look after the child of a poor neighbor and whose own child dies in consequence. This stands in curious contrast to *The Light That Came* and *Through Darkened Vales*, in which the doctor will not even consider an operation to restore sight without cash on the line, and nobody seems to perceive anything reprehensible in such action.

This last point might suggest that the Biographs were more sensitive to personal than to social morality; this, however, was far from being true. Topical references, many of them involving social considerations, abound. Some of these, to be sure, are playful. The "sheath gown," which was apparently supposed to be shocking, is played for laughs in *A Smoked Husband*, as is an extravagant type of millinery in *The Peachbasket Hat*. *The Gibson Goddess* was derived from Charles Dana Gibson's pictures and apparently from a contemporary song, which included the line "Oh! Why do they call me the Gibson Girl?," and in *A Midnight Adventure* a trashy novel is ascribed to Clara Jean Dippy (for Laura Jean Libbey). But Griffith did not confine himself to such matters. *Betrayed by a Handprint* appeals to interest in the comparatively new science of fingerprinting (miscalled palmistry), and *How She Triumphed* reflects the growing vogue of physical culture for women. *The Seventh Day* was announced as having been "inspired by a decision some time ago in the Cook County (Ill.) circuit court." Similarly, *What Shall We Do with Our Old* was "A Story Founded upon an Actual Occurrence in New York City." *The Adventures of Billy* was "Suggested by Press Comment upon the Tramp Evil."

Griffith was also obviously alert to the dramatic usefulness of contemporary science, especially psychology. Perhaps it would be easiest to pile up references to woman's contrariety and changeableness (from the male point of view) and the inscrutability of her choices; in one form or another, this occurs in *A Woman's Way*, *The Cardinal's Conspiracy*, *The Renunciation*, *With Her Card*, *The Primal Call*, *The Female of the Species*, and elsewhere. In *A Woman's Way*, one girl turns upon her rescuers, who have gone through great trouble for her, and suddenly accepts the suitor whom her father's attempt to force upon her had caused all the trouble, and in *The Renunciation* another girl amazes both her "he-man" lovers, who have almost come to a murderous encounter over her, by accepting a marshmallow kind of youngster instead of either of them.

This kind of thing Griffith could have found without the aid of science; there is literary precedent for it running as far back as the Middle Ages. There are other matters, however. *The Honor of Thieves* deals with kleptomania, and both *The Maniac Cook* and *The Restoration* with insanity, to which Griffith returned much later in *The House of Darkness*, which explores the therapeutic value of music. The most interesting films in this connection, however, are *Man's Genesis* and its two-reel sequel, *Brute Force*, though neither shows any scientific knowledge. *Man's Genesis* may have been suggested by such contemporary stories about early man as Stanley Waterloo's *The Story of Ab* and Jack London's *Before Adam*, but it was billed as "A Psychological Comedy Founded upon the Darwinian Theory of the Evolution of Man." Actually it has nothing to do with Darwinism nor the evolution of man either, being a simple story of how Weakhands won Lilywhite away from Bruteforce by inventing the club. In the sequel, which is less appealing, though done on a considerably larger scale (the conflict now is tribal, not merely personal), the cave men coexist with freak animals and a dinosaur who long antedated on the screen both the monsters of *The Lost World* and Siegfried's Dragon. By now the neighboring womanless tribe, bent upon stealing the mates they need for survival, have developed clubs of their own, but the genius of Weakhands triumphs again, this time by inventing the bow and arrow. Contemporary standards in dress and undress being what they are, it is amusing to recall that sixteen-year-old Mae Marsh, then a Griffith newcomer, got the role of Lilywhite because Mary Pickford, Blanche Sweet, and the other established actresses refused to accept a "bare-legged role," and that he rewarded Mae and punished them by also giving her the lead in *The Sands of Dee*, which they all did wish to play very much!

That part of the world which was the contemporary theater was in a class by itself so far as early filmmakers were concerned, but their attitude toward it must have been somewhat divided. On the one hand, they were themselves theater folk, and the prejudice against theatergoing, especially among humble people, was much stronger in America then than it is now, but, on the other hand, they could not have failed to feel the sting in the superior attitude of the "legit" toward the "flickers." Griffith himself was known as "Lawrence Griffith" during his first years in the movies; he was saving "D. W." for the success on the boards toward which he still aspired.

In his films he makes only a limited use of the theater and its people. *Behind the Scenes* employs the stock "show must go on" theme, this time though the poor actress's child is dying. Much later *The Old Actor* was a sympathetic treatment of an actor superseded because of age. In *The Making of a Man* a girl falls in love with an actor, her father is bitterly opposed, and the spectator's sympathies are on the side of the lovers. In *The Dancing Girl of Butte*, a man marries a Western dance hall girl, and the marriage is successful, but in *Oil and Water*, the dancer is unworthy, and in *The Unveiling* a boy's passion for a show girl nearly leads to disaster. The guilt of the actress who is the "other woman" in *Winning Back His Love* is lessened by the fact that she did not know her admirer was married. The show girl in *Two Daughters of Eve* did; she was seeking revenge upon a respectable woman who had been unpardonably rude to her, but she comes to herself finally and finishes much better than she began.

The Ruling Passion seems antitheater by implication, and antifilm too, if anybody stopped to think about it, for it centers on a boy whose imagination, fired by a visit to the theater, rigs up a situation that nearly has fatal consequences. I have already spoken of the man in *Brutality*

The Woman from Mellon's. Billy Quirk, Mary Pickford, George Nicholls

who sees himself in Bill Sikes, and the father in *As in a Looking Glass* comes to his senses through watching his son imitating his drunken tantrums. But the most significant use of the stage in the Biographs is in *A Drunkard's Reformation*, where Arthur Johnson, through witnessing a performance of Charles Reade's *Drink*, which was based on Zola's *L'Assommoir*, is saved by seeing what is in store for him unless he changes his ways. (The scenes showing the play within the film create an interesting kind of double illusion.) The only direct reference to the movies in the Biographs, so far as I can determine, is in an 185-foot short of 1909 (on the same reel with *The Welcome Burglar*), called *Those Awful Hats*, which was simply a bit of comic propaganda against the wearing of large headgear in the nickelodeons.

The most pervasive social concern in the Biographs, as that term is generally employed today, can only be referred to; otherwise half the films would have to be cited, for they are saturated with sympathy for the sufferings of the poor in a world in which not only were goods and opportunities inequitably divided (this is still true today) but in which society had not yet accepted even such inadequate responsibility for the underprivileged as it has come to acknowledge since. It must not be forgotten that, generally speaking, early films were made for those Americans who could not afford to pay more than a nickel for a show, and there was never any question where their sympathies would lie. Of course this does not mean that the filmmakers were insincere. As a matter of fact, they, and especially their actors, were themselves "poor people" during most of our period, for filmmaking had not yet begun to yield rich rewards. Radicalism was frowned upon however. *Waiter No. 5* might venture to present revolutionary activity in faraway Russia with sympathy, but in such films as *The Voice of the Violin* and *The Iconoclast* discontent is frowned upon, and anarchism, socialism, and communism all combined into a kind of dangerous witch's brew.

Griffith's most specific propaganda in behalf of any reform was directed against alcoholism; this interest runs all through his career to his last disastrous "talkie," *The Struggle*. Again, the audience must be considered. Drink and, to a lesser extent, gambling (compare, for example, *The Last Deal*, where the cure administered to the husband by his wife's uncle is neither convincing nor moral) was the Number One Enemy of the poor; when the workingman drank, his wife and children starved and wore rags. *A Drunkard's Reformation* was the first of these films, and it was followed by at least sixteen others, though I do not mean that in all of these it was the main element. In *A Drunkard's Reformation* Arthur Johnson is saved by a temperance play to which he has taken his

daughter, but in *What Drink Did* the swinishness of another film father, David Miles, leads to his child's death in the saloon that she has entered to try to persuade him to come home. In *Pippa Passes* Griffith used only three episodes as against Browning's four, and one of these is his own, directed against pub-crawling, while in *The House with Closed Shutters* the hero (or antihero) is deliberately made an alcoholic. In *The Message of the Violin* the young musician is saddled with a drunken father.

There is no reason to question Griffith's sincerity in his temperance films, but one must also understand that he was as much opposed to prohibition as to alcoholism. Unfortunately there were those in the Biograph circle for whom this combination of convictions did not work out successfully in the long run. Griffith's principal attack on reformers was to be made in *Intolerance*, where the whole portrayal of the "uplifters," powerful as it is dramatically, must seem absurd and unfair to anyone who knows what such figures as Jane Addams and Lillian Wald were even then accomplishing. In one of the first of the Jones pictures, *Mrs. Jones Entertains*, we are supposed to be amused when the temperance ladies get drunk on rum and thoroughly enjoy it, though they do not know what they have been drinking. At the very end of his Biograph years, Griffith returned to the attack with greater elaboration in a two-reeler called *The Reformers, or The Lost Art of Minding One's Business*. Unfortunately for Griffith's argument, this film only shows that one's children are likely to go astray if they are not carefully supervised, but this proves nothing about the "causes" to which their parents were devoted, one way or the other.

Gangsterism appears in *The Inner Circle*, the famous *Musketeers of Pig Alley* (often cited along with *The Mother and the Law* as prefiguring the later gangster film), and the much less well known but certainly not inferior *Bobby the Coward*. *A Corner in Wheat* and *One Is Business; The Other Crime* denounce stock market manipulation and political corruption. *The Fatal Hour* touches white slavery, *The Song of the Shirt* sweated labor. Prison reform is involved, at least by implication, in *A Convict's Sacrifice*. *Thou Shalt Not* tries to alert people to the need for tuberculosis therapy, a comparatively new thing when the picture was made, and even a melodrama like *The Medicine Bottle* urges the clear and proper labeling of dangerous drugs. *For His Son*, in which a doctor supplies the exorbitant demands of his playboy son by inventing a soft drink called Dopokoke—which earns him great wealth and makes Grand Guignol cocaine addicts of both the son and the doctor's secretary, later the son's wife, may strike modern viewers as more comic than terrible, but it still involves a commentary on the building up of great fortunes by means indifferent to public welfare. A more specialized subject is that of the dangers involved in the use of the "third degree" by the police and convicting people on the basis of circumstantial evidence. Griffith devoted at least five Biographs to this—*Tragic Love*, *A Misunderstood Boy*, *Was Justice Served?*, *Conscience*, and *The Burglar's Dilemma*—and returned to the theme in *Intolerance*. It must, then, have interested him considerably.

American Indians made up the principal minority group represented in the Biographs, and the treatment of them was almost consistently sympathetic. The Bulletin on *The Song of the Wildwood Flute* was quite justified in its claim that "the Biograph has always endeavored to depict the redman as he really is, and not as cheap literature would portray him."

It was *The Redman and the Child*, released July 28, 1908, that marked Griffith's discovery of the Indian as a source of cinematic material, and of course it was the great success of that early film that sent out the call for more than thirty successors. Indian pictures used natural backgrounds for the most part, and with early studio resources as limited as they were, any material that afforded an opportunity to film objects of natural beauty at will was a boon. A number of Griffith's films that deal with the sea are famous: *Lines of White on a Sullen Sea*, *The Unchanging Sea*, *Enoch Arden*, *The Mender of Nets*, *The Lesser Evil*, and *The Sands of Dee*. But there are, after all, not many of these in comparison to the Indian pictures. Add *Where the Breakers Roar*, *Fisher Folks*, *The Ruling Passion*, *A Child's Remorse*, and *The Sorrowful Shore*, and you have almost completed the list of the films in which the sea plays an important role.

In the pictures that concern Indian characters alone, Griffith was of course obliged to make Indians "bad guys" as well as "good guys." He perpetuated a number of Indian stereotypes, such as the Indian's impassivity and indifference to pain, as well as his implacable determination to avenge a wrong and his loyalty unto death to anyone who had befriended him. And of course Indian backgrounds and customs are often as inaccurately portrayed as the same kind of thing in the costume films. The essential thing to remember, however, is that even when, as in *A Tale of the Wilderness*, *Billy's Stratagem*, *A Temporary Truce*, *The Massacre*, and *The Battle at Elderbush Gulch*, Indians do dreadful things, they are generally either avenging a wrong or, like the renegade Negroes in *The Birth of a Nation*, under the domination of a white man who is much worse than they are; in the relations between Indian and white, the initial wrong is nearly always on the part of the white. In *Rose O'*

Salem-Town, Indians save a white girl from being put to death as a witch. In *My Hero*, Indian Charlie succors a pair of babes-in-the-wood sweethearts who have fled from unsympathetic parents, and in both *The Broken Doll* and *Iola's Promise* an Indian girl dies out of loyalty and gratitude to whites. Griffith's most famous Indian films include *The Mended Lute*, *The Indian Runner's Romance*, *Ramona*, and *The Song of the Wildwood Flute*. *The Yaqui Cur*, which I have discussed elsewhere, must have been, by all means, the most unusual Indian picture. Oddly enough, *A Pueblo Legend* (the only two-reeler in which Mary Pickford ever appeared), with which the greatest pains were taken, seems to have been one of the least successful. This picture goes back to the Southwest in the days before the Spaniards came. It was made in the pueblo at Isleta, New Mexico, with the aid of trappings borrowed from the Museum of Indian Antiques at Albuquerque, but the company almost got run out of town while making it, and nobody ever seems to have cared much for the finished product.

One asks at once is Griffith equally generous to other minority groups. Everybody knows how, in later days, he resented the charges of Negrophobia leveled against *The Birth of a Nation*, and other repercussions followed the use of foreigners in any unsavory aspect. "From now on," he once declared, "all my villains are going to be Americans." There is a "low-down Negro" in *The Girls and Daddy*, but the old-style plantation Negro, faithful to "Massa," appears in *His Trust* and *His Trust Fulfilled* as well as in *Swords and Hearts*. Many minority groups appear but briefly in the Biographs. *Schneider's Anti-Noise Crusade* has German racial humor of a kind formerly accepted without malice but now considered offensive. Jews are treated with understanding in *Romance of a Jewess*, filmed "in the thickly settled Hebrew quarters of New York City," which has a tragic ending, in *The Honor of Thieves*, and in *A Child of the Ghetto*. The title of *That Chink at Golden Gulch* might be defended as reflecting the language of the whites in the picture rather than that of the producers, and the Chinaman himself is almost a saint.

Some other groups are less generously treated however. The child-stealing gypsies in *The Adventures of Dollie* are stereotypes, and something similar appears again in *An Awful Moment*, *What the Daisy Said*, *The Spanish Gypsy*, and *A Romany Tragedy*. Some of the same irrational intensity ascribed to gypsies—hot blood, revengefulness, etc.—are often attributed to Italians also (in the early films there was a tendency to call them Sicilians) and to Spaniards and Mexicans. There are evil Sicilians in *One Touch of Nature*, *The Cord of Life*, and *At the Altar*. In *Little Italy* and *Italian Blood* have good Italians as well as bad, and both good and bad Mexicans appear in such films as *The Vaquero's Vow* and *A Lodging for the Night*. There is a kindly Italian in *The Rocky Road* and some stock material in *The Italian Barber*. *The Inner Circle* deals with the Black Hand, or Mafia. Spanish-speaking people appear in an undesirable light in *A Siren of Impulse*, *Heaven Avenges*, *Black Sheep*, and *A Temporary Truce*; an early Indian picture, *The Red Girl*, has a Mexican villainess. On the other hand, the Latins are kindly treated in *The Thread of Destiny* and *In Old California*. *The New Dress* has a Mexican heroine; *Her Sacrifice* glorifies a Mexican girl. *The Greaser's Gauntlet* (another now offensive title) accepts the title character's admirable qualities, and in *The Two Sides* a Mexican laborer returns good for evil.

The fundamental spirit of Griffith's work is religious as well as ethical. His characters believe in God and pray to Him. Self-sacrifice is always a virtue, and there is rejoicing over the sinner who repents. In view of these considerations, the number of Biographs that have a distinctively religious theme or in which the church as an institution plays an important part is surprisingly small—about fifteen in all, as nearly as I can tally. *The Greaser's Gauntlet* stresses the efficacy of a mother's prayers, *A Child's Faith* that of a child's. It is interesting that as early as 1909 the Salvation Army was willing to cooperate in filming *The Salvation Army Lass*. Taking the veil is involved in *A Baby's Shoe*, *A Decree of Destiny*, and *The Long Road*. In an historical film, *The Cloister's Touch*, both a wronged husband and a repentant duke enter an order, and in the French Revolutionary film, *The Oath and the Man*, a priest persuades a husband to forgo vengeance on his wife and a nobleman. There are noble priests also in *The Way of the World* and *In Life's Cycle* (though a Protestant, Griffith seems to have had a preference for portraying Catholic clergymen). In *A Strange Meeting*, however, a girl thief is redeemed through a mission minister, and in *The Converts* a young man who had pretended to be an evangelist for a lark makes a true convert and through her finds redemption. The minister in *To Save Her Soul*, however, is an unpleasant fanatic. In *Resurrection* of course the religious element was present in the original story.

I have counted between thirty-five and forty Biographs with what might in some sense be called a tragic ending, though not always according to a strictly classical definition. How clearly Griffith and/or Biograph defined tragedy may be something of a question. *The Female of the Species* was subtitled "A Psychological Tragedy," whatever that may be, but the tragedy that threatens in it is averted. The bereaved wife in the stranded desert party is tempted to kill the girl whom she wrongly suspects of

having seduced her late husband, but she changes her mind when her softer nature is, not too convincingly, awakened by the finding of an Indian baby. Thirty-five or forty tragedies is not a high percentage out of 450 films, but when we take into consideration the resistance to tragedy in popular art, it still seems a respectable number. Perhaps the best known of these films are "1776" or *The Hessian Renegades*, *Lines of White on a Sullen Sea*, *The Last Drop of Water*, *Iola's Promise*, and *The Sands of Dee*.

Calamity takes many forms in these pictures, and irony often breaks in. In *The Fight for Freedom* a comparatively sympathetic killer is carried out at the end to hang, and his wholly innocent wife is killed by a bullet. In *The Girl and the Outlaw* a wayward heroine is killed while doing a good deed. In *Lines of White on a Sullen Sea* a faithful fisher girl dies when her lover proves unfaithful, and in *The Mountaineer's Honor* a mother shoots her son, with his consent, to save him from hanging. In *A Convict's Sacrifice*, a man gives himself up, and is slain, to force his now indigent benefactor to receive a reward for his capture. The "bad" husband in *The Last Drop of Water* dies in the desert to save the good man who, he knows, loves his wife. In *The Expiation*, a drunken husband, awakened, kills himself to free his wife to be happy with the man she loves, but she, not to be outdone in generosity, now refuses her lover!

Out-and-out supernaturalism Griffith seems to have essayed in only one Biograph, *The Hindoo Dagger*. *The Devil* was apparently not so designed, for we are specifically told that "the Devil is intended to illustrate psychic force" and again that he "is the embodiment of our evil inclinations warring with the pure." *The Blind Princess and the Poet* is allegory, however, while *Love Among the Roses*, a "fantasia" whose "personages" are "more mythical than real," at least skirts allegory.

Symbolism was more frequently and significantly employed. There is no lute in *The Mended Lute*; it is the ruptured relationship between three Indians that is mended; one wonders how many in the nickelodeon audiences understood the title. *The Two Paths* is subtitled "A Symbolism" and *The Modern Prodigal* "A Story in Symbolism Showing the Result of Youth's Egotism," and the Bulletin declares of *The Eternal Mother* that "this is rather a symbolism than a picture of the material."

In *The Modern Prodigal*, which deals with the corruption of an ambitious country boy in the wicked city (his adventures there are passed over), his return to his village in convict garb, and his redeeming himself when he saves the sheriff's son from drowning at the risk of arrest, the symbolism is largely superimposed. The action itself is

THE RULING PASSION

The Result of a Youngster's Visit to the Theatre

L ITTLE BILLY has been taken to the theatre by his parents and as a result becomes stage-struck. At a children's party Billy plays stage manager and drills the children in some of the scenes he has witnessed. Later in the day while playing on the lawn the idea strikes him to play the drama with realism, so they go down to the shore and use a rowboat for a pirate ship, seizing his sister and placing her aboard. This is considered great, until the boat breaks from its mooring and little brother and sister are carried by the rough sea far out from the shore. As his parents are away on a visit to the city, it is some time before Billy can secure aid. Upon their return, Papa, after an exciting sail in a motor boat rescues them.

 # BIOGRAPH

Released Aug. 7, 1911

The Biograph Bulletin for *The Ruling Passion*, reproduced with Bitzer's notations from *Biograph Bulletins: 1908–1912*, edited by Eileen Bowser, by permission of the publishers. Copyright © 1973 by Farrar, Straus & Giroux, Inc. Edna Foster is shown playing the role of a boy, as usual. Information concerning the doings of this actress since her Biograph days seems to be unavailable and would be greatly appreciated by the authors of this book. Billy Bitzer's identification of the other child as Gladys Egan is highly questionable.

straightforwardly realistic and is universalized largely through Biblical subtitles, references, and parallels. *The Two Paths* is considerably more daring. There are naturalistic elements in this film also, notably Dorothy Bernard's harrowing death scene. But Griffith cannot possibly have expected the scenes in which the Satanic tempter (and he is deliberately made up to look like Satan) enters the room where the two girls are working and, after some extraordinary eyework, beckons first to the "good" girl, who spurns him, then to the "bad" one, who rises and leaves with him, apron and all, nor the scenes of gilded revel to which he conducts her, to be taken literally; thus regarded, they would be worse than absurd. As Daumier-like cartoons, giving the *sense* of what happens when girls go wrong, these scenes are not without their effectiveness however. Even the workbench of the carpenter whom the "good" girl marries is less a real workbench than a symbol of honest toil; we never see him do anything but run his plane along one single piece of wood!

Griffith was working for people who had never heard of "expressionism" in the theater; perhaps, indeed, he had not heard of it himself. Nevertheless he has here achieved it, and if he did not often go quite so far as in *The Two Paths*, we do still often find him headed in the same general direction. For all his bent toward realism, he was forever straining at its limitations, and the two modes of expression were not always mutually exclusive. There is a great deal that at least borders upon expressionism even in what may at first seem the wholly naturalistic modern story of *Intolerance* (*The Mother and the Law*). Many of the things Mae Marsh does are obviously intended to be taken not as the particular actions of one young woman in this particular situation but rather as an expression of the spirit of faithful womanhood itself. There was much criticism during the years of Griffith's greatest fame, about the way he made his girls "flutter" (Mary Pickford once told George Pratt: "Mr. Griffith always wanted to have me running around trees and pointing at rabbits, and I wouldn't do it"), and I do not pretend that I think this one of his most effective devices or that it was always judiciously employed. But as a means of expressing the exuberant spirits of happy youth, it does have more validity than it can have for those who see it in straightforward realistic perspective.

Film historians have written so much about the "Griffith last-minute rescue" (which, incidentally, is by no means always successful) that a person who did not know his films at first hand might well gather the impression that he used this device in every other film. This is far from being the case. Not having had an opportunity to see all the Biographs, I cannot vouch for my figures, but I am sure that there are fewer than fifty examples in 450 films. What has made the last-minute rescue particularly memorable in Griffith films is his skill in intercutting between the endangered party or parties and the rescuers (Kemp Niver counts thirty-five two-to-five-second cutbacks as early as *The Lonely Villa*), which develops extreme tension. This device was apparently first employed in *The Fatal Hour*, released August 18, 1908, in which a gun has been rigged so as to fire and kill a bound girl when the hands of the clock reach a certain point. Sometimes parallel actions introduced independently are brought into previously unsuspected vital relationship with each other. The rescuers are delayed or impeded by accidents, and suspense is increased by what *almost* happens; in *The Medicine Bottle* the little girl *almost* gives the poison to grandmother before mother arrives home to prevent her, and in *The Cord of Life* the door whose opening will cause the baby suspended in a basket outside the window to drop is *almost* opened. Nobody who has seen *Intolerance*, *Way Down East*, and *Orphans of the Storm* can need to be told that Griffith did not abandon this device in his Biograph days.

Children or girls are the usual victims; the late *Death's Marathon*, in which Blanche Sweet tries to hold her husband Henry Walthall, who has announced his intention of committing suicide, on the telephone until his friend arrives, is exceptional, and this rescue attempt is unsuccessful. In *The Lonely Villa* and *A Woman Scorned* several persons are in danger from burglars, and there are three films—*The Gold-Seekers*, *With the Enemy's Help*, and *The Wanderer*—that have a race between the legitimate owner of a mine and a claim jumper. The right man wins in *The Wanderer*, but the homeless and heroic young man who had made his victory possible is not rewarded. In *Her Terrible Ordeal* the race is with time, not a mortal opponent; the secretary is locked into the office strong room to which the boss alone knows the combination, and the tensest moment occurs when he returns to pick up something he had forgotten and goes away again without knowing she is there. In the farcical *They Would Elope*, the boy and girl only imagine themselves pursued, as their parents are quite in sympathy with their plans. In *Fools of Fate* the husband overtakes the man with whom his wife is eloping, and, the situation being clarified, both renounce her, but when she attempts to return home she finds that her husband has killed himself, and in *Saved from Himself*, which is wholly an indoor film, there is no chase whatever, but the chase type of tension is achieved by the repentant hotel clerk's attempt to get the money he has stolen back into the safe before it is called for.

We have a child or children in a sinking boat (*The

Ruling Passion), in danger of eating doped ice cream at a picnic (*The Old Confectioner's Mistake*), in danger of being murdered by tramps (*The Adventures of Billy*), and in a house about to be blown up by a bomb (*The Inner Circle*). Children are suspended out of windows in *The Cord of Life, The Miser's Heart,* and *A Terrible Discovery,* while *In a Hempen Bag* has a baby who narrowly escapes being drowned in a bag that was intended for a cat (there is much less consideration for animals here than is usual in Griffith films).

Not to exhaust the subject, a girl is menaced by a lunatic in a rowboat (*Where the Breakers Roar*); by a contraption rigged up by a disappointed suitor to kill her at her wedding (*At the Altar*); by poisoned candy (*The Drive for Life*); by fire (*Rose O' Salem-Town* and *The Goddess of Sagebrush Gulch*); by a demented youth holding her at the point of a pistol in the little country school where she teaches (*A Country Cupid*); by a mutinous crew on shipboard (*The Lesser Evil*); by a fugitive who forces her to help him escape in her motor car (*A Beast at Bay*); by being held hostage in a deserted well-box (*A Temporary Truce*); and by burglars in a number of films.

The commonest means of rescue employed are a man's own two feet (and, in some cases, fists after he arrives) and the automobile, but in *The Lonely Villa* the car breaks down (a not uncommon occurrence in those days) and a gypsy's horse and wagon takes its place, and in *The Telephone Girl and the Lady* Mae Marsh rides behind her mounted policeman lover, Alfred Paget, to save Claire McDowell. In *The Adventures of Billy* a dog carries the rescue message. In *Where the Breakers Roar* and *The Lesser Evil,* it is boat against boat. In *The Lonedale Operator,* a locomotive speeds to the rescue, and in *The Girl and Her Trust,* which was a more sensational but not more effective remake of the same story, the locomotive pursues a handcart. The race between train and auto in *A Beast at Bay* anticipates *Intolerance,* though this time it does not furnish the climax of the picture. Other things being equal, the more sensational the properties and the more ingenious the gadgets rigged up, the more exciting these pictures are, but Griffith shows considerably greater restraint in developing sensation for sensation's sake than he is always given credit for.

The gadgets are ingenious nevertheless and are often shown in close-ups, as with the monkey wrench that Blanche Sweet has been using as a pistol to hold the robbers at bay in *The Lonedale Operator* and the bullet that Dorothy Bernard tries to explode in a keyhole in *The Girl and Her Trust.* The telephone, a comparatively new contraption in the early Biograph days, plays an important part in a number of films, but any object upon which our attention needed to be focused might be photographed at close range, as the coin in *The Golden Louis,* the hollowed cake of soap in which Florence Lawrence hides the necklace she has stolen in *Betrayed by a Handprint,* or the vest and trunk in which the money is hidden in *The Unwelcome Guest.* Kemp R. Niver has pointed out how in *Politician's Love Story* and *Resurrection* Griffith turns the camera around so that the audience may see what the character has been reading. In the first instance, we see Mack Sennett's hands holding the newspaper, in the second, Florence Lawrence's finger tracing the words she reads in the Bible.

In his famous *Dramatic Mirror* advertisement, Griffith claimed to have "introduced" to film making "the large or close-up figures, distant views . . . , the 'switchback,' sustained suspense, the 'fade out,' and restraint in expression." Much of this is not literally true; Griffith was himself photographed in close-up in films directed by others before he became a director. To listen to many film historians, one would have to believe that the Biographs were tissues of ingenious technical devices, which is far from being the case. But absolute priority in these matters is of very little interest; what counts in art is not who did it first but who does it best. Griffith never used camera tricks to achieve a deliberate show of virtuosity, but he did show an uncanny ability to get his story told in the most effective possible way. Moreover he began to do this early. There are no close-ups of people in *The Adventures of Dollie,* but the horse and wagon come very close to the camera as they go down to the river, and there are some interesting and varied shots of the barrel in which we know the child to be enclosed as it approaches the falls. Neither *The Ingrate* nor *The Country Doctor* is a sophisticated film, but both use fairly lengthy establishing shots to enable us to become acquainted with the characters before the action begins, and one of these scenes in *The Ingrate* includes a long "pan." Griffith has been misrepresented by overemphasis on his technical prowess (as if there were nothing else in his pictures worth talking about); from this point of view, it is fortunate that circumstances have compelled me, in this study, to place my stress elsewhere. His technique was masterly, but he was not its slave, he was its master. In general his storytelling is straightforward, his technique unobtrusive. Manner does not swallow up matter.

The technique was nevertheless subjected to intensive development as time passed. Niver counts thirteen scenes and twelve camera positions in *The Adventures of Dollie* but 130 and thirty-five in *The Girl and Her Trust.* In these matters, Griffith developed much faster than his critics. Thus the *Dramatic Mirror,* which had praised his repose in 1910, was worried by 1911 about the number of

Scenes from *Enoch Arden*, Griffith's second two-reeler, released June 12 and 15, 1911, showing Wilfred Lucas as Enoch Arden, Linda Arvidson (the first Mrs. D. W. Griffith) as Annie Lee, and Frank Grandon as Philip Ray.

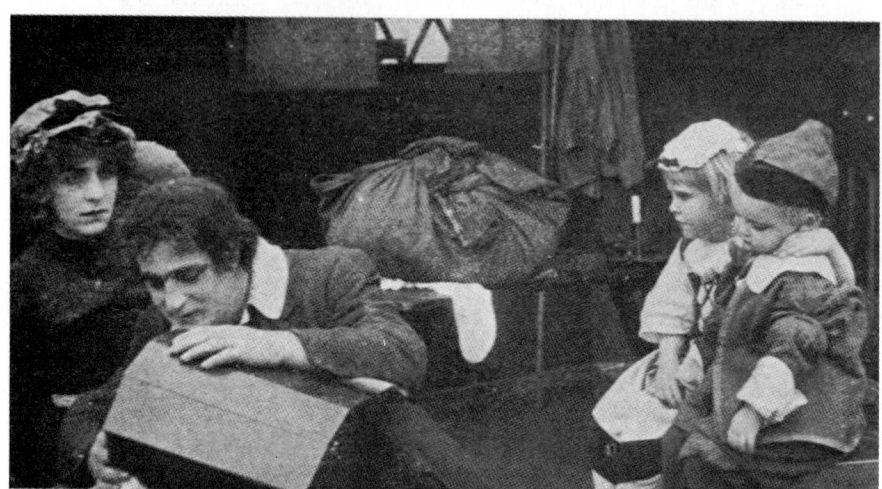

scenes in *A Knight of the Road*. But the real war against Griffith was conducted by *The Moving Picture World*. This began as early as 1909 but was at its height around the time of *The Sands of Dee*, when one Reverend Dr. Stockton, who must have been a busy pastor indeed, went to the nickelodeons, stopwatch in hand, to count the scenes and time them in comparison with those used by other producers! It appeared from this research that the actors were jumping jacks and that the director himself had been "bitten by the lightning bug"; his pictures were not "really drama"; though there was "lots of action," there was "no acting and no chance for any." For such writers, you could not have a harmonious whole if you cut off people's feet, and long shots and close-ups were equally out of order because "on the vaudeville and talking stage, figures of human beings do not expand or contract irrationally or eccentrically"! Edwin S. Porter was the *World* god, and only Edison and Rex films came up to their peculiar standards.[7]

Though it is entirely possible that at times Griffith's cinematic syntax may have got a little out of hand (especially when the operator was in a hurry and ran the film too rapidly), what these strictures really show (and the drama critic Burns Mantle echoed some of them, in a less blatant and more intelligent form, when he was reviewing films for *Photoplay* in the twenties) is that the writer does not understand or really like the cinema; for him a good picture is essentially a photographed play. This was not Griffith's view, even though for him there was no great gulf fixed between the film and the other arts; thus George Pratt has pointed out that the intercutting in *A Corner in Wheat* is straight out of Frank Norris.[8] Griffith was handicapped in Biograph days by the narrow time limits of the single reel format, which obliged him to omit or speed up many developments that might otherwise have been spelled out, and this necessarily sometimes encouraged frenetic tendencies. But if art consists in working within the limitations of your medium and cutting your coat to suit your cloth, he gives us much to admire even here. In *Oil and Water*, the subtitle "His Wife" provides a wholly adequate means of skipping over the courtship, which the film has no time to show and which, in any case, is not what the film is about.

(For this last reason, among others, Henry James, who had hundreds of pages at his disposal, had omitted the courtship of Isabel Archer in *The Portrait of a Lady*.) Again, in *Enoch Arden*, the shipwreck is indicated by a shot of Enoch and his comrades struggling in the water followed by a shot of their being cast upon the shore of the deserted island. The foundering ship we are not shown at all, which was obviously a convenience to the company's treasurer, but since *Enoch Arden* is a film about marriage, not sea disasters, there is, after all, no reason why we should see it. Art consists in what is omitted as well as in what is included; the sculptor cuts away the part of the marble that he doesn't want.

What he needed to do to achieve his purpose, Griffith generally managed to bring off, even in his one-reelers. In the handling of mass action, *A Temporary Truce*, *The Massacre*, and *The Battle at Elderbush Gulch* are about as good as anything he ever did, and we can see *The Birth of a Nation* about ready to turn the corner not only as early as *The Battle* but even earlier in *The House with Closed Shutters*. Despite Mary Pickford's fine performance, *Iola's Promise* is, in some ways, a comparatively primitive film, but the shots involving the wagon train are magnificent. And where in films will you find more masterly composition than in the sequence leading to the killing of the mountaineer by his mother in *The Mountaineer's Honor*?

The Massacre and *The Battle at Elderbush Gulch* have both been analyzed in some detail by my collaborator Anthony Slide (with the active cooperation of Paul O'Dell), in his *Early American Cinema*, from which I quote here at some length [9] in concluding this section.

The Massacre (1912) centres around Blanche, who, after rejecting the passively amorous advances of her guardian, John Bulstrode, explains to him that she is planning to marry Stephen Royston, a young soldier. Bulstrode, who is a retired officer, gives his consent, and decides to join the army once again, but this time as a scout.

The army stages a surprise attack on an Indian village, wiping out all but a handful of its inhabitants. The tribe's chief swears vengeance on the white man and his people.

Meanwhile Blanche and her husband (and, by this time, their baby) feel the urge to move West, and join a wagon train. Blanche's husband is called away from the train on business, and, while he is gone, the train is attacked by the revengeful Indians, who succeed in wiping out the entire party. But a scout manages to get word to the cavalry, who send a detachment to the train's aid. Blanche's husband hears of the attack, and rides off with the cavalry. They arrive to find the whole scene one of complete massacre; but from beneath the body of Bulstrode, killed while defending Blanche and her baby, there appears a

[7] See George Pratt's valuable article, "In the Nick of Time," in the Eastman House journal, *Image*, VI (1957), 52–59, and cf. pp. 90–104 in his *Spellbound in Darkness*. Robert Henderson, *D. W. Griffith: The Years at Biograph*, pp. 165 ff., lists twenty-five "contributions" claimed by Griffith himself or by others for him, though without himself supporting all these claims. Everyone interested in Griffith's technique should consult Kemp R. Niver's *D. W. Griffith: His Biograph Films in Perspective*, where fifty films in which Mr. Niver sees innovations introduced are studied and elaborately illustrated.
[8] *Spellbound in Darkness*, pp. 67–81.
[9] Pp. 128–35. Copyright © 1970 by Anthony Slide; quoted by permission of A. S. Barnes and Company and the Tantivy Press.

hand. . . . Blanche and her baby are safe, protected by the corpse of her former guardian

The closing sequences of *The Massacre* demand closer study simply because of the detail and visual approach to this very simple but extremely effective narrative. Using a device which he had employed many times before in previous films, Griffith gave the film a perspective, a visual depth which distinguished his work from that of his contemporaries. In the scenes in question, we are shown the action that takes place simultaneously in the foreground as well as the background. One complements the other both dramatically and visually, giving us a sense of the geography of the scene as well as serving to economise at the same time as expanding the narrative line. The first scene where this is found comes at the end of the cavalry's gratuitous attack on the Indian village, when the chief and the surviving braves mount the hill and look down on the burning remains of their homes. The chief in the foreground, with his back to the camera, swears revenge on the white man while we can plainly see the ruined village below, still smouldering, and the remains of a cavalry detachment continuing to ride back and forth in the background.

Probably the most impressive sequence in this film is one in which we see the wagon train—in extreme long shot—from the top of a hill overlooking a wide and flat plain. In the immediate foreground we see a prairie dog wander into the picture. A large bear ambles up the hillside toward the camera and frightens the dog away.

The scene shifts to the wagon train itself. We see Bulstrode riding up to Blanche's wagon, thus being reminded of her vulnerability, and that of her baby, while she is without the protection of her husband.

Again, the scene returns to the hilltop, where the bear is still sniffling around the foreground, while the wagon train can still be seen in the distance. Eventually the bear moves out of the picture. Immediately we see what appears to be a second bear; but then we realise that it is in fact an Indian disguised as a bear, spying on the wagon train below. The title, THE INDIANS SCENT THEIR PREY, follows this shot, and we are left with a precise and disturbing picture of the action that is inevitably to follow. This short sequence is so constructed as to communicate all the relevant details quickly and dramatically.

There are several other examples in this film of the "movement on two planes" idea which are worth mentioning while not being exactly akin to the two mentioned above. When the wagon train moves off into Indian territory, in one shot, the following displacement of action-within-the-frame can be recorded: two or more wagons at the beginning of the shot begin to move across the screen in the foreground from left to right, while behind them in the middle distance a line of soldiers march in the opposite direction, across the screen right to left. When the two wagons have gone out of the picture on the right, more wagons pass through the lines of soldiers, still marching across the picture, and lurch towards the camera.

Also, later in the film, the cavalry are seen racing to the besieged wagon train. In one particular shot, they ride furiously across the screen in the background from left to right, turn towards the camera just as they are about to disappear from the frame and ride towards us on the extreme right on the screen. When they reach the immediate foreground they turn abruptly out of the picture on the right. . . .

The story of *The Battle at Elderbush Gulch* concerns Sally (Mae Marsh) and her young sister, who are sent to visit [their uncle]. The trouble begins when the local Indian tribe cele-brates their Feast of the Dogs. Sally, who has brought with her two pet puppies, is told in no uncertain terms by [the ranch owner] that the dogs are to be kept outside the cabin. She therefore puts them, in their basket, outside the door. Before she decides to bring them out for the night, they manage to escape, and, as might be predicted, two passing Indians find them. Sally is beside herself finding them gone, and is even more distressed when she sees the two Indians about to murder both of them.

[Sally's uncle] arrives on the scene to find Sally struggling desperately with the two Indians. He shoots one of them dead, and when Sally runs to safety with her two dogs, the remaining Indian drags off the body of the dead comrade brave. Unluckily . . . the dead Indian is the chief's son. Thus a full-scale retaliatory attack is launched, precipitating one of the most, if not *the* most exciting and impressive, climaxes to be found in an AB.

The Battle at Elderbush Gulch is one of the most complex Biograph films. This is facilitated by the fact that it is in two reels, although Griffith had previously attempted similarly constructed films, with a main narrative supported by subsidiary threads of action, in several one-reel ABs (e.g. *Home Folks*). The main narrative line is that of Sally and the Camerons; but early on in the first reel we are introduced to Lillian Gish and Bobby Harron, portraying a young couple arriving at the town with their baby—and, as the title informs us, the town's first.

When the Indian attack on the town begins, Bobby has arrived for a short visit carrying the baby. Invited into the saloon for a quick drink, he gives the baby to a woman to hold. As the Indians surge through the streets, she in turn passes it to the nearest cowboy. He runs for shelter, and when Bobby runs from the saloon at the sound of gunfire, he is panic-stricken to find his baby nowhere to be seen. Just then he is struck by an Indian bullet, and staggers to the roadside before collapsing.

Meanwhile Lillian has taken refuge . . . in the cabin, Sally and her sister being confined to their sleeping quarters.

Already therefore the sub-plot has divided itself, with Lillian at the . . . encircled cabin, screaming hysterically for her baby; Bobby has been wounded, though we do not know how badly; the baby . . . has disappeared. . . .

Into these threads is now woven another: one man has volunteered to ride to the nearest cavalry outpost with the news of the attack, and throughout the fight that follows we are constantly reminded of his perilous ride.

. . . If the baby is not rescued, Lillian and Bobby are tragic figures and this is not Griffith's plan. If Bobby does not survive the same is true; if the help from the cavalry is not forthcoming, then the whole situation is negated. How the situation is resolved, and how . . . these sub-plots are . . . resolved, are shown with classic simplicity, so that the real complexity of the film is not immediately apparent, nor is that complexity ever allowed to result in incomprehensibility.

After the woman had thrust the baby into the cowboy's arms, he ran with his comrades to the . . . cabin, only to find it already under pressure from the Indians, [and he and others] take refuge in an out-house. . . . All this is, of course, unknown to Lillian who sits dazed in her grief in the cabin.

Sally tries to comfort Lillian, but without success. She suddenly remembers her dogs, who are now kept outside her sleeping-quarters and are hauled in through a specially constructed hatch. . . . She drags them in, and puts them into the bed with her young sister.

Meanwhile the Indians succeed in firing the out-house, and

the cowboys, including the one with Lillian's baby, are forced out into the open. He is shot and fatally wounded. A close-up shows the crying child still held in the cowboy's death-grip.

Sally, in her childish curiosity, looks out and sees by chance the baby with Lillian. She immediately connects the baby with Lillian, and without telling her determines to rescue it. She first urges her sister and the dogs into an old trunk for safety, before clambering out of the dog-hatch. Risking her life, she manages to reach the baby, and return to the cabin. She immediately climbs into the trunk with the child, without telling Lillian that her baby is safe.

Bobby, meanwhile, regains consciousness and stumbles out to the road. The volunteer has also succeeded in reaching the

cavalry and collapses from exhaustion as the detachment mount and ride off in the direction of the town.

The Indians soon have the cabin near submission, for the [besieged] have almost run out of ammunition. As the Indians are battering down the door, a close-up of Lillian shows the gun of an unseen cowboy behind her turned towards her head.

Bobby scrambles out of the path of the approaching cavalry and is picked up by one of the soldiers. They arrive at the . . . cabin in time to fight off the Indians and rescue the whole party within the cabin. Bobby runs in, and is greeted with joy by Lillian. The joy soon turns to distraught grief, however, when she realises that he no longer has the baby. As he tries to explain, the top of the trunk opens, and out pops Sally, her

Two

Biograph Re-issue
Number 8

THE BIOGRAPH

THE BATTLE AT

THE CAST

The waif.....................Mae Marsh
Her uncle.....................Alfred Paget
The ranch owner..........Charles H. Mailes
The young married couple..{ Lillian Gish
{ Robert Harron
{ Kate Bruce
Settlers.................{ W. Chrystie Miller

Directed by
D. W. GRIFFITH

TWO young girls from the East are journeying to make their home with an uncle in the still unsettled West. On the stage coach they fall in with a young married couple bound for the same destination. The entire population of Elderbush Gulch turns out to welcome the stage coach. The young couple and their baby are especial objects of attention. Arrived at their uncle's cabin, the girls reveal that they are not alone. Opening a basket, they produce two ragged little dogs which they have brought from home. The boss hates dogs and issues an ultimatum—" No dogs in my house." So the basket is placed outside the cabin door that night. The dogs escape and run into the arms of two Indians who, having returned late to their camp, have missed a great dog feast. The older girl, bent on smuggling the dogs into her bed, comes out, finds them gone, and, searching for them, encoun-

sister, the two dogs and . . . Lillian and Bobby's baby!

Thus this magnificent film ends, all is well, and even the [ranch owner] becomes fond of Sally and her wretched dogs—the cause of all the trouble—now that she has redeemed herself by this heroic rescue.

The way in which this film is photographed alone makes it of prime importance in Griffith's early work. There are many extremely impressive shots, with "the entire frame filled with sweeping arcs of action." At one point a high-angle shot shows the inhabitants of the town running across a wide flat plain pursued by Indians on horseback, falling from the shots of each other's guns. There are to be found the by-now familiar high-angle shots of the cabin with Indians on horseback circling it and firing on it, seen before in *The Massacre* and *Fighting Blood*. There is a superb sense of chaos as the Indians storm the town, with women and children running to and fro among the panic-stricken cowboys, firing hopelessly at the charging Indians.

The use of parallel action is put to use here with more effect and extraordinary dexterity than before, in part due to the film's elaborate construction. . . .

E. W.

NOTE: A complete list of D. W. Griffith's Biograph films, with their release dates, will be found in the Appendix.

THE BIOGRAPH   *Three*

ELDERBUSH GULCH IN TWO REELS

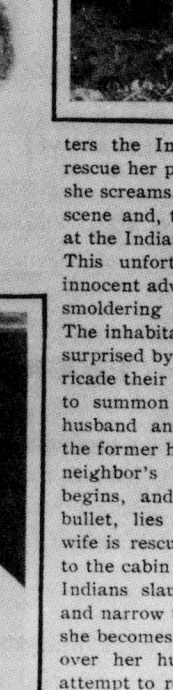

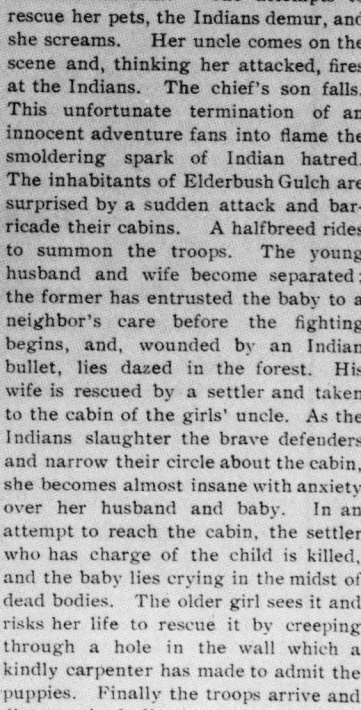

Unquestionably the greatest two reel picture ever produced

ters the Indians. She attempts to rescue her pets, the Indians demur, and she screams. Her uncle comes on the scene and, thinking her attacked, fires at the Indians. The chief's son falls. This unfortunate termination of an innocent adventure fans into flame the smoldering spark of Indian hatred. The inhabitants of Elderbush Gulch are surprised by a sudden attack and barricade their cabins. A halfbreed rides to summon the troops. The young husband and wife become separated; the former has entrusted the baby to a neighbor's care before the fighting begins, and, wounded by an Indian bullet, lies dazed in the forest. His wife is rescued by a settler and taken to the cabin of the girls' uncle. As the Indians slaughter the brave defenders and narrow their circle about the cabin, she becomes almost insane with anxiety over her husband and baby. In an attempt to reach the cabin, the settler who has charge of the child is killed, and the baby lies crying in the midst of dead bodies. The older girl sees it and risks her life to rescue it by creeping through a hole in the wall which a kindly carpenter has made to admit the puppies. Finally the troops arrive and disperse the Indians.

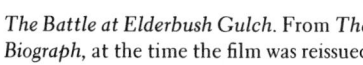

The Battle at Elderbush Gulch. From *The Biograph,* at the time the film was reissued

Wilfred Lucas and Mae Marsh in Griffith's ambitious attempt to probe caveman psychology, *Man's Genesis*, released July 11, 1912.

Blanche Sweet in *Oil and Water*, released February 6, 1913. The showgirl wife reverts to her old ways.

Scenes from *A Temporary Truce*, a neglected two-reel Western, released June 6, 1912.

Scenes from *A Tale of the Wilderness*, one of the few "lost" Biographs, released January 8, 1912, showing Dorothy Bernard and Edwin August.

2

JUDITH OF BETHULIA

SCENARIO: D. W. Griffith, based on the narrative poem "Judith and Holofernes" and the subsequent play, *Judith of Bethulia*, by Thomas Bailey Aldrich, which were based on the Book of Judith in the Old Testament Apocrypha

TITLES: Frank Woods

PHOTOGRAPHY: G. W. Bitzer

FILM EDITOR: James Smith

LENGTH: 4 reels

PRODUCTION/DISTRIBUTION: American Biograph

RELEASED: March 8, 1914

BLANCHE SWEET (*Judith*)

HENRY B. WALTHALL (*Holofernes*)

MAE MARSH (*Naomi*)

ROBERT HARRON (*Nathan*)

LILLIAN GISH (*the young mother*)

DOROTHY GISH (*the crippled beggar*)

KATE BRUCE (*Judith's maid*)

G. JIGUEL LANOE (*the eunuch, attendant on Holofernes*)

HARRY CAREY (*a traitor*)

W. CHRYSTIE MILLER

GERTRUDE ROBINSON

CHARLES HILL MAILES

EDDIE DILLON

(Lionel Barrymore, Marshall Neilan, and Antonio Moreno are often credited with appearances in *Judith of Bethulia*, but Blanche Sweet points out that they were not with the Biograph Company when the film was made.)

THE STORY

The city of Bethulia, in the hill country of Judea, whose walls are fifty cubits thick, guards the approaches to Jerusalem. Here, among others, dwells Judith, the rich widow of Manasses, noted for her piety and honored by her people.

The city's water is drawn from a well outside the wall, and one day the well is captured by troops under the command of Holofernes, "the Bull of Assur," a captain of the great Nabuchodonosor, whom the story regards as an Assyrian, though the actual Nebuchadrezzar was King of Babylonia; this is a mistake which goes clear back to the Apocrypha. Some of the Jews are killed, and Naomi, beloved of Nathan, is carried off, but the enemy fails to achieve entrance into the city. By day and by night, the army of Assur storms the walls, but they are beaten off, and Holofernes finally settles down in his tent, where he

devotes himself to "Bacchanalian festivities" and the infliction of cruel punishments, including crucifixion, upon such of his followers as have shown the white feather, and waits for famine of food and water to force Bethulia to surrender.

Judith's agony of spirit is accentuated by the trust the people have in her and their looking toward her for succor. Finally she conceives an idea which she regards as an inspiration from the Lord. After a period of agonizing prayer in sackcloth and ashes, she attires herself like a courtesan and, attended by her handmaid, goes to Holofernes' camp, where she promises to betray Bethulia to him. Completely captivated, he gives her the freedom of the camp, surrounds her with luxury, and finally begs her to come to Nineveh with him when the campaign is over.

Judith is now attracted by Holofernes; he "seems noble in her eyes." But she "wrestles with her heart" and remains loyal to her people. Having begged and won the boon of serving as his exclusive handmaid for a night, she makes him drunk and cuts off his head.

This she and her handmaid take to Bethulia just as the endurance of the Jews is reaching the breaking point. The "captains of Assur" are "as men bereft" by the death of their commander, and the utterly demoralized army flees. Nathan saves Naomi from death by fire in the tent where she has been tied up by her captors, and Judith is hailed as the savior of her city.

Judith (Blanche Sweet) and Holofernes (Henry B. Walthall), with his attendant (G. Jiguel Lanoe)

Judith and her attendant (Kate Bruce) in the camp of Holofernes

Bethulia under siege

Naomi (Mae Marsh) in captivity

CRITICISM

"A fascinating work of high artistry" was the phrase Louis Reeves Harrison, in *The Moving Picture World* of March 7, 1914, used to describe *Judith of Bethulia*, Griffith's first feature-length production, and the film that many consider the director's rehearsal for *The Birth of a Nation* and *Intolerance*. Contemporary reviewers were awed by its majesty. *Variety* (March 27, 1914) wrote: "It is not easy to confess one's self unequal to a given task, but to pen an adequate description of the Biograph's production of *Judith of Bethulia* is, to say the least, a full grown man's job." Audiences today are equally perplexed by *Judith of Bethulia*, not because of its splendor, but because it is hard to appreciate its initial impact.

Certainly, prints available today do not do it justice, but that is a minor matter. What now makes *Judith* seem so dated is that styles—particularly styles of acting—have changed so much. The acting in the film is almost classical in nature; we who have been nurtured on the relaxed nonacting of today's stars fail to appreciate these performances of sixty years ago. So much has changed; it is all too easy to snigger.

Yet Blanche Sweet's performance as Judith, to all those who will take the time to study it, is stunning. In many scenes the camera remains steadfastly upon her face. She appears to do nothing, hardly a facial muscle stirs, and yet she tells her audience everything. Two scenes that vividly demonstrate this are those when "did Judith wrestle with her heart, for Holofernes now seemed noble in her eyes" and when she tries to cast away "the sinful passion" of her love for the invader. In both scenes the actress uses few gestures. When she pulls out all stops, as in the sackcloth and ashes sequence, and the camera shows a close-up of her anguished face, then all attempts at analysis and study are useless. The mental anguish her face registers is overwhelming. It is hard to believe that the actress one is watching is only seventeen years old.

One other actress stands out. Mae Marsh, although seen in only a few brief scenes, gives a strong indication of the acting greatness she was to achieve in *Intolerance*. Robert Harron, however, is badly miscast; his gestures are all too reminiscent of a brash American youth, and he even sports a twentieth-century moustache.

The battle scenes in *Judith* are, perhaps, the biggest disappointment. The staging is quite frankly a mess, and there is every sign of a small group of people desperately pretending to be a crowd. It is this initial disappointment which makes an audience today overlook Griffith's technique, in particular his skillful editing. This is best exemplified by his superb use of crosscutting in the scene in which the Assyrians ambush some of Bethulia's townspeople as they attempt to get water from the well.

It is interesting to note that Griffith was unable completely to get away from the conventions of the theater. Immediately after the title identifying Prince Holofernes, the viewer is shown two bushes, which part, like a stage curtain, to reveal Henry B. Walthall, completely unrecognizable behind his beard, as Holofernes at the head of his army.

D. W. Griffith shot *Judith of Bethulia* in California in the summer of 1913, after completing *The Battle at Elderbush Gulch*. Release of both films in America, together with the two-reelers *The Massacre* and *Brute Force*, was delayed by the Biograph Company, unsure of audience reaction, until 1914, although all were released in Europe within months of their completion.

In February of 1917, the Biograph Company released, on a states'-rights basis, *Her Condoned Sin*, which was *Judith of Bethulia* lengthened to six reels. According to *The Moving Picture World* (January 3, 1917), "New subtitles have been given the whole production. These are unusual in their artistry. Over dark atmospheric backgrounds, selected from the negative, subtitles have been imposed. The effect is stunning. Out of regard for the opinions of exhibitors, many of whom had complained that *Judith of Bethulia* as a title lacked those psychological qualities of appeal for which showmen as a class have such a keen sense, the enlarged production is released under the name of *Her Condoned Sin*."

A.S.

BLANCHE SWEET ON *JUDITH OF BETHULIA*

D. W. Griffith was in a transition period, growing in scope and importance. At seventeen I had reached an emotional capacity.

Henry Walthall had a more mature acting ability, but Holofernes was a stalwart warrior and Walthall was not a tall man. Griffith did not debate the point long. "Don't worry. Wally will play him tall."

Judith of Bethulia, a great tragedy, told in verse and play form, was waiting to be transferred to film by Billy Bitzer's inventive photography, never before so lustrous.

Our fair sized company of actors would all participate, some even playing two and three parts, beards and distance concealing identity. But the Company that had the final word was the Company that paid the company of actors. American Biograph produced and released to exhibitors.

As I remember, Griffith's clarion call for a $50,000 production caused many a fainting spell in the front office. A $50,000 tragedy! Unheard of! Never been done!

Crazy! Griffith was to be called that many times over in the years to come. He was also called innovator! Great! Genius!

With cast and company's adrenalin coursing we started the interiors of Holofernes' camp in the studio at Pico and Georgia Streets, Los Angeles, while the exteriors were built at Chatsworth, San Fernando Valley. The high walls and massive gate of the beleaguered starving city. Only a few years later Griffith would build higher ones, but the Chatsworth walls were as Babel.

Before dawn we took a train—company, crew, and extras—to where long wagons and four horse teams waited, and Judith-to-be hopped up on a front seat, driving to and from location each day. We were ready by sunup for work. It has been told truly that Judith of the bare body, simple shift and little else had a many-splendored bruise on her thigh, for I followed the action on a horse, riding sort of side saddle, with one leg necessarily thrown over the Western saddle pommel.

Mae Marsh and Robert Harron as the young lovers by the well, Dorothy Gish as the girl at the wall, Lillian Gish as the young mother with her baby, the old people in the street within, soldiers manning the walls—all these were Judith's people to be cared for and to sacrifice for.

The sun beating down and dust in our mouths, we finished the battle scenes and left the West for the East.

The year before Biograph had started building a new studio in the Bronx for Griffith to expand in, according to his ideas. Sundays we had clambered over the half-finished construction, dreaming, planning things to be, teetering over and through beams and joists, barely avoiding broken legs or necks. *Judith* was in the talk stage then.

In 1913 we moved into the new studio to film the interiors of Judith's house. During one sequence Nance O'Neil arrived. A famous stage tragedienne, she had played Judith, and I believe Griffith had acted with her in some other play. He came to me and whispered, "Show her." So, with Billy quietly cranking and Griffith close by, Judith knelt before the close angled camera and played the sackcloth and ashes scenes for all the world and a great director. *Judith* was the first, last, and only motion picture Griffith ever made at the studio he had dreamed up.

In 1965 I did an NBC Special about New York-made films at the very same studio, and I pointed to the shadowy corner of that big stage where it seemed I could hear Griffith whispering and the camera cranking.

—Reprinted by permission from *The Silent Picture*, No. 5 (Winter 1970).

3

THE BATTLE OF THE SEXES (1914)

Based on *The Single Standard* by Daniel Carson Goodman

PHOTOGRAPHY: G. W. Bitzer

FILM EDITORS: James Smith and Rose Richtel

LENGTH: 5 reels

PRODUCTION: Reliance-Majestic

DISTRIBUTION: Mutual/The Continental Feature Film Company

NEW YORK PREMIÈRE: April 12, 1914

RELEASED: April 12, 1914

LILLIAN GISH (*Jane Andrews*)

OWEN MOORE (*Frank Andrews*)

MARY ALDEN (*Mrs. Frank Andrews*)

FAY TINCHER (*Cleo, the siren*)

ROBERT HARRON (*the son*)

DONALD CRISP

THE STORY

Frank Andrews, a prosperous businessman, is living happily with his wife and a grown son and daughter when he is captivated by a "siren." The husband is swept completely off his feet, and the effect on his wife is so disastrous that the daughter determines to kill the "other woman."

Armed with a revolver, she goes to the siren's apartment, but instead of killing her, she herself is captivated by the woman's sweetheart. Arriving opportunely, the father is shocked, and the shock brings him to his senses. "You, my daughter—what are you doing here?" She replies, "My father, what are you doing here?" The question brings the father to his senses; he now realizes that he himself must live by the same code he expects his daughter to live by, and they leave the apartment together.

CRITICISM

Griffith filmed Daniel Carson Goodman's *The Single Standard* twice, first in 1914 as his initial production away from Biograph, and again in 1928. The latter has survived intact, but all that remains of the first version is a short extract in the collection of George Eastman House. Both films were equally trashy, the one made as a quickie to finance the newly reorganized Reliance-Majestic Company, the other in a desperate attempt by Griffith to achieve a box-office success.

The 1914 version was almost entirely shot in a tiny loft converted into a studio at 29 Union Square. G. W. ("Billy") Bitzer, now under a three-year personal contract as Griffith's cameraman, remembered: "There was an-

other cradle of the movies, but a slum one compared to the more pretentious 14th Street Studio." Here Griffith gathered together his principal players, and shot *The Battle of the Sexes* quickly for under $5,000 (Miss Gish remembers the time as five days).

Although the film is lost, a clear intimation of the content of *The Battle of the Sexes* may be found in the following comment from the *New York Dramatic Mirror* of April 15, 1914, which has for us today the added interest of illustrating the semiliterate style all too common in trade journals of bygone days.

The play consists of a prologue and four other reels. The first marvel that strikes home, after the play is finished, is how could

D. W. Griffith directing *The Battle of the Sexes*. Lillian and Dorothy Gish are shown in the center, Donald Crisp and Robert Harron third and fourth from right.

he see that there were five reels of action. For the plot, the old social triangle does not seem to invite any great length of treatment. Besides that, there are only three principal sets used. There is in all scenes a richness and evenness of lighting that established the relation of the different sets in the same house. The sets were lavish, but, above all, they were true to the higher social sphere. There were besides a hall and the two parlors of the opposite apartments, only a section of *thé dansant* and several of the bedrooms in the apartments. That was all the setting. They were used innumerable times, but hardly noticeably. The reels under the skillful hand seemed to glide along smoothly and imperceptibly, needing no explanations except where it was thought best to heighten the effect of some strong scene. Its meaning "got across" without effort. Every scene meant something in the vital development of the narrative. The interpretation of the ... cast was, on the part of the mother, the daughter, the other woman and the son, an eventful piece of artistic work. It is hard to tell just how much the director had to do with their presentation, but to whomever belongs the credit, let it be given. The outcome was as fine, as delicate, as emotional, as finished a series of interpretations as will be the privilege to witness [sic].

It was originally intended to release the production as *The Single Standard*—indeed, it was so billed at its première at New York's Weber's Theatre—but, for obvious reasons, *The Battle of the Sexes* was considered a better box-office draw. The moral message of the film held any threats of censorship of the title at bay. As *Variety* (April 17, 1914) pointed out, "*The Battle of the Sexes* is a fine, big object lesson. It may patch up many a broken home, and no doubt will be blessed by thousands of women throughout the country, for it's going to punch both ways, the woman who errs and the woman who suffers, besides telling fathers to stay at home, even if the attraction is further away than across the hall."

Quickly and cheaply produced, and well received by critics and public alike, D. W. Griffith's first independent production, *The Battle of the Sexes*, augured well for the future.

A. S.

Lillian Gish as Jane Andrews; Owen Moore as her father; Fay Tincher as the siren

A publicity photograph of Lillian Gish, dating from her Mutual period

4
THE ESCAPE

Based on the play by Paul Armstrong

PHOTOGRAPHY: G. W. Bitzer

FILM EDITORS: James Smith and Rose Richtel

LENGTH: 7 reels

PRODUCTION: Reliance-Majestic

DISTRIBUTION: Mutual

NEW YORK PREMIÈRE: Cort Theater, June 1, 1914

RELEASE DATE UNKNOWN

BLANCHE SWEET (*May Joyce*)

MAE MARSH (*Jennie Joyce*)

ROBERT HARRON (*Larry Joyce*)

DONALD CRISP (*"Bull" McGee*)

OWEN MOORE (*Dr. von Eiden*)

F. A. TURNER (*Jim Joyce*)

RALPH LEWIS (*the senator*)

"TAMMANY" YOUNG (*McGee's henchman*)

THE STORY

A prologue shows how carefully nature guards the reproduction of microbes. From the lowest forms of animal life, we work upward, and are shown the care that goes into the breeding of pigs and racehorses. From the orderly racing stables, the viewer is taken to a dancing party where mating is governed by impulse. When the boy asks, "Give me your daughter," the father queries, "Can you support her?" When the response is yes, boy gets girl without any consideration as to whether the boy is mentally or physically sound.

Two sisters, May and Jennie Joyce, are introduced. May, the prettier and stronger of the two, is attracted to "Bull" McGee, a bully, but she escapes from tenement life on the advice of Dr. von Eiden, a surgeon, who visits the tenement to dress a gash on the forehead of May's brother, Larry, which had been inflicted by their father, and which transforms him from a normal boy to a cruel sadist.

Consumptive Jennie, who is envious of her sister's good looks, is fascinated by Bull, and they are married. A year later a baby is born. While Jennie is out buying medicine, Bull arrives home drunk and stumbles over the crib, crushing the life out of the puny child. Jennie substitutes a wax doll for her dead baby.

Nor are things going well for May. Penniless and with no prospect of finding work, she becomes the mistress of a wealthy man, who after a time offers to marry her. But whatever else May lacks, she has a deep sense of the responsibility about bringing children into the world. She leaves the man and tries to bring some cheer into the life of her sister. Bull now plans to sell his wife to a dance hall. He delivers her into the hands of a gang of thieves and procurers, from whom she is rescued only to die in her sister's arms. An operation restores Larry to kindly sanity, and we leave May ready to marry the doctor, who, throughout the film, has been her wisest counselor.

CRITICISM

The first Reliance-Majestic feature, on which D. W. Griffith began production, in December 1913, was *The Escape*, based on the play by Paul Armstrong, which dealt with the now repugnant, but then popular, subject of eugenics. However, it was not bad breeding that resulted in halting production on *The Escape*, but rather Blanche

Sweet's falling ill with scarlet fever, apparently contracted from some dirty, secondhand clothing that she was required to wear in her role as May Joyce.

While Blanche was recovering, the director shot *The Battle of the Sexes* in New York, and then took the company out to California, where his leading lady joined him to complete *The Escape.* This originated the doubtful, but nonetheless amusing, story that Robert Harron, as Larry Joyce, opened a door in one scene of the film in New York, and that when he came through it he was in California.

Although *The Escape* is a lost film, it is not difficult to piece its content together from contemporary reviews. After a scientifically inclined prologue, designed to demonstrate how carefully nature guards the reproduction of microbes "in contrast to the procreatic carelessness of humans," the story of misery and poverty in a tenement house and life in the underworld gets underway.

The Escape, from all accounts, was a thoroughly unpleasant production. It had Robert Harron as a cruel sneak wringing the neck of a kitten, and Donald Crisp stomping his baby to death and selling his wife, played by Mae Marsh, to a gang of thieves and procurers. And over the entire plot loomed the deplorable suggestion that those of a sick mind or body be denied the right to marry and raise children.

However, the story appealed to Griffith, possibly because of its having been a successful stage play. Harry E. Aitken, the financial head of Reliance-Majestic and its distribution arm, Mutual, was also pleased with the drama. He wrote Griffith, on April 15, 1914: "I expect to put out *The Escape* with more publicity in magazines and newspapers than perhaps any film has ever had."

The publicity notwithstanding, *The Escape* did not gain nationwide praise. If the film were available for appraisal today, I suspect most viewers would agree with *Variety* critic Sime, who wrote on June 5, 1914: "You wouldn't know just what to call *The Escape*—and it's just as well not to call it—let it sleep, as they say in vaudeville. . . . The Mutual or Mr. Griffith or both are foolish, one would say, to waste the ability and energy of an able director of the Griffith stamp upon a scenario like *The Escape.*"

A. S.

Mae Marsh as Jennie Joyce

Owen Moore, Robert Harron, Blanche Sweet

Ralph Lewis, with Blanche Sweet

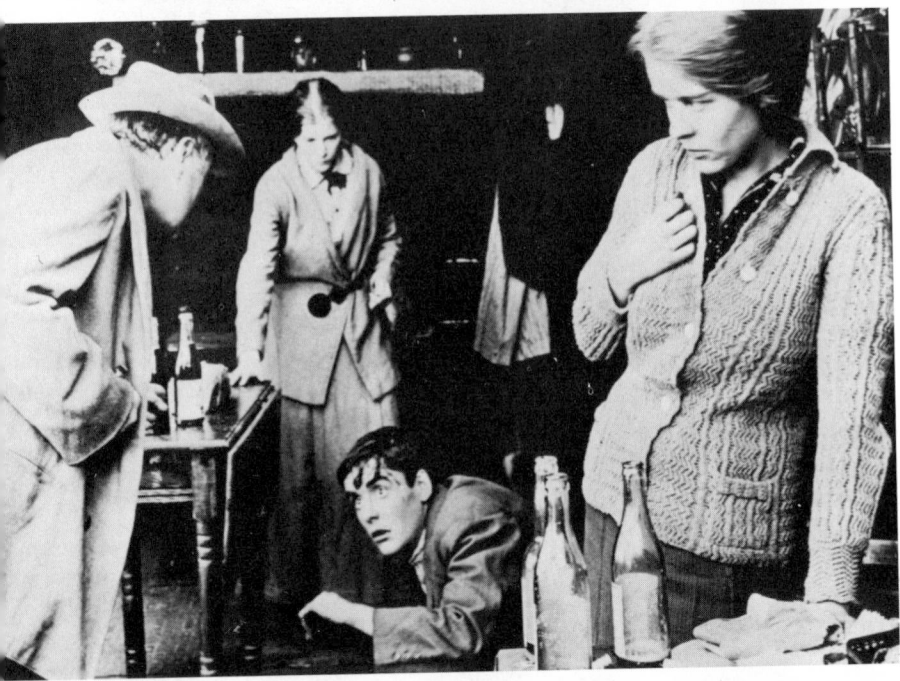

5

HOME, SWEET HOME

SCENARIO: H. E. Aitken and D. W. Griffith

PHOTOGRAPHY: G. W. Bitzer

FILM EDITORS: James Smith and Rose Richtel

LENGTH: 6 reels

PRODUCTION: Reliance-Majestic

DISTRIBUTION: Mutual

LOS ANGELES PREMIÈRE: Clune's Auditorium, May 4, 1914

NEW YORK PREMIÈRE: May 17, 1914

RELEASE DATE UNKNOWN

Prologue and Epilogue

HENRY B. WALTHALL (*John Howard Payne*)

JOSEPHINE CROWELL (*his mother*)

LILLIAN GISH (*his sweetheart*)

DOROTHY GISH (*his sister*)

FAY TINCHER (*the worldly woman*)

The First Story

MAE MARSH (*Apple Pie Mary*)

SPOTTISWOODE AITKEN (*her father*)

ROBERT HARRON (*the Easterner*)

MIRIAM COOPER (*his fiancée*)

The Second Story

MARY ALDEN (*the mother*)

DONALD CRISP, JAMES KIRKWOOD, and JACK PICKFORD (*her sons*)

FRED BURNS (*the sheriff*)

The Third Story

COURTENAY FOOTE (*the husband*)

BLANCHE SWEET (*the wife*)

OWEN MOORE (*the tempter*)

EDWARD DILLON (*the musician*)

BETTY MARSH (*the baby*)

Also appearing in *Home, Sweet Home* were W. H. Long, John Dillon, Earl Foxe, Teddy Sampson, F. A. Turner, W. E. Lawrence, George Siegmann, Ralph Lewis, Irene Hunt, and Howard Gaye.

THE STORY

At the beginning of the film, John Howard Payne is seen in his youth, deeply loved by his mother and his sweetheart, both of whom are grieved by his wildness and irresponsibility. He leaves home to go on the stage, where he meets success but becomes dissipated. In England he becomes well known as both actor and playwright; in France he writes the song "Home, Sweet Home." Disappointed in love, he dies, miserable and alone, in Africa.

From here we proceed to the story of "Apple Pie Mary," a lunch counter girl in a Western mining camp. She falls in love with, and is loved by, a young Easterner, who

leaves her to return East to his fashionable life, but is drawn back to her as his true love by the sounds of "Home, Sweet Home," as played by an itinerant musician on an accordion.

The next episode concerns fratricidal strife and hatred between two sons of a widowed mother. They quarrel fiercely and both are killed. The bitterness and despair that results almost costs the life of the mother also, but she is recalled to life and reconciled to it by hearing "Home, Sweet Home."

The third story, "The Marriage of Roses and Lilies," deals with a young wife's temptation to be unfaithful to her husband. This time the song which reawakens her better nature is played by a great musician on the floor below.

The purpose of these episodes is to show that, in spite of the errors of Payne's life, he created something which remained behind him in the world as a force for good in the lives of human beings. His mother in heaven is comforted by this thought. We see Payne suffering in a place of punishment, from which he is drawn out and up to union in heaven with his mother and sweetheart, while his song continues its blessed ministry on earth.

Above: Mae Marsh with Robert Harron as the Easterner

Above right: Mae Marsh as Apple Pie Mary

Right: Miriam Cooper as the Easterner's sweetheart

Opposite page:

Top: Henry B. Walthall as John Howard Payne

Far left: Walthall as Payne, Lillian Gish as his sweetheart, Josephine Crowell as his mother

Left: Lillian Gish as the dead sweetheart

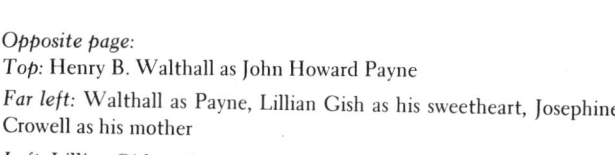

Donald Crisp and James Kirkwood as the fratricidal brothers, with Jack Pickford (between them) as "the Dull Boy"

Blanche Sweet and Courtenay Foote, with their children

CRITICISM

"This will be the first great all-star production for the film and will show more effectively than anything else I can imagine the size and strength of Mr. Griffith's great company in Los Angeles." Thus declared Harry E. Aitken of *Home, Sweet Home* in March of 1914.

Not only did *Home, Sweet Home* feature more Griffith players—Griffith never referred to them as stars, and neither did they so regard themselves—than any film before, but it also might be considered a natural forerunner to *Intolerance*, with its three separate stories, even though such stories were not intercut as in the later production.

The three stories are framed by a prologue and epilogue depicting the life, death, and afterlife of John Howard Payne, the author of the lyrics but not the music—a point that the film does not make clear—of the popular song "Home, Sweet Home." It should also be pointed out that Payne's life was in no way so tragic as Griffith's film implies; when he died he was American consul in Tunis,

and most certainly not living in abject poverty. The John Howard Payne sequences are to *Home, Sweet Home* what Lillian Gish rocking the cradle is to *Intolerance*. Interestingly, Griffith uses the device of a window rising in the foreground as Payne (Henry B. Walthall) and his mother (Josephine Crowell) are first glimpsed, almost like a stage curtain.

One can well understand why the sentiment of "Home, Sweet Home" should have appealed to Griffith, a man whose marriage to Linda Arvidson had long since broken up, who had no real home, and who was fighting adversity to create a work of film art and a production in whose outlook he vehemently believed, *The Birth of a Nation*. Remembering his many fine films, let us hope and pray that, when Griffith came to meet his God, like Payne, "for countless services like these shall not his faults be forgiven."

The three stories in *Home, Sweet Home* differ considerably as to interest and effect. Undoubtedly, the weakest of the three is the second, featuring a mother (Mary Alden) and her three sons (Donald Crisp, James Kirkwood, and Jack Pickford). It is silly, overly melo-dramatic, and totally unconvincing. As *Variety* (May 22, 1914) noted, "This episode was a bit far-fetched."

The third story, featuring Blanche Sweet and Owen Moore, and subtitled "The Marriage of Roses and Lilies," has a fair amount of charm, but requires little of its leading players, and, as the *New York Dramatic Mirror* (May 20, 1914) commented, is "a trifle disappointing in its obviousness."

The highlight of *Home, Sweet Home* is the first story, "Apple Pie Mary," and the credit for much of the success of this episode must be given to Robert Harron and Mae Marsh. As far back as the Biograph *The Sands of Dee*, it was obvious what a fine dramatic acting pair they were, but, here, in *Home, Sweet Home*, they were given the opportunity to play light comedy, and like everything else they did, they did it superbly. There is a totally charming scene in which the two part, and try to find mementos to give each other. Mae Marsh proudly tells Harron, "I got no picture to give you but this Christmas Card looks like me," while Harron announces, "You can keep my glasses." When he returns, his first glimpse of Mae shows her wearing those same glasses, and what a timid, scared mouse they make of her!

Louis Reeves Harrison wrote of Mae Marsh in *The Moving Picture World* (May 30, 1914): "The first episode offered a delightful comedy relief and gave opportunity to one of the best comediennes ever seen in photodrama,

Mae Marsh as 'Apple Pie Mary.' She fascinated the audience as completely as if she had been before them in person, the thousands present laughing at her delicately conveyed mental processes. She has the art of picturing thought to a degree that argues her own intensity and intelligent grasp of all she is required to convey, going even beyond that into spontaneous delineations of her own."

Interestingly, prior to the first screening of *Home, Sweet Home*, this sequence had been released, on April 18, 1914, as a separate story, titled *Apple Pie Mary*, but with a slightly different plot line. Instead of returning to marry Mae Marsh, Harron (here called Burford Dane) marries Miriam Cooper, and only visits Mae again on her deathbed, when she forgives him "with a sad smile playing about her lips and dies with his baby playing at her bedside."

Where *Home, Sweet Home* really falls down is in its final sequence in which John Howard Payne rises from the pit of evil, fighting Master Carnality, Master Brutality, and Master Worldly, to reach his sweetheart in the clouds of Heaven. It is all rather ludicrous today, but at the time it was accepted and acceptable. The *New York Dramatic Mirror* (May 20, 1914) commented: "The producer braves an ignoble fate in this part, the step from the sublime to the ridiculous being so easy to take, but by using every resource of the camera in presenting some wonderful cloud effects and angelic hosts, gives us a fitting climax to a photoplay unusual."

A. S.

6

THE AVENGING CONSCIENCE

SCENARIO: D. W. Griffith, suggested by "The Tell-Tale Heart" and other works by Edgar Allan Poe

PHOTOGRAPHY: G. W. Bitzer

FILM EDITORS: James Smith and Rose Richtel

LENGTH: 6 reels

PRODUCTION: Reliance-Majestic

DISTRIBUTION: Mutual Film Corporation

NEW YORK PREMIÈRE: The Strand Theatre, August 2, 1914

RELEASED: August 2, 1914

HENRY B. WALTHALL (*the nephew*)
BLANCHE SWEET (*his sweetheart*)
JOSEPHINE CROWELL (*her mother*)
SPOTTISWOODE AITKEN (*the uncle*)
GEORGE SIEGMANN (*the Italian*)
RALPH LEWIS (*the detective*)
MAE MARSH (*maid at the garden party*)
ROBERT HARRON (*the grocer's boy*)

THE STORY

The hero of the film has been brought up by an uncle who expects him to become a great writer and resents any interference with his work. The most serious threat comes from a girl whom the young man calls Annabel after Poe's Annabel Lee. When the girl comes to the house, the uncle brutally insults her and accuses her of running after his boy like a common wanton. This brings the situation to a head, and the young people agree to give each other up, though both are very unhappy about it, and the young man worries himself into a morbid state of mind. Watching spiders, ants, etc., he begins to think of nature as a great murder machine and conceives the idea of himself killing the uncle who stands in the way of his happiness.

He concocts what seems to him a foolproof plot, enticing his uncle away on a fake errand from which he returns unperceived by the townsfolk. Upon his return, the nephew chokes him to death and hides his body in the fireplace wall, "each brick so cunningly replaced that no human eye can detect the fraud." Then he diligently inquires for him among the neighbors, but nobody has seen him since he left on his errand. Unfortunately, however, a disreputable Italian has witnessed the murder through the window (him the nephew must begin to pay blackmail as soon as he has come into his inheritance), and

one suspicious soul interests a detective in the uncle's disappearance.

Meanwhile the young man, tortured by guilt, begins seeing his uncle's ghost, has visions of heaven and hell and of the tables of the Law, with the stress on "Thou Shalt Not Kill," and exhibits all the signs of derangement. Enlisting the Italian as an ally, he prepares a refuge for himself in a cabin, with an underground passage to permit his escape. When the detective comes to question him, he has a fit of hysterics. He retreats to his cabin, but the forces of the law converge upon it, and when he attempts to leave it, he finds that his enemies have been there before him and that the trapdoor has been fastened. Hereupon he hangs himself, but the law breaks in before he has strangled and cuts him down. Meanwhile Annabel, in despair, throws herself over a cliff. Then he wakes up.

When his uncle walks into the room alive, he is overjoyed, and they are wholly reconciled. Annabel, who comes to tell him that she loves him and will marry him even if he is disinherited, arrives opportunely and is included in the reconciliation. The last scene shows the honeymooners in a scene suggestive of the way Griffith ended both *The Birth of a Nation* and *Intolerance*. This time Pan plays his pipe and friendly animals and half-naked children come out of the woods.

The uncle (Spottiswoode Aitken) orders his nephew's sweetheart (Blanche Sweet) from the house.

The nephew (Henry Walthall) and the Italian (George Siegmann)

Walthall and Aitken, with Ralph Lewis as the detective

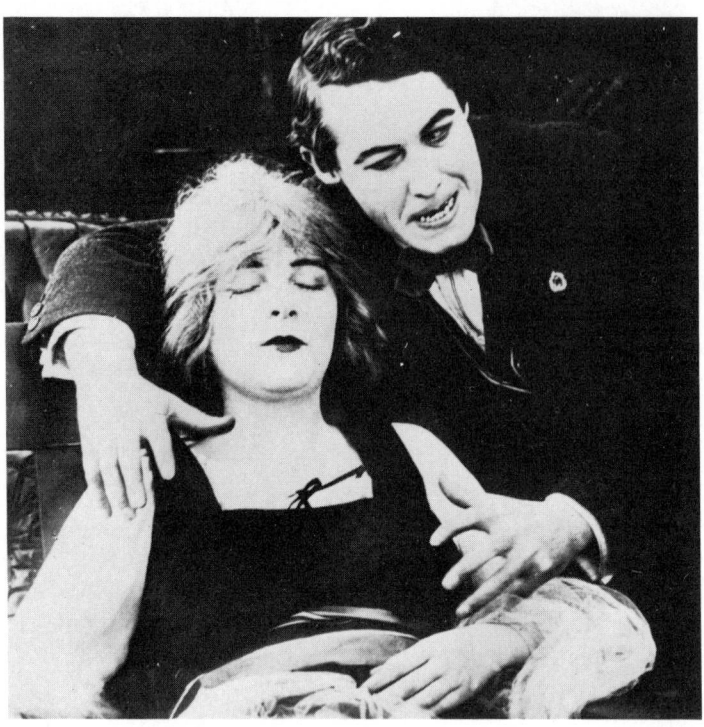

CRITICISM

The Avenging Conscience is by all means the oddest of all D. W. Griffith's feature films. On the one hand, it is a psychological thriller which anticipated such German films of the 1920s as Arthur Robison's *Warning Shadows*; on the other, many passages are as awkwardly done as anything one might find in the pseudo-sophistication manifested in some circles of "advanced" picture making today.

There is an immense amount of going and coming throughout, on the part of nearly all the characters, and in the first part they wander about at some length at an outdoor party being held in the beautiful gardens of a great estate, which has nothing to do with the story and which, one suspects, must have been included because Griffith had access to the estate and embraced the opportunity to put it on the screen. In addition to the guests, Mae Marsh, as a waitress, and Robert Harron, as a butcher's boy, wander into the film at this point and then wander out again. When the detective and the Italian are introduced, subtitles warn us that we shall see them again and that they will have something to do with the story. But the blackmailing accomplishes nothing, and the succeeding alliance between the nephew and the blackmailer is incredible. The ghost is well managed, but the visions, while no doubt involving much ingenious camera manipulation, are not particularly impressive. Nor are the numerous literary quotations in the captions often apropos. The nephew's reading Poe's "The Tell-Tale Heart" is relevant since it prepares for the crime he dreams he commits, but the quotations from "Annabel Lee," etc. seem forced.

These are heavy debits, but there are entries on the credit side. Though one may have some difficulty in explaining how it is achieved, the film does have a brooding intensity, creating a sense of impending doom which is impressive, and this reaches a climax in the second half, which is better unified than the first. But for the student of Griffith's work, perhaps the most interesting thing about *The Avenging Conscience* is the way a psychological pursuit is here substituted for the physical chase so often associated with his films. It is true that the latter element does not altogether drop out. The detective's myrmidons surround the cabin much as the Indians circled about others in *The Battle at Elderbush Gulch* and other films, but this does not last long and not much is made of it. Essentially the pressure which the detective brings to bear upon the nephew is mental, which is certainly appropriate to a film much of whose story exists only in the mind. With proper musical accompaniment, the scene in which the two men sit together, with the nephew clenching his hands, the detective's foot and pencil tapping, and the pendulum of the clock swinging would be nerve-racking even today, and that quite without reference to the violence and supposed supernaturalism which appear at its climax.

E.W.

Sincerely,
Blanche Sweet.

Sincerely Yours
Henry B. Walthall

7

THE BIRTH OF A NATION

SCENARIO: D. W. Griffith and Frank E. Woods, based on Thomas Dixon's novel and play *The Clansman*

PHOTOGRAPHY: G. W. Bitzer

ASSISTANT CAMERAMAN: Karl Brown

FILM EDITOR: James Smith

MUSIC ARRANGED BY: Joseph Carl Breil and D. W. Griffith

COSTUMES: Robert Goldstein

LENGTH: 12 reels

PRODUCTION/DISTRIBUTION: Epoch Producing Corporation

RIVERSIDE (CALIFORNIA) PREVIEW (AS *The Clansman*): The Loring Opera House, January 1, 1915

LOS ANGELES PREMIÈRE: (AS *The Clansman*): Clune's Auditorium, February 8, 1915

NEW YORK PREMIÈRE: (AS *The Birth of a Nation*: Liberty Theatre, March 3, 1915. Released on a road-show basis. (Reissued in 1930 in a shortened version with a sound-track consisting of music and sound effects)

LILLIAN GISH (*Elsie Stoneman*)

MAE MARSH (*Flora Cameron, the Little Sister*)

HENRY B. WALTHALL (*Colonel Ben Cameron, the Little Colonel*)

MIRIAM COOPER (*Margaret Cameron*)

MARY ALDEN (*Lydia Brown, Stoneman's mulatto housekeeper*)

RALPH LEWIS (*the Hon. Austin Stoneman, Leader of the House*)

GEORGE SIEGMANN (*Silas Lynch*)

WALTER LONG (*Gus, a Renegade Negro*)

ROBERT HARRON (*Tod Stoneman, also as two Negro soldiers*)

WALLACE REID (*Jeff the blacksmith*)

JOSEPH HENABERY (*Abraham Lincoln*)

ELMER CLIFTON (*Phil Stoneman*)

JOSEPHINE CROWELL (*Mrs. Cameron*)

SPOTTISWOODE AITKEN (*Dr. Cameron*)

GEORGE (ANDRE) BERANGER (*Wade Cameron*)

MAXFIELD STANLEY (*Duke Cameron*) [1]

JENNIE LEE (*the faithful mammy*)

DONALD CRISP (*General U. S. Grant*)

HOWARD GAYE (*General Robert E. Lee*)

SAM DE GRASSE (*Senator Charles Sumner*)

RAOUL WALSH (*John Wilkes Booth*)

EUGENE PALLETTE (*a fallen foe to whom Ben Cameron gives succor*)

ELMO LINCOLN, OLGA GREY, WILLIAM DE VAULL, TOM WILSON

(Bessie Love is often credited as having played in *The Birth of a Nation*, and there is indeed an actress who looks much like her, playing one of the townspeople who stare from the windows at the Negroes rioting in the streets, but Miss Love denies having been in the production. Director John Ford claims to have been one of the Ku Klux Klansmen.)

(An unauthorized three-reel condensation, titled *In the Clutches of the Ku Klux Klan*, was released early in 1916, and a lawsuit followed. In February 1918, Victor Kremer released, on a states'-rights basis, *The Black Boomerang* as an answer to *The Birth of a Nation*.)

[1] In some lists the actor who played this role is called John French.

THE STORY

After brief opening shots dealing with the introduction of slavery into this country and the controversies later occasioned by it, *The Birth of a Nation* introduces a Northern family, the Stonemans, and a Southern, the Camerons. The Stoneman family consists of Austin Stoneman, "Master of Congress" (obviously suggested by Thaddeus Stevens, whom the film regards as the chief agent of Southern woes during Reconstruction), his daughter Elsie, and two sons, Phil and Tod. Instead of a mother there is a mulatto housekeeper, who is obviously ambitious and who, it is strongly suggested, is or becomes Stoneman's mistress. In the Cameron household are father and mother, their son Ben, his two sisters, Margaret and Flora, and two younger sons, Wade and Duke. Ben Cameron and Phil Stoneman have had previous acquaintance, and the first real incident of the film is the visit of the Stoneman boys to Ben's home in Piedmont, South Carolina, where Phil and Margaret Cameron fall in love and Tod and Duke become "chums." Ben too falls in love with Elsie Stoneman's picture, which he snatches from Phil and refuses to return, carrying it with him thenceforward everywhere, even when he goes to war.

During the visit to Piedmont, the imminence of civil war is rumored, and once it has been concluded, the film moves toward the beginning of hostilities. The Cameron and the Stoneman boys are soon in uniform. With nobody at home but Dr. Cameron and the women, Piedmont is raided by guerrillas: Confederate troops arrive barely in time to drive them off, and the Cameron home is nearly burned.

Tod Stoneman and both the younger Cameron boys die in the war, Tod being shot down in the moment of an encounter with Duke on the battlefield. "The torch of war" is applied to "the breast of Atlanta." Sherman marches to the sea. Confederate troops have a few grains of parched corn as their daily ration. In the last days of the war, Ben Cameron, now "the Little Colonel," leads a heroic charge against a Union trench, commanded over by Phil Stoneman, where he rams the Stars and Bars into the mouth of a cannon. Stoneman recognizes him and drags him wounded into the trench.

Ben is sent to a military hospital where Elsie Stoneman is a nurse and soon succeeds in winning her affection. When his mother comes North to see him, Elsie takes her to see Lincoln, who pardons Ben, unjustly under sentence of death as a guerrilla. The young Stonemans are present in Ford's Theater the night Lincoln is assassinated. By this time Ben has returned to his nearly ruined home, and he and his family, as representative of the Southern people, have bravely gone to work to repair the ravages of the war. But they are greatly discouraged when the news of Lincoln's death arrives. "Our best friend is gone," says Dr. Cameron. "What will become of us now?"

Lincoln had rejected Stoneman's plea for vengeance upon the "rebels." "I shall treat them," he declared, "as if they had never been away." But his death changes the situation, and Stoneman and his allies proceed relentlessly to "put the White South under the heel of the Black South." Whites are disfranchised; illiterate Negroes dominate the South Carolina legislature; outrages are committed and criminals acquitted by black juries. Stoneman goes South with Elsie and Phil, makes Piedmont his headquarters, and engineers the election as Lieutenant Governor of a conscienceless mulatto, one Silas Lynch, who is loyal neither to him nor to the Negro race but only to his own advancement and aggrandizement. Stoneman, blind to the man's true character, swears to make Lynch, as the symbol of his race, the equal of any white man alive.

Brokenhearted over the Southern anguish, Ben Cameron sees some white children frighten Negro children on the beach by putting sheets over their heads and pretending to be ghosts; thus he conceives the idea of the Ku Klux Klan, "to protect the Southern country." Lynch lusts after Elsie Stoneman, whom he aspires to marry, not only because he desires her but because such a marriage would be the crowning sign of his advancement. The younger Cameron girl, little Flora, has also been unfortunate enough to attract the attention of a renegade Negro, Gus, and one day, when she injudiciously goes alone to the spring for water, he confronts and pursues her: to escape him she jumps from a cliff and is killed, but not before, dying in her brother's arms, she has named her assailant. Though Lynch's minions had "scored first blood" against the Klan, Klansmen now move in on Gus, who had hidden in a gin mill, slay him after a "trial" full of mumbo jumbo, and deposit his body on Lynch's doorstep.

The situation has now become very tense indeed, and various instances of conflict between the races are shown. Elsie, though still in love with Ben, has been estranged from him by the discovery that he is a Klansman. Dr. Cameron is arrested when Klan costumes are found in his house, but is rescued by his faithful servants (ex-slaves), with the help of Phil Stoneman, who kills a Negro in the process. With Phil, all the Camerons take refuge in a cabin inhabited by two Union veterans and the little daughter of one of them. Elsie, who has accidentally witnessed the shooting, goes to Lynch, in her father's absence from Piedmont, to beg a pardon for her brother, and now, for the first time, learns Lynch's intentions toward her. When she scorns him, he turns vicious and detains her forcibly. Stoneman, returning, is all for intermarriage in theory, but when it turns out to be his own daughter who is involved, his attitude changes. Elsie's screams are overheard not only by her father, now himself held captive, but also by some disguised Klan spies, who notify their comrades, and the Klansmen ride to the rescue not only of Elsie and Stoneman but also of the Camerons, besieged in the little cabin. This is the climax

a

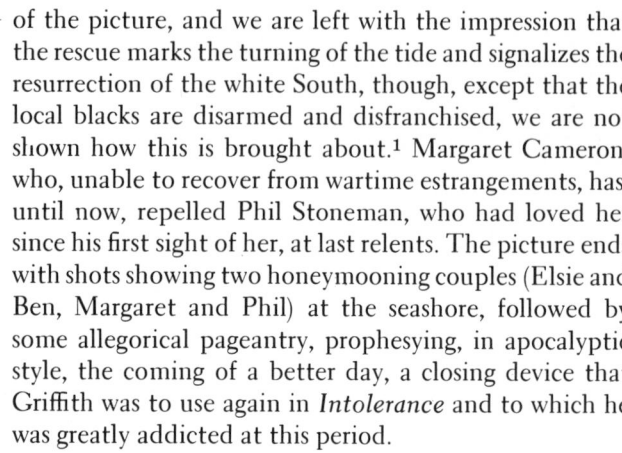

of the picture, and we are left with the impression that the rescue marks the turning of the tide and signalizes the resurrection of the white South, though, except that the local blacks are disarmed and disfranchised, we are not shown how this is brought about.[1] Margaret Cameron, who, unable to recover from wartime estrangements, has, until now, repelled Phil Stoneman, who had loved her since his first sight of her, at last relents. The picture ends with shots showing two honeymooning couples (Elsie and Ben, Margaret and Phil) at the seashore, followed by some allegorical pageantry, prophesying, in apocalyptic style, the coming of a better day, a closing device that Griffith was to use again in *Intolerance* and to which he was greatly addicted at this period.

[1] There is, however, apparently reliable testimony that, as it was originally shown, the film's vision of the future included the promise of wholesale deportation of American blacks, a kind of development of the "colonization" schemes favored by early American abolitionists. This is known to have been Thomas Dixon's solution for the "Negro problem," and he insisted that it was also Lincoln's. The present writer saw *The Birth of a Nation* in 1915 and has no recollection of any such scene, but he might of course have forgotten it. We know that a good many scenes were cut in response to criticism and/or censorship demands, and this may very well have been one of them. The modern Ku Klux Klan is reported to own a print of *The Birth of a Nation* containing the deportation scene, but they apparently prefer not to answer inquiries about it.

Lillian Gish as Elsie Stoneman (*a*) ready for a journey and (*b*) facing the menace of Silas Lynch

b

Mae Marsh as the Little Sister

Miriam Cooper as Margaret Cameron

Howard Gaye as Robert E. Lee

Raoul Walsh as the assassin John Wilkes Booth

The first shot in *The Birth of a Nation*, depicting the introduction of African slaves into America

An idealized picture of life on the old plantation.
In the center: Ben Cameron (Henry Walthall),
Margaret Cameron (Miriam Cooper), and Phil
Stoneman (Elmer Clifton).

Ben Cameron leaves Piedmont for the war.

Dr. and Mrs. Cameron (Spottiswoode Aitken and Josephine Crowell) waiting for the Klansmen to rescue them from the beleaguered cabin at the end of the film

Henry Walthall and Lillian Gish as the Little Colonel and Elsie.

CRITICISM

The Birth of a Nation was an aesthetic achievement, a monument, and a cultural and sociological phenomenon; there is no other film of which such a statement can be made with equal truth and force. When René Clair said that "nothing essential has been added to the art of the motion picture since Griffith," he was stating a simple truth, but he would have made almost as good sense if he had said "since *The Birth of a Nation*."

There had been good pictures before, many more of them than the average "cinemaphile," perhaps even more than the average (dreadfully average) critic of today, has even begun to realize. Griffith himself had made more of them than any other man, but he had established no monopoly of them. All over the land there were people of all ages, hundreds of thousands of them, who, for some years now, had loved the movies as hardly anybody loves them today, and for whom they had created a world derived from, yet distinct from, this material world we inhabit—a world through which they might enlarge and

intensify their everyday experiences by entering, almost at will, as human beings had long been finding enrichment in the kindred superimposed worlds of music, literature, and the plastic arts. But though there were some honorable exceptions among them (intelligent, penetrating people, lovers of life, with a capacity to judge that which came before them by a direct, intuitive apprehension of its essential being, instead of merely trotting out stock responses in blind obedience to the labels they encountered), generally speaking this company was composed of unsophisticated, comparatively uncultivated people, who were content to enjoy with no special capacity for analyzing their enjoyment or establishing critical categories. In 1915, in other words, the notion that the motion picture was a serious, respectworthy art form, perhaps *the* characteristic art form of our time—not only a new way of telling a story but a new way of responding to life itself—had not occurred to many. There had been a foretaste of what was to come in one aspect in the form of a few ambitious spectacles, mostly of Italian origin—notably *Quo Vadis?* and *Cabiria*—but though these films might overwhelm by their magnitude, this was about as far as they went. *Cabiria*'s strong man, Maciste, was about the only *person* anybody remembered from any of them. They did not seize upon the emotions or concern themselves with matters that were vital to twentieth-century American audiences; neither did they awaken controversy.

The Birth of a Nation was different. It brought the motion picture out of the nickelodeons, which it had hitherto largely though not exclusively inhabited, into the "legitimate" theater, where it was presented at the "legitimate" level of prices and seen by a great many people who had hitherto known very little about films. Composed of an aggregation or a conglomerate of all the cinematic devices which a vital and developing art had been devising over the years, it flung them into the faces of thousands who had not hitherto known of their existence. It concerned itself with the great crisis of American history, then only fifty years behind us (many of the people who saw *The Birth of a Nation* in 1915 were the children or grandchildren of men who had died in the Civil War), and it tied this up with matters which were still of social concern. Pulsating with a vitality which still thrills more than half a century afterwards, it was crowded with characters whom one loved and hated. As it compelled distinguished men and women to take a stand for or against it, it became impossible to deny its power or that of the medium it represented. Certainly it was not the first film to raise problems, but until now the enemies of the motion pictures had generally concerned themselves with the effect which they, or the places in which they were shown, might have on immature minds. Children might see something they ought not to see. Their belligerent impulses might be stimulated. Or, pleasure itself being still seriously suspect under the Puritan work ethic, moviegoing might lead to idleness and an unwholesome desire for stimulation. None of these worries was altogether irrational; there were cases in which all these undesirable results were obtained. But *The Birth of a Nation* went beyond all this. Here was a film with an idea. With it the motion picture became a weapon in the battle for men's minds, and the attacks on it made this particular specimen of it a gambit in the struggle for freedom of thought and expression.

Nobody but a fool has ever questioned the greatness of *The Birth of a Nation* as cinema. Technically Griffith does here almost everything that can be done in pictures, and while it is true that the average spectator cares nothing about technique as such, it is also true that he is powerfully affected by it, and that it conditions and creates the things for which he does care. A. R. Fulton speaks of the film's "masks, vignettes, split screens, and other devices" and describes how Griffith "not only cuts shots before they are ended but also juxtaposes long, medium, and close shots—thus obtaining variety in the spatial length of the shots," at the same time varying their "temporal length." Someday we shall have books that contain complete scene-by-scene descriptions of both *The Birth of a Nation* and *Intolerance*, with at least one sample frame from each shot; in the meantime we must make out as best we can with such analyses as Theodore Huff's of the assassination of Lincoln scene and of Lynch's final encounter with Elsie Stoneman.[1] The enemies of the film have always shown the most arrant Philistinism imaginable in their complete indifference to its quality as a work of art. But art does not exist in a vacuum. It was made for and by man, not man for it. Therefore it is quite as shortsighted to pretend that its social and sociological aspects are of no importance. This film inspired riots and near-riots from the time it was first shown, and there are many communities where no one would dare exhibit it publicly today. Nothing could be sillier than to pretend that it is pure chance that this has happened with *The Birth of a Nation* rather than with *The Gold Rush* or *Civilization* or *Tess of the Storm Country*.

The literary foundation of *The Birth of a Nation* (it seems a sacrilege to use the word "literary" in this connection) must be sought in the novel and play *The Clansman*, by the notorious Negro-hating clergyman, Thomas Dixon.[2] Nobody outside the Ku Klux Klan could take Dixon seriously today (that much progress at least we have made). In his time he had more reputation, and the reader of early reviews of *The Birth of a Nation* is startled when he often finds the picture spoken of as Dixon's film, with no mention made of Griffith! It was called *The Clansman* during its initial run at Clune's Auditorium in Los Angeles, but it was *The Birth of a Nation* from the time it opened in New York, though the story that Dixon suggested the great title spontaneously while watching a showing unreel, on the ground that *The Clansman* was not a big enough title for so great a film, may be apocryphal. Russell Merritt cites an advertisement in the Los Angeles *Times*, February 9, 1915, in which it is called "The Clansman—or—THE BIRTH OF A NATION," but a Clune's program dated September 19 still calls it only *The Clansman*, more than six months

---

[1] See Fulton, *Motion Pictures*, pp. 91–97; Lewis Jacobs, *The Rise of the American Film*, pp. 180–85.

[2] The program claimed, and it has been commonly believed, that Griffith took additional material from another novel of Dixon's, *The Leopard's Spots*. In his excellent article, "Dixon, Griffith, and the Southern Legend," *Cinema Journal*, Vol. XII, No. 1 (1972), 26–45, Russell Merritt denies this; everything in *The Birth of a Nation* that seems to come from *The Leopard's Spots* had already appeared, Merritt contends, in the dramatic version of *The Clansman*. I have made no independent investigation of this point.

after the New York opening. Though born in North Carolina, Dixon was not an unreconstructed Confederate. Instead he was a passionate admirer of both Webster and Lincoln; in 1920, in a play called *A Man of the People*, he was to glorify Lincoln as "the savior, if not the real creator, of the American Union of free Democratic States." This is exactly the point of view of *The Birth of a Nation*, foreshadowed in *The Clansman* (the novel) at the point where we are told of Elsie Stoneman that "she began to understand why the war, which had seemed to her a wicked, cruel and causeless rebellion, was the one inevitable thing in our growth from a loose group of sovereign States to a United Nation." To the end of his days, however, Dixon remained an unabashed racist of the deepest dye. As he saw it, American civilization was a white civilization, and the Negro could not be assimilated into it. The nation could not survive half white and half black.

When Griffith was attacked for alleged racism in *The Birth of a Nation*, he seemed both surprised and hurt, and there is considerable evidence to support the view that he was sincere in this. Certainly he has nowhere committed himself to Dixon's extremist views. In *The Greatest Thing in Life* he was to have Robert Harron kiss his dying black "buddy" in the trenches, so that the boy might, in his delirium, suppose himself dying in his mother's arms, and in *The White Rose* it is a Negro family that succors Mae Marsh in her distress. In *The Birth of a Nation* itself he insists that the film is not meant to reflect on any race or people of today. There are good Negroes as well as bad in the film; the real villains are white, and Griffith goes to some pains to show that even the worst of the blacks have been misled by unscrupulous whites for their own advantage. In the interview with Walter Huston which was filmed as a Prologue to the 1930 reissue of *The Birth of a Nation* with sound, but apparently never used for that purpose, Griffith described how his mother sat up nights during Reconstruction days, sewing costumes for the Klan, as the Camerons do in *The Birth of a Nation*, and he added, "The Klan was necessary *in those days*." The clear implication seemed to be that its modern revival was not necessary. A careful comparison between the film and Dixon's own writings will show better than any words of mine could how different Griffith's spirit was from Dixon's. In *The Leopard's Spots* the character who had caused the death of Flora is *burned alive!* [3]

This is not of course equivalent to saying that there is no justification for criticizing *The Birth of a Nation* on the racist score. Griffith may have "loved" Negroes, and I am sure he meant just what he said when he told Lillian Gish that since the Civil War they had advanced at a more rapid rate than any other race in recorded history, covering in decades the ground that it had taken white men centuries to traverse. But for all his goodwill, he was still an old-time Southerner, whose memories went back to post-Reconstruction days, and he could no more have avoided this than he could alter the basic tastes in literature and drama that had been formed in the same environment. It is Negroes who keep their "place" and make no trouble for the whites who are praised in *The Birth of a Nation*. The intelligent spectator understands that even the worst of the blacks in the picture behave as they might be expected to behave in view of their conditioning, not because they are Negroes but because they have been exploited and underprivileged human beings, and Griffith, who understood the importance of conditioning, must have been quite aware of this. But he must also have known that not all his audiences were going to be intelligent.

In view of all the circumstances involved, I would suggest that his insistence that he had created an historical spectacle probably deserves to be taken at something closer to face value than is generally done. The Civil War and Reconstruction periods involved deep passions and profound cleavages. Confronting all the difficulties involved in putting them on the screen, Griffith might of course have decided that the subject was "too hot to handle" and therefore let it alone. But if he were going to make a picture about it, he would have to tell "the truth," as he saw it; he would have to establish a point of view. The view that he chose was the Southern view, modified by the pro-Lincoln, pro-Unionist outlook that he and Thomas Dixon shared. Only, actually, he did not choose it but was chosen by it; no other view would have been possible for him.

He approached the production, as James Agee so finely said, with "absolute passion, pity, courage, and honesty." Was it "the truth"? If this means the whole truth, of course it was not. Human eyes perceive truth only in flashes. This applies even to "scientific" historians, who are never less scientific than when they forget it, but it applies even more to creative artists. Agee went on to compare *The Birth of a Nation* to Brady's photographs (on which its Civil War scenes were modeled), Lincoln's speeches, and Whitman's poems, and these do not embrace the whole truth either. The film "seems to me," he says, "to be a perfect realization of a collective dream of what the Civil War was like, as veterans might remember

[3] For further consideration of this matter, see Wagenknecht, *The Movies in the Age of Innocence*, pp. 103–4.

it fifty years later, or as children, fifty years later, might imagine it." And that, I suspect, is exactly what a great film ought to be.

Only of course it is not the war portion of *The Birth of a Nation* that has occasioned controversy. If the film had been confined to Part I, ending with the assassination of Lincoln, it would never have got into trouble, and there have always been those who insisted that a great masterpiece was marred when *The Birth of a Nation* went into its second half. Incidentally, Part I is almost pure Griffith, with little or no Dixon in it. Merritt, to be sure, insists that the historical tableaux are essentially Dixon, but Griffith does show his affinity to this type of presentation in other films. The battle scenes have never been surpassed, but they were produced cannily, out of considerations of economy, with far fewer participants than the spectator supposes he sees, and they play a smaller role in the film than their great fame might lead one to expect. Moreover the purpose of their portrayal is "that war might be held in abhorrence." One caption reads: "*War* claims its *bitter, useless* sacrifice." Another—"War's peace"—precedes a shot of corpses on the battlefield. And the original program carried a note:

Armies seldom settle disputed questions of state. But where they accomplish this much, in the wake of conflict arise newer and more terrible questions. But for the hatred engendered in the Civil War, the sufferings of the Reconstruction period would never have been known.

The war and the Reconstruction were clearly linked, then, in Griffith's mind, and different as Part II is from Part I, they fuse into an impressive whole in the spectator's viewing experience; sacrificing one section to the other is a perilous business. Whatever one may think of the real Klan, the Klansmen do furnish superb movie material, and Griffith's crosscutting, building up to a tremendous climax, is seen at its best in the final sequences.

It would not be quite correct to say that *all* the characters are vivid to us (I think we never see the younger Cameron sons very clearly), but I quite agree with Gilbert Seldes that "the second half of the picture is filled with a kind of idyllic poetry," in spite of its melodrama, and that "the whole countryside is peopled with characters who come to life no matter how briefly we see them." There is no arguing about Henry Walthall as "the Little Colonel," Lillian Gish as Elsie Stoneman, or Mae Marsh as the Little Sister, but Miriam Cooper, though the perfect physical type for Margaret Cameron, is handicapped by the iron reserve she is forced to maintain through the whole second half, and I think Elmer Clifton as her lover

makes less of an impression than Robert Harron as his younger brother, though the latter dies early in the film. It may sound sadistic to say that the scenes leading up to the death of the Little Sister partake of the "idyllic poetry" which Seldes refers to, but I think they do, and this is due not only to Mae Marsh's charm and the marvelous rightness of her acting but quite as much to the sensitive use Griffith makes of natural beauty in this sequence, thus softening what might easily have been an almost unbearable effect. It is a tribute too to Griffith's humanity, as well as to Walter Long's acting skill that, terrible though Gus's role is, we cannot avoid feeling some pity for him as he skulks, fear-stricken, in the gin mill and writhes at last in the clutches of his inimical captors. When the picture was first released, there was criticism, especially in the South, of the casting of Josephine Crowell as Mrs. Cameron because, it was said, she did not look like a Southern lady. Mrs. Crowell was not perhaps the perfect image of how the Southern lady thought she ought to look, but her acting was both skillful and deeply felt, and one sympathizes with her very deeply in the successive woes that are rained upon her.

E. W.

When *The Birth of a Nation* was in its heyday, the title of the film, printed as shown here, appeared on the billboards and in the newspapers of every city where the film was shown.

8

INTOLERANCE

SCENARIO: D. W. Griffith

PHOTOGRAPHY: G. W. Bitzer

ASSISTANT CAMERAMAN: Karl Brown

FILM EDITORS: James and Rose Smith

MUSIC: D. W. Griffith and Joseph Carl Breil

IN CHARGE OF SET CONSTRUCTION: Frank ("Huck") Wortman

PROPERTY MASTER: Ralph DeLacey

ASSISTANT DIRECTORS: Arthur Berthelon, Allan Dwan, Erich von Stroheim, W. Christy Cabanne, Tod Browning, Jack Conway, George Nicholls, and Lloyd Ingraham

LENGTH: 14 reels

PRODUCTION/DISTRIBUTION: Wark Producing Corporation

RIVERSIDE (CALIFORNIA) PREVIEW: The Loring Opera House, August 6, 1916

NEW YORK PREMIÈRE: Liberty Theatre, September 5, 1916. Released on a road-show basis

Of All Ages
LILLIAN GISH (*the Woman Who Rocks the Cradle*)

The Modern Story
MAE MARSH (*the Dear One*)

FRED TURNER (*her father*)

ROBERT HARRON (*the Boy*)

SAM DE GRASSE (*Arthur Jenkins*)

VERA LEWIS (*Mary T. Jenkins*)

MARY ALDEN, PEARL ELMORE, LUCILLE BROWN, LURAY HUNTLEY, and MRS. ARTHUR MACKLEY (*the "Uplifters"*)

MIRIAM COOPER (*the Friendless One*)

WALTER LONG (*the Musketeer of the Slums*)

TULLY MARSHALL (*a friend of the Musketeer*)

TOM WILSON (*the kindly policeman*)

RALPH LEWIS (*the Governor*)

LLOYD INGRAHAM (*the Judge*)

BARNEY BERNARD (*attorney for the Boy*)

REV. A. W. McCLURE (*Father Farley*)

MAX DAVIDSON (*the kindly neighbor*)

MONTE BLUE (*a striker*)

MARGUERITE MARSH (*a guest at the ball*)

JENNIE LEE (*woman at dance of Jenkins's employees*)

TOD BROWNING (*owner of the racing car*)

EDWARD DILLON (*the chief detective*)

CLYDE HOPKINS (*Jenkins's secretary*)

WILLIAM BROWN (*the warden*)

ALBERTA LEE (*the wife of the kindly neighbor*)

The Judaean Story
HOWARD GAYE (*the Christ*)

LILLIAN LANGDON (*Mary, the mother*)

OLGA GREY (*Mary Magdalene*)

GUNTHER VON RITZAU and ERICH VON STROHEIM (*Pharisees*)

BESSIE LOVE (*the bride of Cana*)

GEORGE WALSH (*the bridegroom*)

The French Story
MARGERY WILSON (*Brown Eyes*)

EUGENE PALLETTE (*Prosper Latour*)

SPOTTISWOODE AITKEN (*Brown Eyes's father*)

RUTH HANDFORTH (*Brown Eyes's mother*)

A. D. SEARS (*the mercenary*)

FRANK BENNETT (*Charles IX*)

MAXFIELD STANLEY (*Monsieur La France, Duc d'Anjou*)

JOSEPHINE CROWELL (*Catherine de Médicis*)

GEORGIA PEARCE [i.e., CONSTANCE TALMADGE] (*Marguerite de Valois*)

N. E. LAWRENCE (*Henry of Navarre*)

JOSEPH HENABERY (*Admiral Coligny*)

MORRIS LEVY (*Duc de Guise*)

HOWARD GAYE (*Cardinal Lorraine*)

LOUIS ROMAINE (*a Catholic priest*)

The Babylonian Story
CONSTANCE TALMADGE *(the Mountain Girl)*

ELMER CLIFTON *(the Rhapsode)*

ALFRED PAGET *(Belshazzar)*

SEENA OWEN *(Attarea, the Princess Beloved)*

CARL STOCKDALE *(King Nabonidus)*

TULLY MARSHALL *(High Priest of Bel)*

GEORGE SIEGMANN *(Cyrus the Persian)*

ELMO LINCOL *(the mighty man of valor)*

GEORGE FAWCETT *(a Babylonian judge)*

KATE BRUCE *(a Babylonian mother)*

LOYOLA O'CONNOR *(Attarea's slave)*

JAMES CURLEY *(the charioteer of Cyrus)*

HOWARD SCOTT *(a Babylonian dandy)*

ALMA RUBENS, RUTH DARLING, and MARGARET MOONEY
  (girls of the marriage market)

MILDRED HARRIS and PAULINE STARKE *(favorites of the harem)*

WINIFRED WESTOVER *(the favorite of Egibi)*

GRACE WILSON *(the first dancer of Tammuz)*

LOTTA CLIFTON *(the second dancer of Tammuz)*

AH SINGH *(the first priest of Nergel)*

RANJI SINGH *(the second priest of Nergel)*

ED BURNS *(the charioteer of the priest of Bel)*

JAMES BURNS *(the second charioteer of the priest of Bel)*

MARTIN LANDRY *(auctioneer)*

WALLACE REID *(a boy killed in the fighting)*

CHARLES EAGLE EYE *(barbarian chieftain)*

WILLIAM DARK CLOUD *(Ethiopian chieftain)*

CHARLES VAN CORTLANDT *(Gobyras, lieutenant of Cyrus)*

JACK COSGROVE *(chief eunuch)*

(Sir Herbert Beerbohm Tree, Douglas Fairbanks, Owen Moore, and Frank Campeau have been named as extras in *Intolerance*. The authors of this book cannot vouch for this, but E. W. has often wondered whether Tree might not be the Pharisee who drops the stone at "Let him that is without sin among you" in the Judaean story. This man is an actor of authority, whoever he may be, and he looks a little like Tree in his Fagin makeup. Ruth St. Denis is generally credited as having been the solo dancer in *Intolerance*, but shortly before her death she vehemently denied this. Colleen Moore is also often credited with a bit part in the production, but this is totally incorrect.)

THE STORY

*I*ntolerance is a "film fugue," comprising four separate, interwoven stories, unified by their common concern with the theme of man's inhumanity to man. The Babylonian story deals with the fall of Babylon to the Persian conqueror Cyrus the Great in 538 B.C. The Judaean story treats the life of Christ. The French story centers on the Massacre of St. Bartholomew's Day in Paris, August 23-24, 1572. The modern story is set in an American mill town and the slum area of an American city.

The Judaean and French stories are comparatively undeveloped. The first presents only three episodes in the life of Christ: the miracle at Cana, the incident of Christ's mercy toward the woman taken in adultery (both related only in the Fourth Gospel), and the Crucifixion. The intolerance of the Pharisees toward Jesus is stressed throughout.

In the French story, Catherine de Médicis and her allies are pitted against the Huguenot (Protestant) party, headed by Admiral Coligny. Both sides are intolerant, but it is Catherine who takes the lead in pestering her reluctant son, King Charles IX, into signing the order for the massacre. There is a brief glimpse of the wedding proces-

sion of Catherine's daughter, Marguerite de Valois, whose union with Henry of Navarre was supposed to aid in establishing peace between the two groups, but nothing is made of this dramatically, and the story centers on a Huguenot family—father, mother, and two daughters—and Prosper Latour, the accepted lover of the elder daughter, Brown Eyes. On the eve of the wedding, all these persons perish in the massacre.

Nabonidus, King of Babylon, who is more interested in archaeology than in government, and his son Prince Belshazzar, lover of the Princess Beloved, are kindly people, living in happiness and splendor in Babylon and opposing any kind of religious persecution. Belshazzar is adored from afar by the Mountain Girl, of violent temper and generous heart, herself loved by the Rhapsode, in the service of the High Priest of Bel, who, not sharing Belshazzar's live-and-let-live tendencies, opposes the introduction of the worship of Ishtar into Babylon and conspires with Cyrus to turn the city over to him.

The first attack by the Persians is repelled after a terrific battle on the walls (the great gate of Imgur-Bel cannot be forced), but Cyrus returns while the Babylonians are still rejoicing in their victory. This time the treacherous priests have opened the gates from within, the city is taken, and both Belshazzar and the Princess commit suicide to avoid capture. This does not happen, however, without the Mountain Girl's having been apprised of the danger through her contacts with the Rhapsode. Stealing a chariot, she drives to Cyrus' camp, where her fears are confirmed, and then races the Persian army back to Babylon. She arrives in time to give the warning but not early enough to effect the closing of the gates. In the ensuing fighting, she is killed.

In the modern story, Jenkins, a wealthy millowner, pours large sums of money into the Jenkins Foundation, which is supposed to benefit the poor but actually only gives a company of self-righteous intolerant women a chance to impose their ideas on others. The Boy and the Dear One both live in the mill town, with their respective fathers, though the young people are not acquainted there, as does also the girl later known as the Friendless One. The Boy's father is killed when company guards fire upon strikers at the Jenkins mill, and the Friendless One too is left alone by the strike, we are not told how.

The survivors of the strike all gravitate to the same slum district in a neighboring city. The Dear One keeps house for her father in a tenement flat, where they are fairly contented in their poverty until he develops a heart condition, but the Boy, unable to find employment, becomes a petty thief in the service of a small gangster known as the Musketeer of the Slums, into whose clutches poverty also delivers the Friendless One.

As a blind for his operations, the Boy conducts a newsstand outside the tenement in which the Dear One lives and is strongly attracted to her as soon as they meet. Her father opposes any contact between them, but after his death, the Dear One marries the Boy. Now determined to live cleanly, like his wife, he breaks with the Musketeer, quarreling with him in the process; in revenge the Musketeer has stolen goods planted on him and he is sentenced to a term in prison.

The Dear One comforts herself in his absence with her newborn child, but her happiness is soon shattered when the representatives of the Jenkins Foundation decide that the convict's wife is no fit mother and take the baby from her to put him in an institution.

After the Boy has been released, the Musketeer meets the Dear One and, finding her attractive, promises to use his alleged influence to recover her baby. Unfortunately the Friendless One becomes aware of his interest and is violently jealous. Arming herself with the revolver which the Boy had returned to the Musketeer when withdrawing from his band, she follows him to the Boy's flat and shoots him through an open window while he is struggling inside with the Dear One and the Boy, who had been warned by a friend that the Musketeer had been seen entering the flat.

Having thrown the gun into the room, the Friendless One escapes without being apprehended, and the weapon being known to have belonged to the Boy, he is convicted and sentenced to death. A kindly policeman who believes in his innocence makes stalwart attempts to enlist the aid of the Governor but to no apparent avail. No progress is made until the latest possible moment when the officer becomes suspicious of the now repentant Friendless One and confronts her. She breaks down and confesses, after which she, the Dear One, and the officer pursue the Governor's train in a racing auto, board the train, and secure an order to stay the execution. There follows another race with time, and the party arrives at the jail only after the black cap has been placed over the Boy's head. As we have not been told anything about the life of the Friendless One before she came to the city, so we are not told what happens to her after she has confessed the murder.

Howard Gaye as the Nazarene

The One Who Rocks the Cradle (Lillian Gish)

"Be ye as harmless as doves."

The miracle at Cana. Mary, the mother (Lillian Langdon),
behind the Christ.

Christ saves the woman taken in adultery (Olga Grey).

Griffith directing a crowd scene in a Jerusalem street

54412

Griffith with the doves on the Judaean set

The Court of France

Catherine de Médicis and her co-conspirators.

Catherine urging her son Charles IX (Frank Bennett) to authorize the
Massacre of St. Bartholomew's

Brown Eyes (Margery Wilson), her lover Prosper Latour (Eugene Pallette), her father (Spottiswoode Aitken), her mother (Ruth Handforth), and her little sister. For some strange reason, the name of the girl who played the sister seems never to have been given in any *Intolerance* cast. The editors of this book would welcome any information any reader might have concerning her. Incidentally, little girls did not wear short dresses in sixteenth-century France.

Brown Eyes (Margery Wilson) and Prosper Latour (Eugene Pallette)

The massacre.

The death of Brown Eyes

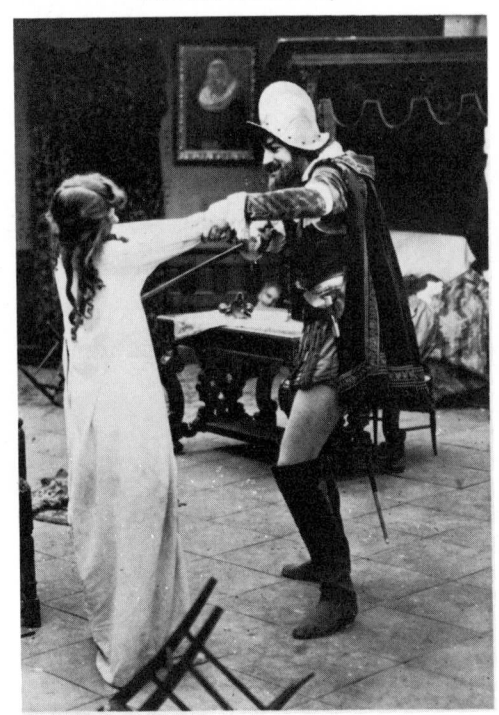

The Dear One (Mae Marsh) in her new tenement home

The Dear One and the hopeful geranium

The Boy (Robert Harron) and the Dear One meet.

The Dear One leads the Boy in the straight and narrow path.

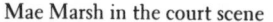

The Boy's trial for murder

Mae Marsh in the court scene

Remorse of the Friendless One after killing the Musketeer of the Slums. Not all of this material appears in the film.

Flagging down the Governor's train after the confession of the Friendless One.

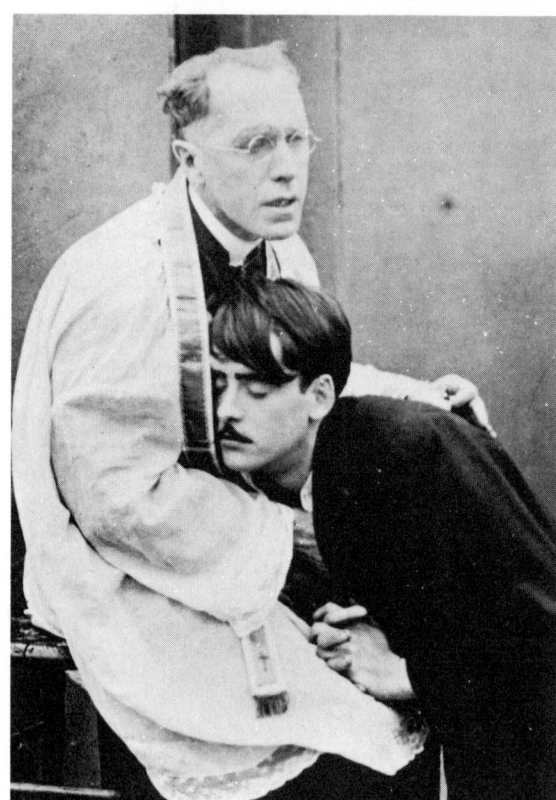

Father Farley (Rev. A. W. McClure) comforts the Boy on his way to the gallows.

The Governor's pardon saves the Boy.

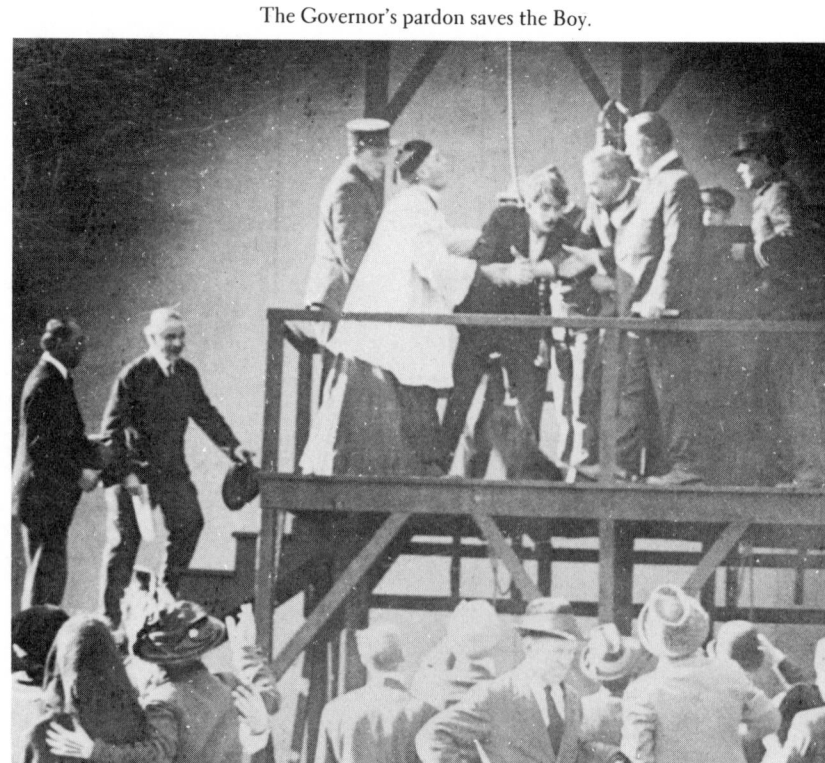

The Princess Beloved (Seena Owen)

Belshazzar (Alfred Paget)

Belshazzar on the Walls of Babylon

Belshazzar defies the High Priest of Bel (Tully Marshall).

Belshazzar's Banquet Hall.

Moods of the Mountain Girl (Constance
Talmadge)

The Mountain Girl and the Rhapsode (Elmer Clifton)

Opposite page:
Above: Cyrus moves against Babylon.
Below: The city attacked

Cyrus in camp

Fighting on the walls

Night fighting

A new weapon against Cyrus

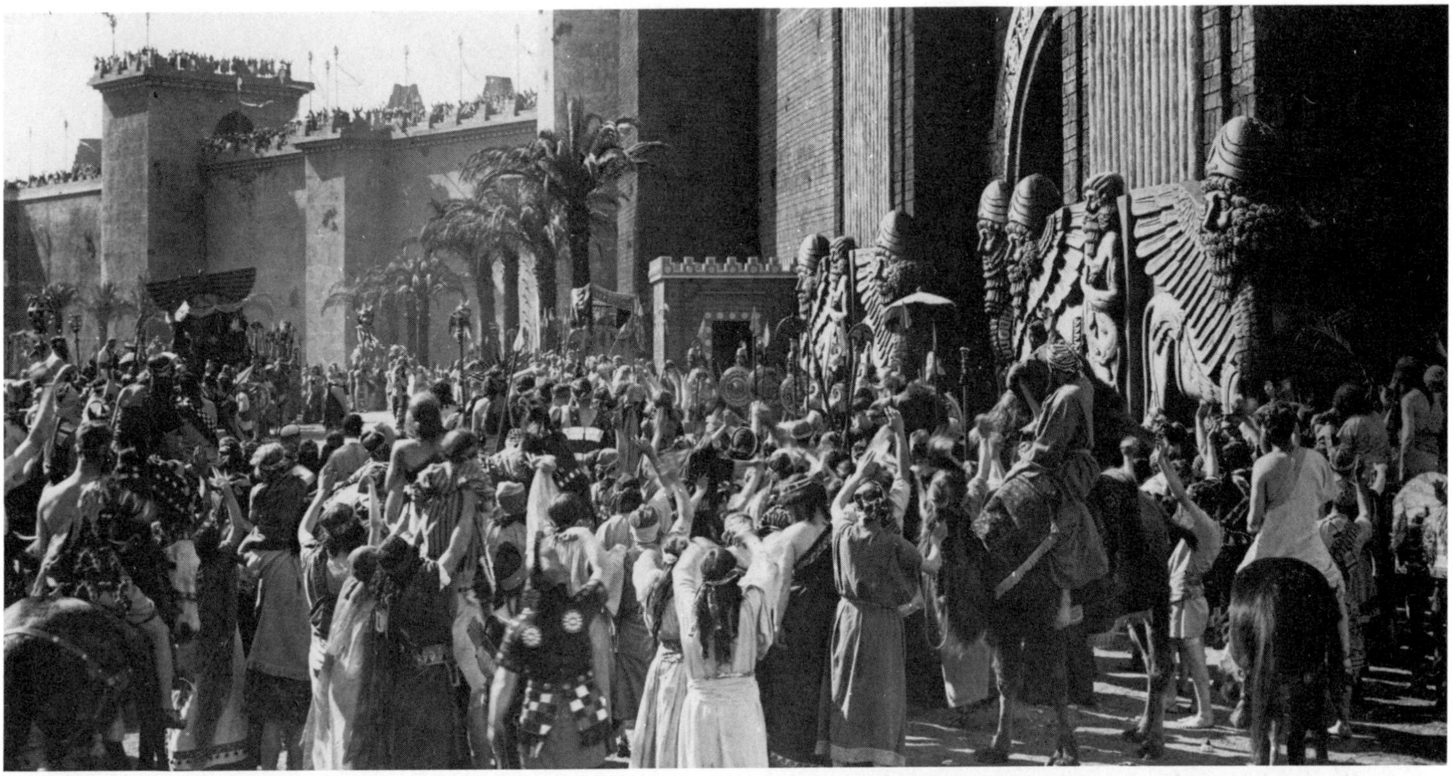

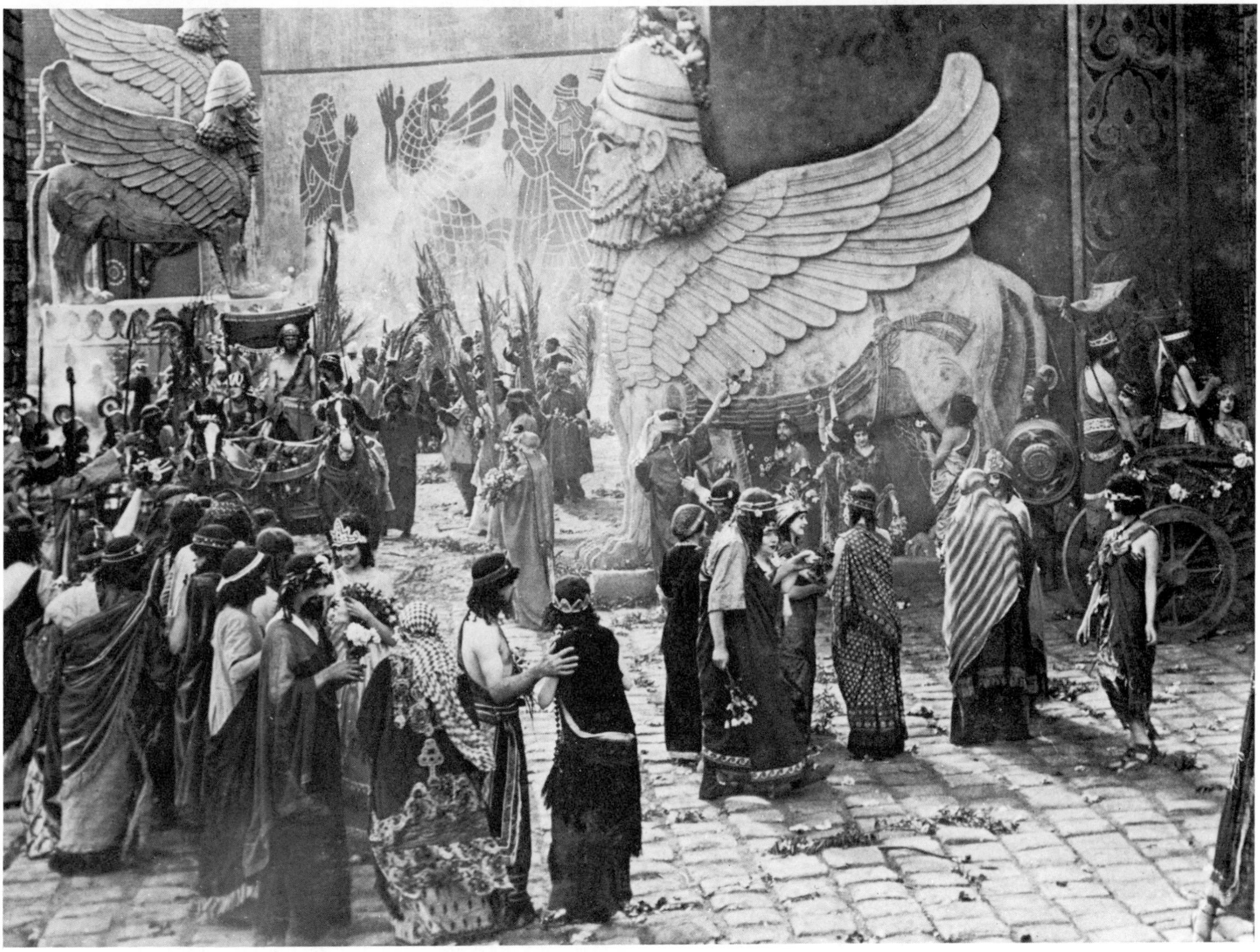

Sacrifices for deliverance and victory

The Mountain Girl brings Belshazzar news of the attack

The Banquet Hall in shambles

CRITICISM

There are a good many of us who will never be convinced that *Intolerance* is not the greatest of all motion pictures, "the end and justification," as Iris Barry has said, "of that whole school of American cinematography based on the terse cutting and disjunctive assembly of lengths of film, which began with *The Great Train Robbery* and culminated in *The Birth of a Nation* and in this."

This is not to say that it is a flawless work of art. On the contrary, it has enough faults to wreck any film except a very great one. It is full of melodrama and half-baked sociology, and it sometimes forces the note in an attempt to achieve unity by making intolerance the root of all woes. Though so great an authority as A. H. Sayce was tremendously impressed by the Babylonian section, the simplification of the struggle between Babylonia and

Persia as a confrontation of "good guys" against "bad guys," with the fall of Babylon a calamity for civilization, would be difficult to substantiate; one wonders too how the Temple of Love and the festival and orgy scenes were supposed to support the hypothesis of Babylonian superiority! The conflict between the various acting styles employed is sometimes troublesome. Mae Marsh, Robert Harron, and others in the modern story are naturalistic, but Constance Talmadge as the Mountain Girl is obviously giving a performance and a very good one at that. Though we know Griffith's own attitude toward Catherine de Médicis to have been one of considerable charity and understanding, Josephine Crowell presents her in the film as more demon than woman, while such figures as Christ, Belshazzar, and the Princess Beloved are very

85

nearly reduced to immobility, being permitted hardly any more action than if they were posing for their portraits. Some matters, too, such as the degree of the Rhapsode's involvement in the treachery of the High Priest of Bel, are left unpardonably obscure. But none of this counts for much against the film's scope, power, passion, and humanity.

It was of course so colossal a failure commercially that it cast its shadow over all the rest of Griffith's career, a fact which stands in amazing contrast to its tremendous reputation and influence. Its influence on film spectacle was not limited to Ince's *Civilization*, Tourneur's *Woman*, DeMille's *Joan the Woman* (the first of his big spectacles), to say nothing of the two *Ben-Hurs*, several *Cleopatras* and many more, but extended to France (Abel Gance), Germany (Fritz Lang), and above all to Russia, where Lenin toured it through the country for a decade and the great directors of the burgeoning Russian cinema used it as their textbook.

Though the abstract title of the film was probably unfortunate, especially coming as it did after the greatest title in motion picture history, *The Birth of a Nation*, whose eloquence still rings down the years, its commercial failure has never been adequately explained. The stock explanations, which practically every writer on films parrots from his predecessors, are that the use of four interwoven stories puzzled the simple spectators of 1916, that the intensity of the film and the restlessness and pace of its last two reels wearied them, and that its temper was antipathetic to that of a nation that was preparing to make the world safe for democracy by joining in the bloodiest war that human idiocy had thus far achieved and by this means destroy war forever. "There is so much in it," wrote Iris Barry; "there is too much of it; the pace increases so relentlessly; its intense hail of images—many of them only five frames long—cruelly hammers the sensibility; its climax is near hysteria."

But none of this really seems to cover the case. Even the Woman Who Rocks the Cradle, the recurrent shots of whom Griffith uses to symbolize life's progress and continuity and to mark transitions from one age to another, has been boggled over. One gentleman objected that she had nothing to do with the story, yet she obviously has everything to do with it, for all the characters are her children. Another objected that to an audience the image of a woman rocking a cradle could only mean that a baby was coming, but babies are generally rocked after birth, not before. Alexander Woollcott found "grotesque incoherence of design and utter fatuity of thought" in *Intolerance*, and Heywood Broun confessed to preferring the contemporary Annette Kellerman swim spectacle, *A Daughter of the Gods*, because it contained a story that

could be followed. Surely a man does not often have a better chance than that to make a fool of himself, for the truth is that anyone who had trouble following *Intolerance* might also be expected to have trouble with "Little Red Riding-Hood"; I could name you a dozen one-reel Biographs which presented greater difficulties but which the nickelodeon, often largely juvenile, audiences seem to have taken in their stride. Frederick James Smith was quite just when he pointed out in the *New York Dramatic Mirror* that the trouble with people like Woollcott was that they did not know how to watch a motion picture or understand the difference between stage and screen technique. As for the war, everybody who lived through those years knows that the American nation as a whole was not burning with zeal to embrace the conflict in 1916; if this had been so, Woodrow Wilson would not have been reelected because "he kept us out of war." Indeed, if the war had any influence upon the immediate fate of *Intolerance*, my own guess would be that people stayed away from it, not because their mood was militaristic but because they were getting enough of war in the newspapers. But all speculation of this kind is guesswork, no matter where it comes out.

One thing is clear, however: the graduates of the nickelodeon were much better equipped to understand *Intolerance* in 1916 than most of the people who went to see it only because it was being presented in "legitimate" theaters. For while the film was creative, even revolutionary, in its technique, it had long roots in cinema history and especially in Griffith's own. This was never better pointed out than by the reviewer in the Boston *Evening Transcript*; Griffith cannot often have encountered so well informed an evaluation of his work, and he must have rubbed his eyes to find it in such a definitely "upper class" newspaper. One wonders whether Amy Lowell read it in nearby Brookline; along with Hardy's *Dynasts* and Carlyle's *French Revolution*, *Intolerance* may well have influenced her *Can Grande's Castle*.

The [general] effect is naturally a stunning departure from the customary moving picture, developed though it is from Mr. Griffith's own invention, the "flash back." But it is not so much a departure from Mr. Griffith's past as many will think. Just as the two different stories told, one following another, in the two halves of *The Birth*, may be traced technically to his earlier Biograph films, *The Battle* and *The Battle at Elderbush Gulch*, so you may find "studies" for the various parts of *Intolerance* in other films made in those almost prehistoric but immortal days when the future of the photoplay and of Mr. Griffith was being made at the old Biograph studios. The slum life of the modern story in *Intolerance* was handled in half a dozen films like *The Musketeers of Pig Alley*, blending the romance of the "gunman" with an intimate realism of treatment. The fall of Babylon had its prototype in *Judith of Bethulia*. The Christ story has figured in a dozen bits of allegory in photoplays of other periods. The Renaissance of Charles IX is almost wholly novel to the screen but Griffith has handled Italian costumes of that period in *The Perfidy of Mary* [1] and *The Blind Princess and the Poet*. There is even a bit of Griffith's old "Pickford stuff" . . . in the girl from the mountains who descends upon Babylon, displays her tempestuous talents in the marriage market, and ends by driving a rocking chariot to the relief of the city.

The element of propaganda was just as evident in the old Biograph days. Mr. Griffith has always been fascinated by the ability of the film to show, both in action and in printed "leaders," an ethical point of view. He taught a sort of cave-man psychology in *Man's Genesis* . . . ; he showed the eternal struggle of the scholar-husband and the light-minded dancer-wife in *Oil and Water*; he made a sort of *Everywoman* of the films in *The Blind Princess and the Poet*; and the list might be continued almost indefinitely.

Intolerance was "A Drama of Comparisons," depicting "Love's Struggle Throughout the Ages." It began with the modern story, which in its original form had been made independently. The other three stories were an afterthought, prompted in part by Griffith's resentment of what he considered the intolerance that had been shown toward him by those who had opposed the exhibition of *The Birth of a Nation* and partly perhaps by his feeling that *The Mother and the Law* alone was not big enough to be issued as a successor to that film.

But the changes and additions did much more than transform *The Mother and the Law* into a giant spectacle. They universalized the theme, leaving the hero and the heroine no longer merely this man and this woman but Humanity, the helpless Little Man, who, in every age, asks only to be allowed to enjoy his simple life in peace, and whose happiness is forever being wrecked by the exploiters who break in upon him and enslave him to make him the tool of their cruelties and selfish aggrandizement, the instruments of their meaningless greed and hate and lust. "The little factory couple in the modern street scene called The Dear One and The Boy," wrote Vachel Lindsay, "seem to wave their hands back to Babylon amid the orchestration of ancient memories. The ages make a resonance behind their simple plans and terrible perplexities." Many years later, A. Nicholas Vardac expressed the same idea more elaborately:

The young wife rushing to save her unjustly condemned husband from the gallows was . . . of only contemporary importance, but its dramatic and thematic significance was lifted out of all time and presented as an eternal verity through the intercutting of the culminating events of the other three spectacles: Christ struggling toward Calvary, the Babylonian mountain girl racing to warn Belshazzar that his priests had

betrayed him, and the Huguenot fighting his way through the streets on St. Bartholomew's Day to save his sweetheart from massacre by the French mercenaries.

This, surely, provided abundant justification for Griffith's not setting forth events "in their historical sequence, or according to accepted forms of dramatic construction," but, as he says, "as they might flash across a mind seeking to parallel the life of the different ages."

Griffith had been known for his ingenious manipulation of shots for a long time and his capacity to break a scene up into shots that enable us to see it, sometimes with incredible speed and convenience, from different points of view. Paul O'Dell, whose analysis of the action of *Intolerance* is the best available substitute for seeing the film itself, has analyzed the murder sequence in detail, finding that it runs about five minutes and comprises 111 shots. In this film, moreover, Griffith intercuts not only within each story but between the stories, so that at last everything coexists in a kind of Eternal Now. Like Shakespeare, Griffith also knew the difference between dramatic time and actual time, and the time element in *Intolerance* is handled so skillfully that nobody is ever troubled by the fact that it seems to be taking as long to carry the Boy to the gallows as was required for the whole Fall of Babylon and Massacre of St. Bartholomew's.

The French story is closed somewhat earlier than the others, and the Christ story is useful primarily for the grandeur of its associations; if He too was a victim of intolerance, then indeed we are dealing with a cosmic theme, and all who suffer innocently are, in Biblical parlance, filling up His sufferings. At at least one point the parallelism may be open to objection: however innocent the Boy in the modern story may have been, many must experience a faint sense of blasphemy when his march to the gallows is juxtaposed to Christ's walk along the Via Dolorosa. Yet even this might be defended by citing His own words that "inasmuch as ye have done it unto the least of these, ye have done it unto me," and many of the other juxtapositions do shed a light on the significance of what is being presented that could have been achieved in no other way. I for one must admit my indebtedness to Paul O'Dell's penetrating note on the placing of the Boy's return to the Dear One after his first term in prison in juxtaposition to Belshazzar's feast in the Babylonian story:

The link between the Boy's return and Belshazzar's feast is not so slight or arbitrary as it might at first seem. In both cases the atmosphere is one of rejoicing and anticipation of more settled times ahead; and in both cases there is also a sense of loss—the Boy is confronted with the seizure of his child whom he has never seen—and in both cases also, the hope for the future is soon to be destroyed, quickly, and unexpectedly.

[1] An error, surely; see the stills from *The Perfidy of Mary* in Lillian Gish's *Dorothy and Lillian Gish*, p. 21.

The magnificence of the Babylonian sequence in *Intolerance* can hardly be overstated. I cannot vouch for its historical accuracy, but its dramatic power is overwhelming. It revives the glory of the ancient world and stimulates the imagination as few films have even attempted to do it. Yet *Intolerance* could not move us as it does for this reason alone. The final justification of the film is that it makes us care for human beings and what they represent. If we grant that Griffith fails to extend to Pharisees the same charity that he rightly and gladly proffers to publicans, grant his unfairness to settlements and foundations, grant that the specific measures he advocates and opposes may well occasion intelligent dissent, he was still everlastingly right in his basic contention that charity stinks when it is given without love, and we know this better now than we did in 1916. Unfortunately it is still true in these latter days that many persons' idea of justice is "an eye for an eye, a tooth for a tooth, and *a murder for a murder*," that war is "the most potent weapon forged in the fires of intolerance," and that conquerors still cry, "Kill, kill, kill, and to God be the glory, world without end, Amen." When D. W. Griffith made *Intolerance*, he was thinking of the film as a universal language, directed toward understanding and good will and offering the hope of amelioration of ancient wrongs. It did not turn out that way, but that was not Griffith's fault. And though it is now the fashion to call him naïve for having believed, one may still be pardoned for continuing to feel that his naïveté may entitle him to a higher place in the New Jerusalem than the disillusioned sophistication of those who have succeeded him.

Thus the final greatness of this great film lies somewhere beyond its heroic scope, the grandeur of its sets, or its appeal to the imagination. It even lies beyond the technical innovations that were so far ahead of their time that for many years they were thought of as having originated much later with the Germans and the Russians. It is a great thing to be able to manipulate and control multitudes to achieve a dramatic effect, but it is greater to be able to deal with individual human beings so as to draw out of them such acting as deepens the humanity of all who see them. Griffith certainly does not leave us indifferent to the people in the French and the Babylonian stories. Take the wonderful moment in the French story in which the priest draws the fleeing Huguenot child under his robe and into his house, indicating to her pursuers that she had fled down the street. This was more than an attempt to placate Catholic viewers; it was an affirmation of Griffith's belief that there is decency and humanity in men belonging to all parties and all creeds.

Yet when all is said and done, the greatest triumphs in this kind are won in the modern story. Mae Marsh's anguish in the courtroom scene has been praised often enough though not too highly, but surely her greatest scene, and Harron's too, comes at the very end, when they clasp each other again after he has been brought down from the gallows. This is a moment so true and so perfectly handled that one can hardly view it, no matter how often he may have seen the film, without tears, and surely it is one of the finest things that have ever been filmed. Moreover, though the attention is rightly focused on the principals, it is not the least of the virtues of this scene that the minor characters in it—the Governor's wife, the priest, and at least one of the prison officials—are drawn into its emotional pattern and make their contributions to its overwhelming total effect. Can it be that they represent ourselves? Here is humanity naked and unashamed—not of sin, which is flaunted often enough—but of love and innocence, which we so often fear and try so desperately to conceal. Surely something like this was the effect Griffith dreamed of and hoped that his film might create in the hearts of the world.

E. W.

The Fall of Babylon and *The Mother and the Law*

For the D. W. Griffith Repertory Season at New York's George M. Cohan Theatre, in the summer of 1919, the director took two stories from *Intolerance* and presented them as solo features. Following their New York premières, both films were released on a states'-rights basis.

The first to emerge as a separate film was *The Fall of Babylon*, which opened on July 21. Griffith took the basic story as it had appeared in *Intolerance*; slightly reedited it; shot some additional footage, largely of Constance Talmadge as the Mountain Girl and George Fawcett as a Babylonian judge; and added a new ending. Instead of meeting death by a Persian arrow, the Mountain Girl escapes with the Rhapsode, and goes with him to her old home in the mountains.

For the première of *The Fall of Babylon*, the director

devised an entirely original form of presentation. The curtain rose on a totally dark stage, on which was a globe representing the earth, and a woman (Betty Kaye) representing ancient Babylon. On the globe was projected film of New York City. Then began the film proper, showing Babylon in all its splendor, and introducing the Mountain Girl and the Rhapsode. Then, as the *Moving Picture World* (August 2, 1919) explained: "During a feast given by Belshazzar to his favorite, the action is transferred from the screen to the stage by a clever arrangement of lights, and the dance which follows seems an appropriate part of the story. It is called the shawl dance, and, as performed by Kyra, is a remarkable exhibition of grace and dexterity."

The presentation returned to the film at the point where Cyrus, King of the Persians, is introduced. Before the end of Act One of the program, at which the Persians are defeated, there was one further cutback to the stage, when Margaret Fritts and Samuel Critcherson, as the Mountain Girl and the Rhapsode, sang a duet.

Act Two began with the stage set to represent a hall in the Babylonian Palace, and with a dance by Betty Kaye. The film, then, reopened with the Feast of Belshazzar. There was one further stage sequence, immediately prior to the fall of the city, at which point Kyra performed the Dance of Undulation.

As Edward Weitzel commented in the *Moving Picture World:* "The novelty of the method [of presentation] will commend it, and D. W. Griffith is to be applauded for his willingness to try something new and to add to the scope of the screen." Of the film itself, Julian Johnson in *Photoplay* (October, 1919) wrote: "It was most interesting to me as a reminiscence of my original enthusiasms, as I view them in longer focus, for where has there ever been such painting, such sculpture, such complete reconstruction of a civilization not only dead, but forgotten?"

The Mother and the Law was first screened on August 18, 1919, minus—some might say thankfully—any stage presentation. As with *The Fall of Babylon,* Griffith made changes, shooting additional footage, editing other footage, and using film rejected for the story as it appeared in *Intolerance.*

The production contains a number of major changes. The most major, and certainly the most moving of which is the indication of the fate of the baby taken from the Dear One. As a result of insufficient care in the hands of the Jenkins Foundation, it dies. This event results in one of the most emotional moments of the film, in which the Dear One sees her dead baby in the coffin and bids him good-bye. Arthur Lennig movingly describes the scene in his book *The Silent Voice:* ". . . the Dear One is told, 'Owing to your lack of care of the baby before we took it,

it has died.' The lid has been put on the small grey coffin. She asks that it be lifted and looks at the dead child. Then she approaches it, smiles, and touches it lovingly; only when she finds it cold do her eyes take on a look of pain. The scene is one of the greatest of all Griffith's attempts to touch the human heart."

Scenes featuring Mae Marsh with Robert Harron, not in *Intolerance,* include the couple's first date and their honeymoon, which, apparently, took place in a lumberyard. There are also many additional scenes of Robert Harron in prison, breaking rocks and passing an open grave.

When *Intolerance* was first shown in Philadelphia, *The North American* of December 30, 1916, criticized the film for its "libel against a class which comprises some of the cleanest-souled, most unselfish and self-sacrificing women of the nation," and for its "intent to incite popular resentment against social workers, because—drawing the inference from the whole film—because they are dangerous foes of the saloon and the brothel." To counteract criticism such as this, Griffith added an extremely lengthy sequence to *The Mother and the Law,* depicting the valuable work undertaken by the Salvation Army. This sequence included shots of Kate Bruce as a Salvation Army worker comforting an unmarried mother-to-be.

Extant prints of *The Mother and the Law* now end at the freeing of the Boy at the gallows. According to a list of titles in the D. W. Griffith Collection at the Museum of Modern Art, the film originally ended on a happier and cozier note. The final titles were:

"They won't hang him, Father?"

Two Years Later

The little hub of the new universe

"Shu'um toothums!"

Such titles indicate that the Dear One and the Boy were blessed by a second child, but give no indication as to the fate of the Friendless One.

As released in 1919, *The Mother and the Law* is for me one of Griffith's most moving and finest works. With all the splendors and disasters of earlier eras removed, the viewer may concentrate on this simple story of human love and human frailty. No actor and actress of the silent screen have done anything to compare with the playing of Robert Harron and Mae Marsh, and no director has come closer to perfection in realism than has D. W. Griffith in *The Mother and the Law.*

A. S.

9

HEARTS OF THE WORLD

SCENARIO: M. Gaston de Tolignac, translated into English by Captain Victor Marier (both pseudonyms for D. W. Griffith

PHOTOGRAPHY: G. W. Bitzer

ADDITIONAL EUROPEAN PHOTOGRAPHY: D. P. Cooper

TECHNICAL SUPERVISION: Erich von Stroheim

FILM EDITORS: James and Rose Smith

MUSIC ARRANGED BY: Carli Elinor and D. W. Griffith

MISS GISH'S DRESSES BY: Nathan of London

LENGTH: 12 reels

PRODUCTION: Paramount–Artcraft/D. W. Griffith, Inc.

DISTRIBUTION: Released on a road-show and subsequent states'-rights basis

LOS ANGELES PREMIÈRE: Clune's Auditorium, March 12, 1918

NEW YORK PREMIÈRE: 44th Street Theatre, April 4, 1918

ADOLPHE LESTINA (the grandfather)

JOSEPHINE CROWELL (the mother)

LILLIAN GISH (the Girl)

ROBERT HARRON (the Boy)

JACK COSGRAVE (the Boy's father)

KATE BRUCE (the Boy's mother)

BEN ALEXANDER (the Littlest Brother)

MARION EMMONS and FRANCIS MARION (the Boy's other brothers)

DOROTHY GISH (the Little Disturber)

ROBERT ANDERSON (Monsieur Cuckoo)

GEORGE FAWCETT (the village carpenter)

GEORGE SIEGMANN (von Strohm)

FAY HOLDERNESS (the innkeeper)

L. LOWRY (a deaf and blind musician)

EUGENE POUYET (a poilu)

ANNA MAE WALTHALL (a French peasant girl)

YVETTE DUVOISIN (a refugee)

HERBERT SUTCH (a French major)

ALPHONSE DUFORT (a poilu)

JEAN DUMERCIER (a poilu)

GASTON RIVIERE and JULES LEMONTIER (the stretcher bearers)

GEORGE LOYER (a poilu)

GEORGE NICHOLLS (a German sergeant)

MRS. MARY GISH (a refugee mother)

MRS. HARRON (woman with daughter)

JESSIE HARRON (a refugee)

JOHNNY HARRON (boy with barrel)

MARY HAY (a dancer)

NOEL COWARD (boy with wheelbarrow)

ERICH VON STROHEIM (a German soldier)

(A slightly revised "peace edition" of Hearts of the World had its première on August 11, 1919, at the George M. Cohan Theatre, New York.)

THE STORY

On the eve of World War I, two American families are living side by side on the rue de la Paix in a little French village. The Boy, a budding literary genius, the oldest of four sons of a frustrated painter, falls in love with the Girl, who is the only child of the other family Their romance is almost frustrated by the shameless play which the Little Disturber, a street singer from Paris, makes for the Boy, but this crisis is resolved, and the two young people are just on the eve of marriage when war begins. Because he believes that "any country worth living in is also worth fighting for," the Boy, though an American citizen, goes to war with two village companions, the enthusiastic and eccentric M. Cuckoo, who has by this time been accepted by the Little Disturber on the sensible ground that "if we cannot get what we want, we had better want what we can get," and the Village Carpenter; in the army the three think of themselves as the three musketeers.

When the French retreat, the village is shelled. The Boy's father and the Girl's mother and grandfather are all killed, and the Girl is deranged by war's terrors. Clutching her wedding dress, which had been carefully packed away in a trunk, she wanders aimlessly until she comes upon the Boy, badly wounded and unconscious, upon the battlefield; here they spend what was to have been their wedding night together. While she is absent, he is carried off by the Red Cross, and she believes him dead. The Girl and the Little Disturber both find shelter at the village inn, whose female proprietor had long been in league with a German spy, von Strohm, whose attention the Girl had unfortunately attracted before the war. There the Little Disturber nurses the Girl back to health and sanity, and they become good friends.

In time the Boy rejoins his comrades in the trenches; they, like the Girl, have supposed him dead. The villagers, including the Girl, are put to work and brutally punished by German taskmasters. The mother and three small brothers of the Boy take refuge in a cellar in another part of the village, where the mother dies, worn out with hardship and labor, and her sons themselves bury her to save her body from being dishonored. Later the Girl and the Boy's brothers are reunited, and she steals food from the inn kitchen to try to keep them alive.

The French advance again, and the Boy, disguised as a German officer, invades the enemy's lines, and after spending two days in a rain-drenched shellhole, gives the Allies the awaited signal for an attack. The Boy then returns to the village and the inn, where he and the Girl are reunited. She hides him in her room, but he is discovered by the brutal German sergeant who had already beaten the Girl for her inability to perform hard labor; while the sergeant is struggling with the Boy, the Girl stabs his antagonist in the back, which gives Boy and Girl a chance to retreat to an upper floor of the inn, where they barricade themselves in and await what looks like certain death.

Von Strohm, by whom the Girl had already narrowly escaped rape only through the opportune arrival of other German officers at the inn just as he had her cornered, learns what has happened when the sergeant staggers into the room and falls at his feet, and he and his followers locate the Boy and Girl in their retreat. It now becomes a race in time between the ability of the besieged to hold the door against their attackers and the arrival of the French, who are on the point of retaking the village. The Girl begs the Boy to shoot her rather than let her fall into von Strohm's hands. Von Strohm is just on the point of bursting into the room when he is felled by a hand grenade, thrown by the Little Disturber from the stairway, just as the French arrive.

Lillian Gish with Ben Alexander

D. W. Griffith in the trenches

The village before the war, with Dorothy Gish in the center

The Girl (Lillian Gish) and her Mother (Josephine Crowell)

The Boy's Littlest Brother (Ben Alexander) has not yet made up his mind to welcome the Girl into the family.

The Boy (Robert Harron) in the trenches with the village carpenter (George Fawcett)

The Girl, deranged by war's terrors, searches for her bridegroom.

The Girl menaced by von Strohm (George Siegmann)

Right above: The Girl faces the desperate choice between death and falling into the hands of von Strohm.

Right: The Little Disturber (Dorothy Gish) happily reencounters M. Cuckoo (David Butler) after the attack on the inn.

CRITICISM

Hearts of the World, Griffith's most important World War I picture, is the hardest of all his major productions to evaluate fairly today. It was made as a propaganda effort at the suggestion of the British government, then cut and altered when the war ended sooner than many had expected, and it is difficult even for those who saw it in 1918 to recapture the emotion they felt then or distinguish clearly between what Griffith and what history contributed to its effect.

Lillian Gish and her mother crossed the Atlantic on the first camouflaged ship to sail after the United States had entered the war; Dorothy, Robert Harron, and Billy Bitzer followed on the *Baltic* with General Pershing. Both crossings were dangerous. In England and in France, the actors lived through nerve-racking air raids; once at least they were not far behind the front lines. (Bitzer escaped the latter risk because the authorities did not venture to allow a man whose given names included Johann, Gottlob, and Wilhelm to enter France!) Some of the village scenes were shot in England and some in France, but much of the picture was made in California, to which the company returned late in 1917. "The film," says Karl Brown, "was continually switching from Hollywood to France to England and back to Hollywood, all within seconds of running time. A gun was fired in France and its shell shattered a wall on the *Intolerance* lot." Thus some of the war scenes were real, some staged. Of the former, some were shot by Griffith and some came from the camera of one Captain Kleinschmidt and other sources. The real stuff was not less appalling than the imagined, but it was generally less dramatic. Griffith himself remarked that as a drama the war was disappointing. He might well have felt this, for he had done much better himself.

The story in *Hearts of the World* is less interesting in itself than in any other leading film of Griffith's with the possible exception of *America*. The focus of interest falls on the war itself, and the characters are primarily significant as they illustrate its ebb and flow. We catch (staged) glimpses of the House of Commons, the Chamber of Deputies, and 10 Downing Street, and of various high personages of the time, all very interesting then but less so now. The film follows the official propaganda line: the Germans alone were responsible for the war, which was a deliberate blow aimed at "civilization," and the conflict was a plain case of right against wrong, with every German soldier a Hun and every poilu at least a potential Cyrano de Bergerac. In a way, Griffith may at the time have "believed" all this, but if so, he believed it somehow against the bent of his own nature,

which, as his earlier films had proved, was profoundly antiviolence and antiwar. As late as 1916 he had enthusiastically supported Wilson because "he kept us out of war." It is true that the climax of *Hearts of the World* involves even the hero and the heroine in bloodshed, yet the picture begins by questioning whether war "ever settles anything," and it certainly emphasizes the horrors of war rather than its glories. Griffith even introduces the old-line idealistic German who believes that "justice is the only right" against the militaristic doctrine that "might makes right." Lillian Gish has testified to the searing impression that what he saw of war's horrors made upon him, and has said that he never forgave himself for having made the film. Certainly there can be no question concerning her own views. Many years later, when as a member of the America First Committee she was doing her best to keep her country out of World War II, she did public penance in an article, "I Made War Propaganda," in *Scribner's Commentator*, in November 1941.

Nevertheless the film did much for her career and even more for Dorothy's. Since she was still a developing artist (when, for that matter, has she ever ceased to be that?), her Girl was not up to the level of her later performances in Griffith films; neither was it the first adequate revelation of her gifts as an actress, for she had been very fine in a number of previous Biographs, Majestics, and Triangles. But *Hearts of the World* did surround her with a more impressive showcase than she had ever inhabited before. She had played a leading role in *The Birth of a Nation*, but *The Birth of a Nation* was not essentially *about* her; neither did she dominate it. *Intolerance* had, in a sense, revolved around her, but the Woman who Rocks the Cradle was only a symbol, not a character. *Hearts of the World* was the real thing at last—idyllic youthful charm, passion, sensation, even derangement—and from this time on there was never to be any question that she was an artist to be reckoned with.

The great immediate popular triumph was Dorothy's, however, as the Little Disturber in a black wig. The wig, which she retained through the series of popular comedies that followed, and that her success had imperatively demanded,[1] was only the outward sign of the public's

---

[1] *Battling Jane* (1918); *The Hope Chest, Boots, Peppy Polly, I'll Get Him Yet, Nugget Nell, Out of Luck, Turning the Tables* (all 1919); *Mary Ellen Comes To Town, Remodeling Her Husband. Little Miss Rebellion, Flying Pat, Ole Swimmin' Hole* (all 1920); *The Ghost in the Garret, Oh, Jo* (both 1921); and *The Country Flapper* (1922). These films were supervised, but not directed, by Griffith, and all except the last were released by the Famous Players–Lasky Corporation as Artcraft Pictures. (Eileen Bowser suggests, however, that *Ole Swimmin' Hole* may never have been released at all.)

To filmgoers accustomed to thinking of Dorothy Gish in the demure aspect shown in this publicity photograph from her Mutual period, her Little Disturber was a revelation.

pages will already have discovered that Griffith had a way of anticipating a great many trends in motion pictures combined with a tendency to drop them carelessly and leave them for others to exploit. In a sense one may say that the Little Disturber anticipated the flapper films of the twenties, as represented by such stars as Clara Bow and Colleen Moore. But though Dorothy Gish was once startled when a strange woman sitting next to her in a motion picture theater during a screening of *Hearts of the World* confided to her that she was willing to "bet" that "that girl" must be "a bad one," since otherwise she could not act the part so well, the wistfulness was never buried very deep, and the girl turns out at last a very "good one," and heroic besides. Was she a wholly believable character? By the standards of realistic fiction, not quite, and less so, certainly, than some of the girls in the Artcraft series that was to follow. But in theater terms, and as a theatrical creation in the soubrette tradition, the Little Disturber quite deserved the response she evoked and the films that followed were one of the happiest series in cinema history.

Aside from Griffith's use of weapons and other war materials—like the dirigibles which he calls "the eyes of the Allies"—as properties (a development of his more modest use of less lethal objects in earlier films), there is not a great deal of technical interest in *Hearts of the World*, but the scenes set in various locations in and around the inn as the picture approaches its climax achieve great tensity, and the modified "chase" which makes up the closing sequence is possibly the most complicated example of this device in any of Griffith's films. It is not only the lives of the lovers that are at stake but the fate of all the refugees and the future of the village itself. Indeed, as the film is constructed, we pass so quickly from the defeat of the attackers to the victory of the Allies that we almost tend to feel that the war itself was won here! During the process we intercut not only between the lovers and their attackers but also between both and the troops locked in battle outside. Moreover, as if this were not enough, we are also invited to look in on the agonies of the Little Disturber as a helpless onlooker, until finally, anticipating the French army by moments, she is able to make her strike to save her friends.

It is interesting to remember that as late as 1925, no less an authority on matters cinematic than Charles Chaplin told Harry Carr that the three best films ever made were *The Birth of a Nation, Intolerance,* and *Hearts of the World.*

E. W.

discovery of a great comic talent; until now she had hardly been thought of as less wistful than Lillian. Her walk, as famous in its time as Marilyn Monroe's was later to be, was copied from that of a girl she never saw but whom Griffith and Lillian spied on the street one day and followed until they thought they could imitate it well enough to show her how to do it. The reader of these

10

THE GREAT LOVE

SCENARIO: Captain Victor Marier (i.e. D. W. Griffith and S. E. V. Taylor)

PHOTOGRAPHY: G. W. Bitzer

FILM EDITOR: James Smith

LENGTH: Exact footage unknown, printed sources vary in listing films as 5 reels or 7 reels

PRODUCTION/DISTRIBUTION: Paramount-Artcraft

NEW YORK PREMIÈRE: Strand Theater, August 11, 1918

RELEASED: August 12, 1918

ROBERT HARRON (Jim Young of Youngstown)

HENRY B. WALTHALL (Sir Roger Brighton)

GLORIA HOPE (Jessie Lovewell)

LILLIAN GISH (Susie Broadplains)

MAXFIELD STANLEY (John Broadplains)

GEORGE FAWCETT (Rev. Josephus Broadplains)

ROSEMARY THEBY (Mademoiselle Corintee)

GEORGE SIEGMANN (Mr. Seymour of Brazil, formerly of Berlin)

QUEEN ALEXANDRA, LILY ELSIE, LADY DIANA MANNERS, MRS. JOHN LAVERY, BETTINA STUART-WORTLEY, ELIZABETH ASQUITH, VIOLET KEPPEL, THE COUNTESS OF MASSARENE, THE HON. MRS. MONTAGUE, THE PRINCESS OF MONACO, LADY PAGET, SIR FREDERICK TREVES, THE BARONESS ROTHSCHILD, SIR HENRY STANLEY (themselves)

THE STORY

The central character in *The Great Love* is Jim Young, of Youngstown, Pennsylvania, who, fired by stories of German atrocities in Belgium, goes to Canada and enlists in the British army, reaching the trenches in advance of America's entry into the war. Wholly romantic and idealistic in his attitude toward the conflict, Jim would like to make himself the shield and protector of all the women and children of the world. Rejoicing to serve and incur the risks of serving, he believes he has achieved maturity through the war and observes with great interest and admiration not only the military preparations and training that are going forward in England but the way in which English society as a whole dedicates itself to service—aristocrats, great ladies, and all.

On leave after having been wounded, Jim meets and falls in love with an Australian girl, one Susie Broadplains, a clergyman's daughter, who is quite as idealistic as he is and even more innocent. Aside from the menace of the war itself, the only flaw in their happiness is caused by the fact that, once she has inherited £20,000, Susie is diligently pursued by a mysterious and highly aesthetic character named Sir Roger Brighton, an unscrupulous victimizer of women. Though Susie remains faithful to Jim, she is too innocent to be able to see through Sir Roger or completely resist his fascination. Actually, even much more sophisticated persons do not see through him at this time, but ultimately he is exposed as the ally of international conspirators and profiteers and disappears into jail. At the end, we leave Susie and Jim in a white fever of patriotic exaltation, confident that, whatever the future holds, they have found themselves and learned the meaning of life, not only in each other but in their common dedication of themselves to the Great Love, which is that of country and humankind.

97

Lillian Gish as Susie Broadplains

Robert Harron as Jim Young of Youngstown

Susie with Sir Roger Brighton (Henry B. Walthall)

Sir Roger with Susie and Mlle Corintee (Rosemary Theby)

D. W. Griffith in England during the filming of *The Great Love* with Lily Elsie and
Lady Diana Manners

CRITICISM

Griffith first conceived the idea for *The Great Love* in the autumn of 1917. He had shot more war footage for *Hearts of the World* than he had been able to use, and what was more important, he had film of a number of English society ladies, including Queen Alexandra, which he was anxious to use in one way or another. With S. E. V. Taylor, Griffith wrote a story titled *Women and the War*, which subsequently became *The Great Love*.

The highlight of the film, another of the "lost" Griffith features, was undoubtedly, as far as the director was concerned, the footage showing the elite of English society helping in the war effort. Griffith was a snob, and being allowed not only to film such people but also actually to associate with them as an equal must have been one of the proudest experiences of his life.

On his return to the States, he spoke at length on the subject:

I never really knew the full meaning of the word "graciousness" until I went to England and began to produce my picture-plays over there. I was in a rather delicate position. The personages with whom I was working had kindly offered me their services as actors and actresses in my story; they were giving me their most valuable time simply as a courtesy. But a more willing and obliging assembly I have never had.

I was permitted to photograph practically anywhere I wished. I remember one place. It was at a beautiful country place that at one time was one of the favorite spots of King Edward VII. In the back of an arbor was a tree planted there by the Emperor of Germany while on a visit long before the war. The tree still stands and blossoms, but the tablet which commemorates the occasion of the planting has been buried deep in the ground at its roots.

Queen Alexandra was gracious enough to come down to Lady Diana Manners' hospital which she conducts on her country estate and devoted nearly an entire day in arranging the hospital scenes and appearing in them herself. The Queen is greatly interested in the cinema, and showed a familiarity with a number of photoplays, and when they visited *Intolerance*, the first time they had been to the theater in two years, she and the King sent for me to come to their box.

I went to London a total stranger to those with whom I worked. I felt that I could do some good toward letting the world know war conditions and what England and France were doing toward winning it. These ladies and gentlemen who appear in *The Great Love* agreed with me, and although they are directing and supervising the affairs of the empire, they gladly took the time to assist in the making of the picture. It was an honor paid the photodrama which could not be equalled.

The Great Love reunited Griffith with Henry B. Walthall for the first time since *The Birth of a Nation*. According to one of the critics, Walthall appeared over-melodramatic in his acting, compared to his fellow players, which is possibly the reason Griffith decided not to use him again until the coming of sound. The director himself appeared in *The Great Love* as a passer-by in a Paris street-scene; history does not record whether his acting was melodramatic or not.

The production was not particularly well received by the critics. Frederick James Smith described it in *Motion Picture Classic* (October, 1918) as "merely a modern story of the war told in the terms of the old Biograph melodrama." (Admittedly, as Smith at that time was also employed by Maurice Tourneur to write publicity, his opinion might have been somewhat biased, but it was shared by many of his colleagues.) However, as a program picture, and I do not believe that *The Great Love* can be considered as anything other than that, it served its purpose. It entertained the public for an hour or so, and was promptly forgotten.

A. S.

11

A ROMANCE OF HAPPY VALLEY

SCENARIO: Captain Victor Marier (i.e. D. W. Griffith), based on a story by Mary Castelman

PHOTOGRAPHY: G. W. Bitzer

FILM EDITOR: James Smith

LENGTH: 5,905 feet

PRODUCTION/DISTRIBUTION: Paramount-Artcraft

NEW YORK PREMIÈRE: Strand Theater, January 26, 1919

RELEASED: January 26, 1919

LYDIA YEAMANS TITUS (*Auntie Smiles*)

ROBERT HARRON (*John L. Logan, Jr.*)

KATE BRUCE (*Mrs. Logan*)

GEORGE FAWCETT (*John L. Logan, Sr.*)

LILLIAN GISH (*Jennie Timberlake*)

GEORGE NICHOLLS (*her father*)

ADOLPHE LESTINA (*Jim Darkly*)

BERTRAM GRASSBY (*Judas, the city man*)

PORTER STRONG (*the funny waiter*)

ANDREW ARBUCKLE (*the minister*)

FRANCES SPARKS (*Topsy*)

CAROL DEMPSTER (*a girl John Logan meets in New York*)

THE STORY

Happy Valley is in Kentucky, and life there revolves about the Sanctificationist Church. "If we smile at these quaint people, let it be through tears of sympathy. We must remember that from similar places have come the very highest ideals. Sometimes they do backslide, but the dream is upward."

The love John Logan, Jr., feels for Jennie Timberlake makes him wish to stay at home, but his ambitions call him to "the devil and New York." The Sanctificationists try to save him by making him the subject of their prayers at a Sunday service, and for the time they seem to be successful, but he soon backslides and leaves. "In the city, we would like to find John in some magnificent occupation, but facts cannot be altered. His chief ambition is to invent a toy frog that will swim." It takes him seven years to achieve this, during which Jennie has marked off the days on her calendar and at the end of which she accounts herself an "old maid."

Prosperity achieved, John finally returns home to very different conditions than those he had left. His pious father has lost his money, faces want, and is tempted to crime. He attacks a lodger with a view to robbing him and, through an ingenious if not wholly convincing set of circumstances, he is led at one point not only to consider himself a murderer but also to believe that he has killed his son. Neither of these impressions turns out to coincide with the facts, however, and all ends happily for everybody, including John and the long faithful Jennie.

Lillian Gish and George Nicholls.

George Fawcett and Robert Harron

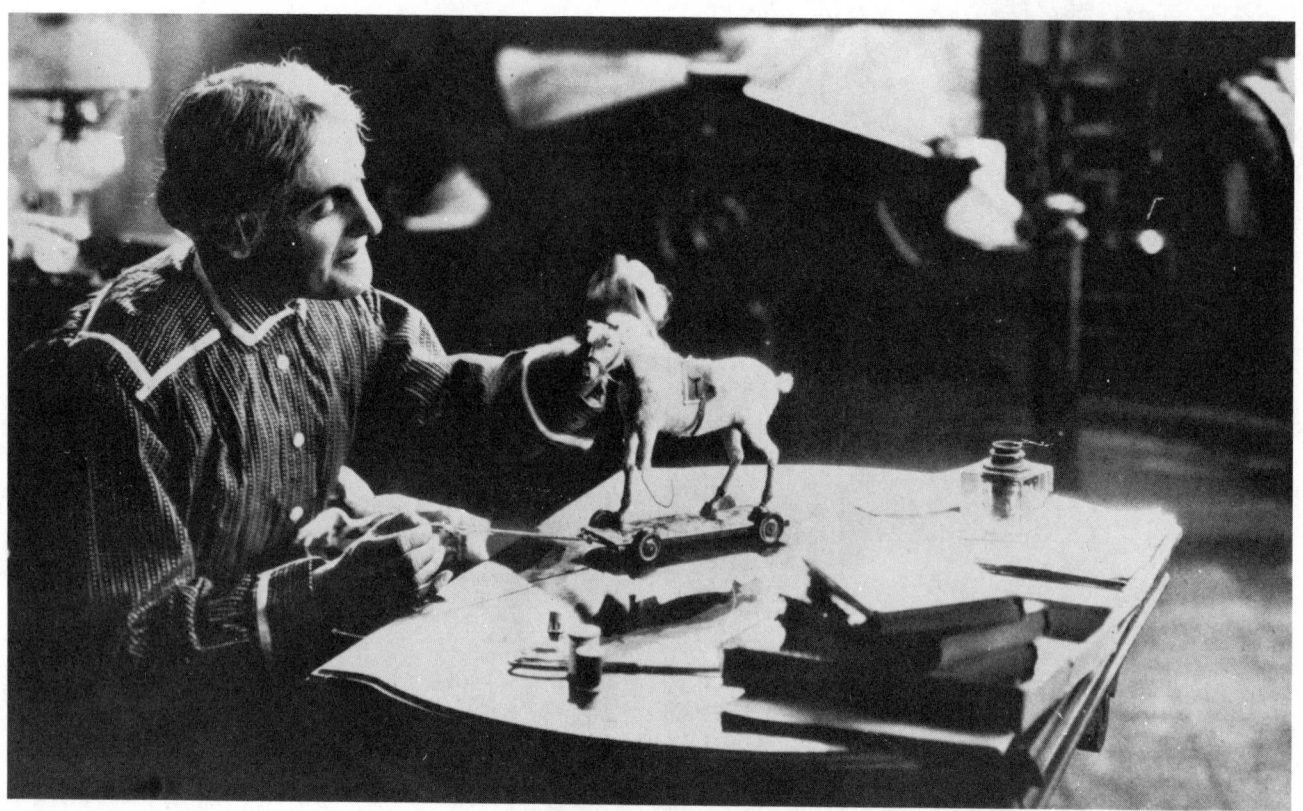

Kate Bruce

Porter Strong and Robert Harron.

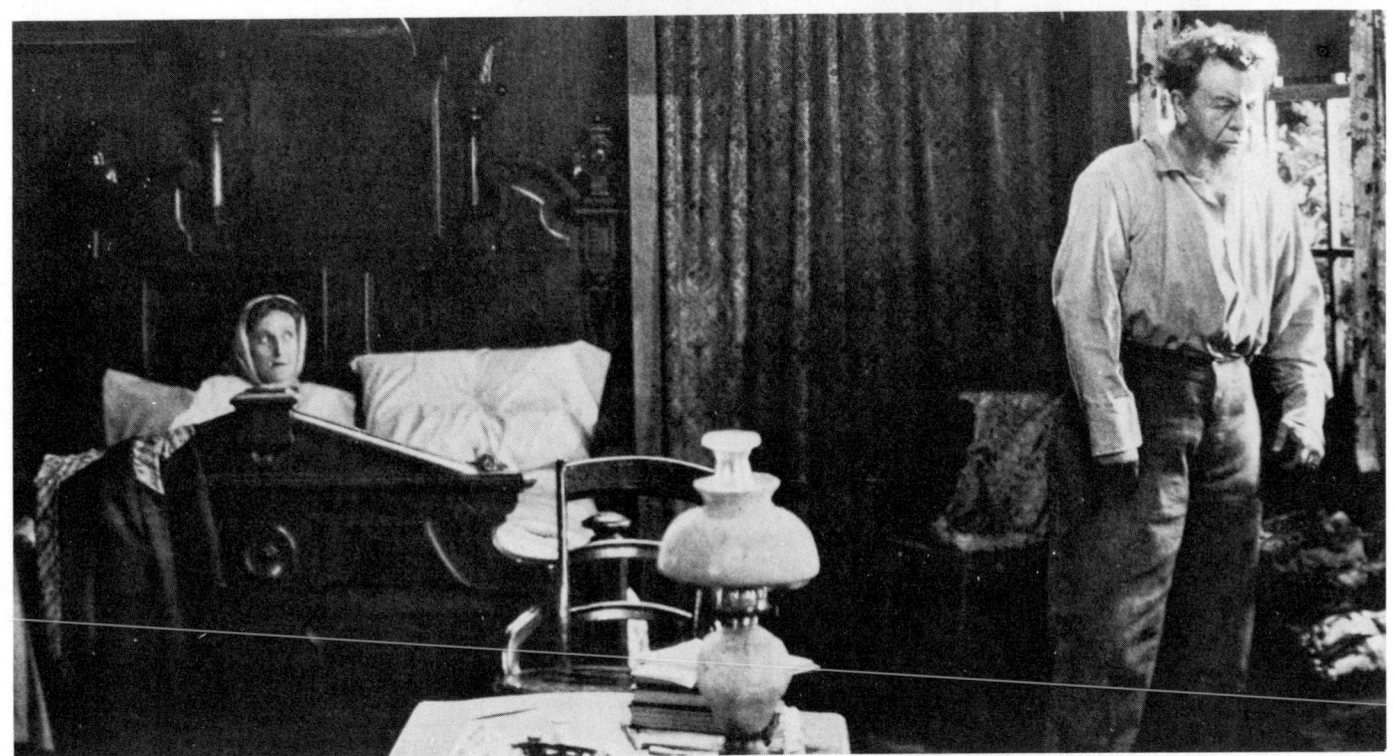

CRITICISM

Writing in *Rob Wagner's Script* (May 11, 1946), Herb Sterne criticized Iris Barry, "a lady who patently rates glister above nuance," and the Museum of Modern Art for failing to appreciate Griffith's so-called minor works. It was this failing—both in appreciation and preservation—that has denied Griffith devotees the opportunity to view *A Romance of Happy Valley* until recently, when it was rediscovered in the Russian film archive. The nitrate print that Sterne was able to screen in 1946 was allowed to rot in the Paramount vaults, as, of course, was the then-surviving print of *The Greatest Thing in Life*.

A Romance of Happy Valley was set in Griffith's home state of Kentucky; as a title asks, "What better place for a romance than Old Kentucky?" Griffith's Kentucky is an idealized rural heaven, where old ladies rock on porches and smoke pipes, and mothers husk corn; where the *Farmer's Almanac* indicates the latest in fashion; where the greatest happiness is owning one's own home; and where the church is "strong for the faith." To the residents of Griffith's Happy Valley, New York is Sodom and Gomorrah, as, indeed, it must have appeared to the director himself when he first journeyed there, just as Robert Harron does in this film, with no friends or money, only ambition.

There is much to delight the viewer in *A Romance of Happy Valley* and much to hold his attention. Virtually nothing happens in the first two reels of the film, and yet one's thoughts and attention never stray from the images on the screen. Its depiction of small-town religion is fascinating, with the entire congregation pleading with Harron to stay in Kentucky, and praying, "Save him from the Devil and New York."

Lillian Gish, as Jennie Timberlake, gives a performance which is almost a straight rehearsal for her role in *True Heart Susie*. Here, she is desperately courting Harron, and trying to persuade him to give up all thoughts of leaving for New York. Here, as in *True Heart Susie*, she is an "old, faithful stupid," who waits eight years for her lover's return. During the years of waiting, the girl's longing for love leads her to hug and caress a scarecrow bearing one of her lover's old jackets. Lillian does have a number of charming moments of comedy, as when she checks under her bed each night for lurking burglars before retiring, or when she ties one end of a piece of string to her father's thumb and the other to her own in order that she may awaken should he need her during the night.

It is hard not to sympathize with John Logan, as played by Robert Harron. Anyone who would devote eight years of his life to inventing a mechanical frog deserves all the sympathy he can get. Harron is a truly dedicated inventor; he would rather spend an evening working on his frog than dancing with Carol Dempster, here making her Griffith debut. Perhaps our sympathies are not really needed, for it is remarkable how much money one can make from a mechanical frog!

Two character actresses stand out in *A Romance of Happy Valley*: Lydia Yeamans Titus and Kate Bruce. The former is the perennial, kindly old optimist with wise advice to Lillian Gish, "Don't frown, child. God smiles from the flowers and the corn and everywhere. You just got to smile back." Kate Bruce, as Harron's mother, delivers a totally restrained performance, best exemplified by the scene in which she discovers that her son has returned. There is no great emotional outburst, just a simple upturned look and a "Thank you, God," delivered without the aid of a subtitle. I cannot help but believe that Lillian Gish's performance in *The Night of the Hunter* is based on Kate Bruce's performance here.

If *A Romance of Happy Valley* has any faults, it is in the final sequences, involving the pure melodramatics of a bank robbery and mistaken identities. Scenes at this point are overlong and distract from the general charm of the rest of the production.

A Romance of Happy Valley is a short work, running only fifty-five minutes, but it is also one of Griffith's finer achievements. It is not incautious to describe it as a little masterpiece. Certainly, had *A Romance of Happy Valley* been as readily accessible to critics as has *True Heart Susie*, it is hard to guess which would have been judged the greater work.

A. S.

12

THE GREATEST THING IN LIFE

SCENARIO: Captain Victor Marier (i.e., D. W. Griffith and S. E. V. Taylor)

PHOTOGRAPHY: G. W. Bitzer

FILM·EDITOR: James Smith

LENGTH: 6,062 feet

PRODUCTION/DISTRIBUTION: Paramount-Artcraft

NEW YORK PREMIÈRE: Strand Theater, December 22, 1918

RELEASED: December 8, 1918

LILLIAN GISH (*Jeanette Peret*)

ROBERT HARRON (*Edward Livingston*)

ADOLPHE LESTINA (*Leo Peret*)

DAVID BUTLER (*Monsieur Le Bébé*)

ELMO LINCOLN (*the American soldier*)

EDWARD PEIL (*the German officer*)

KATE BRUCE (*Jeanette's aunt*)

PEACHES JACKSON (*Mlle Peaches*)

THE STORY

Jeanette Peret is a poor but beautiful girl who sells cigars over the counter for a living. Edward Livingston is a very superior young Southern gentleman. He is strongly attracted to Jeanette but so plainly shows his condescension toward her that she is antagonized. Nevertheless Livingston secretly befriends her father and makes it possible for him to return to France in the hope of regaining his health. Livingston follows, but Jeanette, still repelled by his pride, becomes engaged to marry a grocer, M. Le Bébé, who is a good man but far from a romantic ideal.

Livingston's awakening comes through the war, in which he serves in the American army and learns that there are men worthy of respect in all walks of life. M. Le Bébé dies defending Jeanette against an attack by a German officer, and Livingston signalizes his emancipation from ancient prejudices by kissing his dying Negro "buddy" in the trenches so that he may believe himself in his mother's arms. These incidents clear the way for Livingston's final union with Jeanette.

Lillian Gish as Jeanette

Jeanette and her parents (Adolphe Lestina and Kate Bruce)

Jeanette with Edward Livingston (Robert Harron)

Jeanette with M. Le Bébê (David Butler)

CRITICISM

Of all the "lost" Griffith features, the one whose discovery is most eagerly awaited, and prayed for, is *The Greatest Thing in Life*. In her autobiography, Lillian Gish calls it "one of Mr. Griffith's best films and one of his most neglected." Miss Gish also takes credit for the title, which, apparently, she dreamed up during a lunch of cheese sandwiches and malted milk with Griffith and the publicity man, Harry Carr. The title the director had originally assigned to the film was *Cradle of Souls*.

The Greatest Thing in Life was the third of the Griffith "war" features, and was concerned with the overcoming of snobbery, and, above all, with love, which, of course, is the greatest thing in life. The first three captions—a list of the subtitles of *The Greatest Thing in Life* has survived —indicate its themes:

The story of a young girl and the most important thing to a young girl—Love.
An idealist, who, we are afraid, expects too much of her heroes.

Also the story of an aesthetic young bachelor—too much good fortune has made him selfish and a stranger to his brethren.

Also of a war drum.

Also—but enough.

The most famous scene in *The Greatest Thing in Life* was that in which the selfish Southern snob (played by Robert Harron) kisses the cheek of a dying Negro soldier. This incident occurred in reel six of the production, and was told through two titles:

"Mammy—good-by Mammy—Kiss me!"

To dying ears.
"Here—here's your mammy."

This scene was universally acclaimed on the film's release. Peter Milne in *Picture Play* (April, 1919) wrote: "Harron has never done such an excellent piece of acting as when he learns that race prejudice has no place on the battlefield—when he kisses the cheek of a dying negro calling for his mammy." *Exhibitor's Trade Review* (January 4, 1919) described the kiss as "possibly one of the finest things ever presented on the silversheet."

However, the rest of the film was not so well regarded. "In producing another war picture Griffith does nothing big or unusual enough to justify our confidence in his being the greatest director," wrote Hazel Simpson Naylor in *Motion Picture Magazine* (March, 1919). Her fellow critic, Frederick James Smith, was equally unimpressed. He wrote in *Motion Picture Classic* (March, 1919): "At heart it is the old Griffith chase. It reveals just one thing new, a sort of idealized close-up—with hazy, dreamy outlines, singularly suited to Lillian Gish."

The close-up to which Smith referred was the work of Hendrik Sartov, a portrait photographer, whom Lillian Gish introduced to Griffith. Sartov's contribution to *The Greatest Thing in Life* was small; he was to make a major contribution to future Griffith productions, and eventually to oust "Billy" Bitzer as Griffith's cameraman.

One of the most interesting aspects of the film was the prologue, which preceded the production's Los Angeles première at Clune's Auditorium. Entitled *Voices*, it was personally produced by Griffith, and was stage directed by George Fawcett. Among the players in the prologue were Rudolph Valentino and Clarine Seymour as "The Followers of the Modern Dance" and Carol Dempster as the leader of "The Dancers from the Land of Shadows." Both Seymour and Dempster were to be important in Griffith's future work.

A. S.

13

THE GIRL WHO STAYED AT HOME

SCREENPLAY: S. E. V. Taylor and D. W. Griffith, based on an original story by S. E. V. Taylor

PHOTOGRAPHY: G. W. Bitzer

FILM EDITOR: James Smith

LENGTH: 5,385 feet

PRODUCTION/DISTRIBUTION: Paramount-Artcraft

NEW YORK PREMIÈRE: Strand Theater, March 23, 1919

RELEASED: March 23, 1919

ADOLPHE LESTINA (*Monsieur France*)

CAROL DEMPSTER (*Atoline France*)

FRANCES PARKES (*the chum*)

RICHARD BARTHELMESS (*Ralph Grey*)

ROBERT HARRON (*James Grey*)

SYN DE CONDE (*Count de Brissac*)

GEORGE FAWCETT (*Edward Grey*)

KATE BRUCE (*Mrs. Edward Grey*)

EDWARD PEIL (*the Turnverein Terror*)

CLARINE SEYMOUR (*Cutie Beautiful*)

TULLY MARSHALL (*Cutie's old friend*)

DAVID BUTLER (*August Kant*)

THE HON. JOSEPH SCOTT (*head of the Draft Exemption Board*)

PROVOST MARSHAL GENERAL E. H. CROWDER, GENERAL MARCH, SECRETARY OF WAR NEWTON BAKER (*themselves*)

THE STORY

The Girl Who Stayed at Home deals with the adventures in love and war of two young American brothers of (at the outset) sharply contrasted characters. Ralph Grey is a fine, manly young man, who enlists in the army, against his father's wishes, shortly after America enters World War I. His brother, Jim, a playboy, is drafted against his will but remade, both physically and spiritually, by his army training. Both brothers, who meet in France, make excellent records.

Before the war, Ralph had fallen in love with the daughter of M. France, an unreconstructed old Confederate living in France, but had returned home believing his suit hopeless. Jim's sweetheart is a show girl known as Cutie Beautiful; she is "the girl who stayed at home," and she welcomes the new man back after the war. When the French chateau is seized by the Germans, the girl Ralph loves is in danger of rape, but a decent German saves her by shooting her assailant. The war over, M. France, for the first time, calls himself an American, not merely a Confederate, and his daughter, whose betrothed, a French nobleman, has now died, accepts Ralph.

Clarine Seymour

James Grey (Robert Harron) with the Hon. Joseph Scott

Atoline with Ralph Grey (Richard Barthelmess)

James Grey with Atoline France (Carol Dempster)

Atoline with M. France (Adolphe Lestina)

James and Ralph Grey in the trenches

CRITICISM

The Girl Who Stayed at Home is a little picture by any standard, but it is also a thoroughly disarming one, and deserves far greater attention by critics and historians than it has received.

The Girl Who Stayed at Home was obviously produced with a mind to utilizing war footage shot for *Hearts of the World,* and at the same time as official government propaganda for the draft, and if the film fails, it is in the war sequences, which are all rather tedious. We all know the Americans will arrive, and all will be saved; they have done it on film so many times before and since. However, by the time the production was ready for release the war was over, and Griffith decided to temper its anti-German attitudes severely. He introduced a kindly German, Johann Kant, who, like the American soldiers, has a cherished mother back home, and who, when Carol Dempster is threatened with rape by one of his countrymen, shouts out, "Fight men—not women."

What makes *The Girl Who Stayed at Home* such a delight to watch is its large number of Griffith touches—both big and minor. No one but Griffith would have considered featuring a Confederate soldier (Adolphe Lestina), who, rather than surrender to the Yankees, has sought exile in France, and proudly declares to a bemused American visitor (George Fawcett): "I am not an American. I am a citizen of the Confederate States of America." The heroine, threatened with a fate worse than death, is an old Griffith plot element, as familiar as his use of the subtitle, "Mercy—the woman's part."

Clarine Seymour makes her first Griffith appearance in *The Girl Who Stayed at Home* and Carol Dempster her first in a featured role. Carol Dempster, I must admit, does not make a very good impression. She does far too much jumping around, and, even worse, is featured in a pseudo-Isadora Duncan dance sequence, which must have set back modern dance a good twenty years.

Biased as I am, I must proclaim Clarine Seymour the real hit of the film. I do not believe that she ever had a better role than that of the show girl, Cutie Beautiful, and, in my opinion at least, she transforms a small part into a leading role. As Hazel Simpson Naylor noted in *Motion Picture Magazine* (June, 1919): "Clarine injects life, piquancy, allurement into an image of life and makes of a role a stellar part."

Playing opposite Clarine was Robert Harron as the worthless son of a wealthy industrialist, transformed by the war into a hero. Harron displays a real gift for comedy, looking surprisingly like Charlie Chase, and adopting an astonishing walk, described as "the killing slouch." As fate would have it, both Harron and Miss Seymour were to die, tragically, in 1920. Had they lived, they might have made a wonderful light comedy team.

One of the most delightful scenes in the film is their farewell dinner before Harron is called to the front. Clarine shyly confesses, "I flirted with two men," to which Harron responds, with all the brashness of youth, "Look at me—thirty Janes." By the evening's end, both have declared their love, and Clarine has accepted Harron's engagement ring.

A perfect counterpoint to this scene is the one at the film's close, when Harron arrives home from the war, two hours ahead of time. He comes bounding in through the door, while Clarine falls back in her chair, full of delight that he is back, and at the same time scolding him for not coming at the time that had been set.

In contrast to the scenes between Clarine Seymour and Robert Harron, the Carol Dempster–Richard Barthelmess love affair is strangely tepid; it lacks the joyful emotion of true feeling. Griffith might describe their love as "the young love that will soothe the wounds of the world," but it is the Harron-Seymour love that proclaims joy and hope for the future.

Richard Barthelmess in this, his first Griffith production, gives little intimation of the acting heights to which he was to rise. When he is not merely standing around, he is overacting badly. In one disgraceful melodramatic moment, when his love for Dempster seems doomed, he falls to the ground and begins to claw at the grass. A subtitle describes this as "the tragedy of youth"; the tragedy of bad acting might be a more appropriate description.

After he had completed *The Girl Who Stayed at Home*, Griffith arranged for a screening in Washington, where the production was acclaimed. Representative Edward Keating wrote to the director on March 28, 1919: "*The Girl Who Stayed at Home* is one of the most satisfying pictures inspired by the great world war.... In some mysterious way your camera has caught the spirit which carried America into the war—the spirit which demands justice, equality, and freedom for all the peoples of the earth."

However, not everyone was as pleased with the film. Many considered that it showed the Germans in too favorable a light. One lady complained to the Department of Justice: "I protest the appeal which is made for German sympathy through the showing of a good German soldier taking leave of his mother and her sorrow at later getting word of his death. I object to this [the German mother's] prayer.... The whole picture strikes me as being a clever camouflage for some more German propaganda and I ask that it be investigated."

Complaints such as this, which were echoed by a number of critics, must have irked Griffith considerably. It was a sad reflection on the American people that they should turn a blind eye to the beauty and humanity of a Griffith production, and see only anti-American propaganda. It was not the first time that a Griffith film had aroused such a negative public response, and it most certainly would not be the last.

A. S.

14

TRUE HEART SUSIE

SCENARIO: Marian Fremont

PHOTOGRAPHY: G. W. Bitzer

FILM EDITOR: James Smith

LENGTH: 6,200 feet

PRODUCTION/DISTRIBUTION: Paramount-Artcraft

NEW YORK PREMIÈRE: Strand Theater, June 1, 1919

RELEASED: June 1, 1919

LILLIAN GISH (*Susie May Trueheart, otherwise known as True Heart Susie*)

ROBERT HARRON (*William Jenkins*)

WALTER HIGBY (*William's father*)

LOYOLA O'CONNOR (*Susie's aunt*)

GEORGE FAWCETT (*the stranger*)

CLARINE SEYMOUR (*Bettina Hopkins*)

KATE BRUCE (*Bettina's aunt*)

CAROL DEMPSTER (*Bettina's chum*)

ROBERT CANNON (*Sporty Malone*)

THE STORY

Susie May Trueheart, a country girl, loves her neighbor William Jenkins, but in spite of their good-fellowship together, William is as blind to her in a romantic aspect as David Copperfield was to Agnes. Unbeknownst to William, Susie sells her cow and other possessions to secure the wherewithal to send him away to college to study for the ministry and thus fulfill his ambition to become a man who amounts to something.

After his graduation, William returns, and Susie has the satisfaction of hearing him preach his first sermon. But her hopes are dashed when William is fascinated by a beautiful but frivolous and worthless girl, Bettina Hopkins, a vivacious and flashy young milliner.

Susie swallows her pride and grief to serve as bridesmaid at the wedding, but the marriage is a disaster. Totally unqualified as a minister's wife, Bettina takes to cheating with "sporty" and dissipated friends. After being caught in a terrible storm, she takes ill because of exposure and dies.

Susie, who knows the truth, protects the dead girl's memory and shields William from the pain of knowing his wife's unworthiness by concealing from him the true nature of his wife's excursion, and William vows never to marry again. This is too much for Bettina's aunt, who now tells William who paid for his education, and Bettina's friends enlighten him as to the true character of her excursion. His eyes opened at last, William realizes that Susie is his true love.

It is hard to believe that only a little over half a century ago, a girl of twenty could wear such a hat as is shown in this portrait of Clarine Seymour. But it says much for her beauty that it was not extinguished by its accoutrements.

Susie and William in youth (Lillian Gish and Robert Harron)

In Bettina's (Clarine Seymour's) fascination for William, Susie sees the ruin of her hopes.

Thanks to Susie's generosity, William is now a minister.

William's wayward wife, with her rackety friends

Clarine Seymour with Robert Cannon

CRITICISM

D. W. Griffith's films are actually divided into two groups: the epic and the lyric. Until recently, the weight of critical opinion has regarded Griffith's more ambitious, large scale productions such as *The Birth of a Nation*, *Intolerance*, and *Orphans of the Storm* as more serious works than his less ambitious, more intimate films like *A Romance of Happy Valley* and *True Heart Susie*. Yet the more Griffith I see, the harder I find it to distinguish between the epic and lyric impulses. *Intolerance*, especially the Babylonian sequence, achieves its greatest emotional power through the juxtaposition of history in long shot and intimacy in close-up. Griffith's work, like John Ford's, succeeds in capturing the momentary beauty of an idiosyncratic gesture against the eternally impersonal stone face of history.

All of Griffith's epics, constructed on this dramatic principle, blend history and melodrama into a single narrative fabric. In *Orphans of the Storm*, Griffith uses the French Revolution as a chaotic background for his separation/reunification melodrama. Even in *America*, history and melodrama are inextricably interwoven. Using the Montague family as an immediate and personal microcosm of the American Revolution, *America* combines national with personal catastrophe. In one remarkable sequence, young Charles Montague, who, unknown to his loyalist father, has gone off to fight on the side of the Americans, exposes himself to British fire to get much-needed powder in the battle at Breed's Hill. On his way back to the American trenches, Charles is shot and falls. Griffith cuts to a shot of his sister, Nancy, reading Charles' old letters to comfort their wounded father. Then, Griffith cuts back to Charles who miraculously struggles to his feet, delivers the gunpowder and collapses (dead). Though the cut to Charles' father is partly ironic—since Justice Montague, a Tory, is unaware that his son is fighting against the king—the sequence does illustrate the spirit that lies behind the son's heroism. The shot of Nancy comforting his father seems to give Charles strength; his own letters to his father mysteriously comfort him. Though Griffith conceives of the American Revolution in family terms—i.e., the son revolts against his father—he uses the spirit of the family—the son's love for his father—to animate and guide his revolt.

In comparison with *America*, one of Griffith's more ambitious and didactic pictures, *True Heart Susie*'s uncomplicated simplicity and stylistic directness give it a charming sort of purity. The absence of an historical background and the specificity of detail such a back-ground demands creates a freer, more open structure. Instead of the usual, multiple-plot narrative, *True Heart Susie* tells a single story, avoiding a counterplot's symbolic or metaphoric commentary on the central action. This simplification of the action results in a greater formal simplicity. The film feels less rigidly structured. For example, there is practically no cross-cutting between two separate events for dramatic effect. Nor does Griffith construct separate, dialectic worlds, each with its own internal order and logic, whose conflict gives birth to a new world. For example, in *Broken Blossoms*, the two major sets—Battling Burrows' cold, bare, waterfront shack and the Yellow Man's warm, exotically detailed storetop apartment—delimit the two, polarly different worlds that exist for Lucy in the film. Her home is a place of abuse and unhappiness; the Chinaman's becomes a peaceful refuge from that. After Lucy is cruelly beaten to death by her father, the Chinaman, though he arrives too late to save her life, nevertheless "rescues" her from the grim waterfront setting. After he shoots Burrows, he carries Lucy back to his own apartment where we see them for the last time. The heavily tragic action at the end is lightened by their minor triumphs: Lucy escapes her world and the Chinaman escapes his.

True Heart Susie lacks this Dickensian dialectic of décor: there are no good or evil settings, nor are there conflicting worlds. Rather, Griffith creates a single universe, flawed only by its fragmented separation of one character from another. The opening shot of the film, a high-angle shot of two farm houses separated by a dirt road that runs between them, presents a single community or world, unified in time and space. The subsequent editing which reveals William's father working outside one house with his hoe and Susie's aunt sitting inside the other house sewing, does not oppose worlds as much as characterize separate parts—e.g., male/female, exterior/interior—of a single one.

The introduction of Susie and William at school, like the opening shot, sets up a physical unity whose violation and restoration have their roots in the fragmented nature of the composition itself. Griffith shows William and Susie, standing next to one another in a spelling bee, in a single frame. William misspells "anonymous." Susie, for whom the word has much more meaning, spells it correctly and exchanges places with him in line. In another Griffith film, such a switch in position would, because of the moral rigidity of spatial positioning in his compositions, indicate a dramatic reversal or turning point. The ease with which it is made here reflects the looseness of Susie and William's relationship. Though William and Susie stand together, their differences separate them. Though the difference—Susie spells better—seems slight, it actually foreshadows the greater gulf in awareness that eventually isolates one from the other.

It is hard to analyse the lovers' separation beyond its physical fact. In most melodramas, the characters' separation arises out of an externally imposed design. Their differences in class (*Orphans*) or race (*Broken Blossoms*) prevent their union. Or the action itself, like Henriette's loss of the abducted Louise in *Orphans* or the storm and ice floe that separate David from Anna at the end of *Way Down East*, keeps the characters apart from one another. In *True Heart Susie*, the separation seems to grow out of the characters themselves, out of their blindness (William) and shyness (Susie), out of their own inertia and inability to change the way things are at the start of the film.

The absence of an externally imposed formal structure shifts the dramatic balance between form and content in *True Heart Susie*. Griffith's direction reveals a greater concern for characterization than narrative development. It is through the characters, not the plot, that Griffith expresses and defines the nature of the characters' separation.

The greatest beauty of the film lies in the tremendous performances Griffith gets out of Lillian Gish and Bobby Harron. Their scenes together evoke a sense of emotional disjointedness. Though both are physically alive to one another, the self-containedness of their gestures reveals a deep isolation that neither can easily escape. The way William strokes and twirls his new mustache on his return from college suggests a personal vanity that blinds him to Susie's merits. Earlier in the film, on their way home from school, William and Susie stop by a tree. They look at one another; start to kiss, then draw apart without completing the kiss. Instead, William carves Susie's initials, along with his own, into the tree. The frustrated kiss which recurs throughout the film emphasises not only the physical space but also the emotional gap between them and finds visual resonances in the other barriers which come between the lovers: Susie's fence, the hedge, and the window in the last scene.

The film's settings, both the exterior, rural landscape and the interior, orderly domesticity of Susie's house, set off, frequently in a humorous way, the idiosyncratic actions of the characters. The physical presence of the world of nature works as a foil for the unnatural gestures that appear within it. When William rehearses his first sermon, Susie's impassive rapture in his wild, fire-and-brimstone gesticulation works ironically with the natural setting (a beautiful grove of trees) to underscore the unnaturalness of William's action. Earlier, as Susie and William walk down a country road in long shot, Susie's right foot kicks out. A characteristic trait, the spasmodic foot also betrays externally the inner self-restraint which prevents Susie from fully expressing her love for William. Inside her own home this restraint vanishes and Susie explodes like a firecracker. She jumps around, dances and physically delights in her excitement over a non-committal letter she receives from William away at college. The static quality of her environment makes her frenetic actions appear all the wilder. Her aunt's request that Susie "deport" herself makes her violation of the order of her setting more outrageous.

At the end of the film, William learns of Susie's sacrifices for him and, with a new maturity, goes to tell her of his love for her. He approaches her at her window as she waters flowers with a huge watering can. When he tells her that he loves her, she (inside the house) hides shyly behind the watering can. Finally, William leans through the window and kisses her. Though the ending unites William and Susie, their unification is made only with difficulty. The presence of the window and the watering can between them gives the scene and their actions an awkwardness reminiscent of their earlier scenes together. Yet the composition—combining male and female, exterior and interior—reflects a new stability and balance in their union.

The lack of stylistic sophistication in *True Heart Susie* makes it one of Griffith's purest and most immediate films. There is nothing between us and the characters. In a film built on chaotic adolescent behavior, there is a remarkable simplicity of characterization: Griffith, like Ford, creates characters with a single gesture. The physical presence of the natural countryside throughout the film lyricises the central relationship—it has none of the pressing inner necessity of Griffith's more constricting interior films. In comparison with Griffith's other work, *True Heart Susie* seems unique in its lyrical directness. There is no great story or idea that moves it, but a series of awkward, idiosyncratic gestures and a feeling for the beauty of his characters' love.

John Belton

—Reprinted by permission from *The Silent Picture*, No. 17 (1973).

15

SCARLET DAYS

SCENARIO: S. E. V. Taylor

PHOTOGRAPHY: G. W. Bitzer

FILM EDITOR: James Smith

LENGTH: 5 reels

PRODUCTION/DISTRIBUTION: Paramount-Artcraft

NEW YORK PREMIÈRE: Rivoli Theater, November 10, 1919

RELEASED: November 30, 1919

RICHARD BARTHELMESS (*Alvarez, a bandit*)
EUGENIE BESSERER (*Rosie Nell*)
CAROL DEMPSTER (*Lady Fair, her daughter*)
CLARINE SEYMOUR (*Chiquita, a Mexican dance-hall girl*)
RALPH GRAVES (*Randolph, a Virginia gentleman*)
GEORGE FAWCETT (*the sheriff*)
WALTER LONG (*King Bagley, the dance-hall proprietor*)
KATE BRUCE (*an aunt*)
RHEA HAINES (*Spasm Sal*)
ADOLPHE LESTINA (*Randolph's partner*)
HERBERT SUTCH (*the marshal*)
J. WESLEY WARNER (*Alvarez's man*)

THE STORY

Rosie Nell is a tough dance-hall woman in the Gold Rush days of '49. Her daughter, to whom she is deeply devoted, and who has been reared in ignorance of her mother's way of life, is in a fashionable school in the East, and Nell is saving her money so that she can go East to join her and live respectably.

Nell gets into a row with two other rough women who try to rob her, and, in the course of the fracas, one of these, Spasm Sal, dies of a heart attack. Sal's friends consider Nell a murderess, and she is nearly lynched by a mob, but Alvarez, a bandit chief, saves her.

Nell's enemy, King Bagley, proprietor of the dance hall, and his gang, attack the cabin in which Nell and her daughter are living, and Randolph and Alvarez defend it. When he perceives that the gang is sure to win, the bandit saves the others by giving himself up to the sheriff. The gang is dispersed, but Nell is slain by a chance shot.

Chiquita, the outlaw's Mexican sweetheart, comes to the Sheriff to plead for her lover's life, and the two are able to make a daring escape together on his horse.

Lady Fair with her mother, Rosie Nell (Eugenie Besserer)

Randolph (Ralph Graves), his partner (Adolphe Lestina), Alvarez (Richard Barthelmess), and Lady Fair (Carol Dempster)

Alvarez with Chiquita (Clarine Seymour)

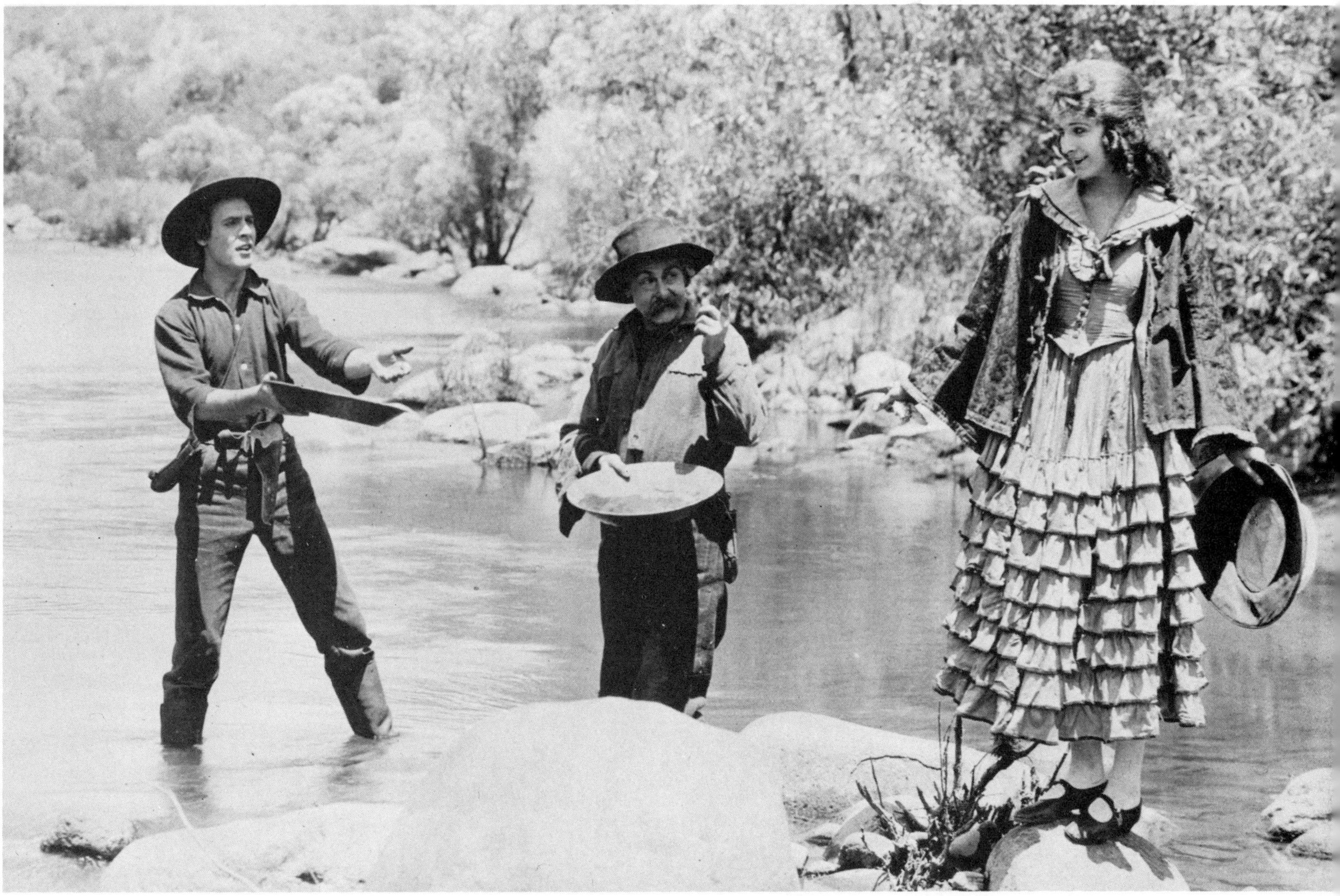

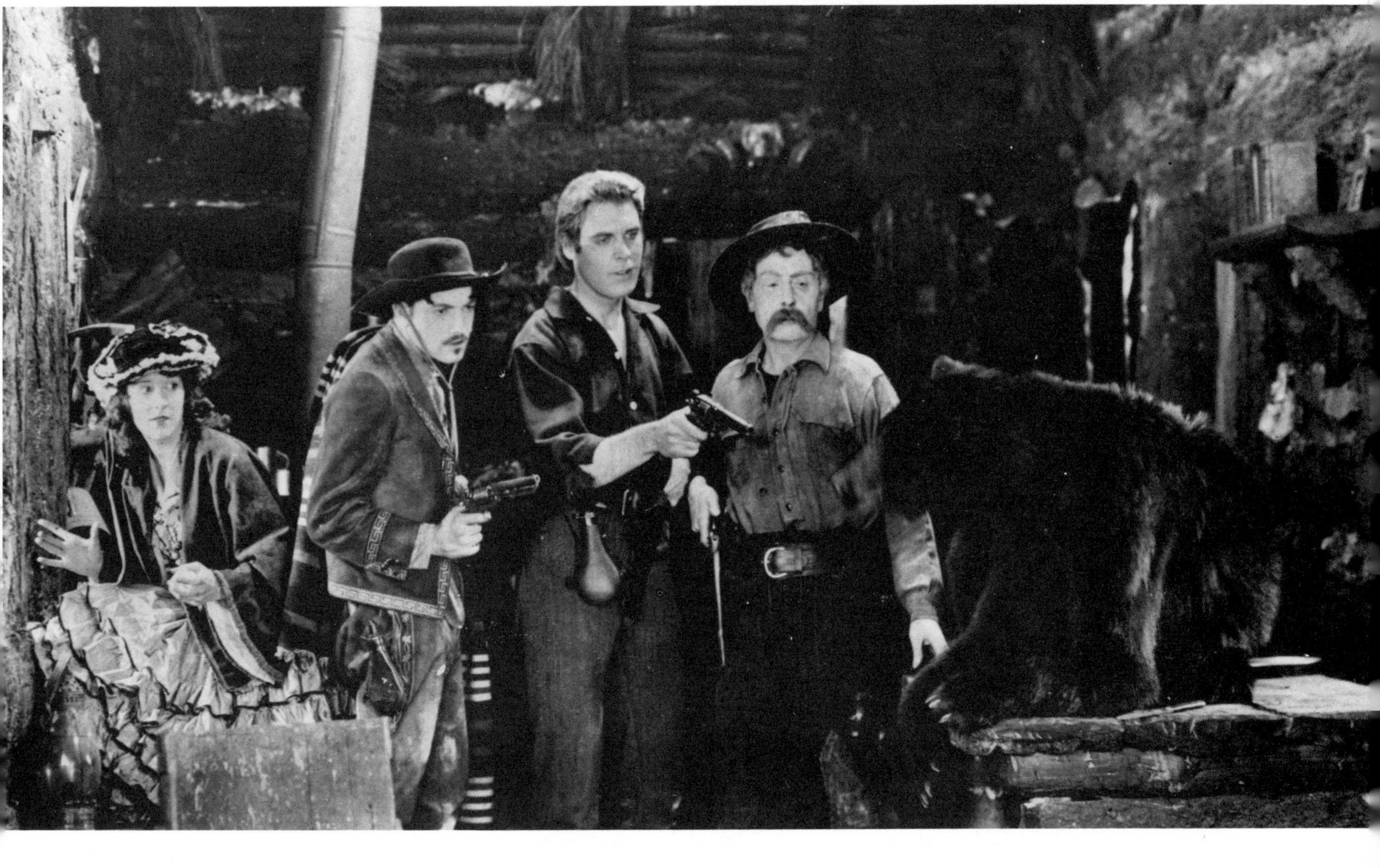

CRITICISM

D. W. Griffith first considered the possibility of directing a Western feature in December of 1918, and asked his associate, S. E. V. Taylor, to come up with a suitable subject. The story which Taylor supplied to Griffith was *Scarlet Days*, set in Arizona in 1849. Griffith promptly changed the locale to California and updated it to 1875; he also decided to base the bandit-hero, Alvarez, upon a true-life Mexican, Joaquin Murietta, and introduced a number of historical incidents dealing with the bandit's career.

For his cast Griffith chose Richard Barthelmess, Carol Dempster, Clarine Seymour, and Ralph Graves. The last was making his Griffith debut, and never looked more handsome and dashing than he did in this production. Eugenie Besserer, in the minor role of Rosie Nell, is particularly impressive, and quite obviously deserves to be remembered for more than her performance as Al Jolson's mother in *The Jazz Singer*. Clarine Seymour also stands out as Chiquita, a Mexican dance-hall girl, with a peculiar habit of fighting not with her hands, or even her feet, but using her head as a battering ram! Only a Griffith heroine, I feel sure, would have resorted to such tactics.

Scarlet Days is a beautiful film to look at, if one can manage to avoid paying too much attention to the acting or the story. Griffith had made the best possible use of the locations he chose in Tuolumne County, California.

Everything else about *Scarlet Days* is bad. The story is as melodramatic as the acting. The interior scenes are particularly jarring, forcing the viewer, as they do, to concentrate on the characters, and forget about the picturesque scenery. Worst of all, *Scarlet Days* is strongly derivative of earlier—and infinitely better—Griffith productions. There is a besieged cabin, as in *The Battle at Elderbush Gulch* and *The Birth of a Nation*, and just as in the latter film, the besieged women hide in the cellar. And just in case the reader should not recall *The Birth of a Nation*, Griffith has Carol Dempster giggle hysterically, in her panic, exactly as Mae Marsh had done four years earlier.

This similarity was not lost on contemporary viewers. *The Morning Telegraph* (November 16, 1919) commented: "Carol Dempster, under Mr. Griffith's direction, is a sort of composite of Lillian Gish and Mae Marsh since she employs a number of Miss Gish's nervous little mannerisms and has one scene which recalls Miss Marsh's big moment in *The Birth of a Nation*."

It really is hard to believe that *Scarlet Days* was made several years later than *The Birth of a Nation*; it looks more as if it had been produced five years earlier. On its release, *Variety* suggested that possibly Griffith had not directed it at all, or, at the least, had not bothered to supervise the editing.

Variety, however, was in the minority in disliking the film; most other critics were impressed. Harriette Underhill, in the New York *Tribune* (November 10, 1919), wrote: "*Scarlet Days* is so exciting that after it is finished you sink back in your green plush chair at the Rivoli and try to make up your mind whether you are glad or sorry that it is over."

D. W. Griffith had directed a number of films with Western themes for the Biograph, but *Scarlet Days* was his only feature-length Western. I wonder if the director was as disappointed with *Scarlet Days* as I was when I first viewed it? Could it be that its failings turned him permanently against the film Western?

A. S.

16

BROKEN BLOSSOMS

SCENARIO: D. W. Griffith, based on "The Chink and the Child" in *Limehouse Nights* by Thomas Burke

PHOTOGRAPHY: G. W. Bitzer

SPECIAL EFFECTS: Hendrik Sartov

ADDITIONAL PHOTOGRAPHY: Karl Brown

FILM EDITOR: James Smith

TECHNICAL ADVISER: Moon Kwan

MUSIC ARRANGED BY: Louis F. Gottschalk and D. W. Griffith

LENGTH: 6 reels

PRODUCTION: D. W. Griffith, Inc.

DISTRIBUTION: United Artists

NEW YORK PREMIÈRE: George M. Cohan Theatre, May 13, 1919

RELEASED: October 20, 1920

LILLIAN GISH (*Lucy Burrows*)

RICHARD BARTHELMESS (*the Yellow Man*)

DONALD CRISP (*Battling Burrows*)

ARTHUR HOWARD (*his manager*)

EDWARD PEIL (*Evil Eye*)

GEORGE BERANGER (*the Spying One*)

NORMAN "KID MC COY" SELBY (*a prizefighter*)

THE STORY

The small-time prizefighter, Battling Burrows, "an abysmal brute, a gorilla from the jungles of East London," lives with his fifteen-year-old illegitimate daughter, Lucy, in a hovel in Limehouse. When he is in a rage over his manager's scolding him for his dissipations, which is often, he relieves his feelings by using the girl as a punching bag. Since he never gives her a decent word, she is so terrified of him that when he commands her to smile, she pushes up the corners of her mouth with her fingers.

One day she spills food over his hand when serving his meal, and though this is due to his own clumsiness, he chooses to believe that it was done deliberately and beats her without mercy. In his absence, she stumbles out of the house and into Cheng Huan's Chinese curio shop, where she faints on the floor.

In China this priestly trained young idealist had conceived the idea of coming to London to convert rude Westerners to the gospel of the gentle Buddha. By this time thoroughly disillusioned, he has become a frequenter of opium dens and gambling hells, but, remaining a poet at heart, he, and he alone in Limehouse, has for some time been an admirer of Lucy's delicate beauty as he has seen her pass his shop in the street. When he finds her, he carries her upstairs, tends her bruises, surrounds her with flowers, dolls, and Chinese finery, and treats her like a princess or a goddess in a shrine.

Unfortunately Cheng Huan's shop is shortly visited on business by a miserable little slum rat who is a hanger-on of Burrows. Hearing a noise above while Cheng Huan is out making change, he tiptoes up the stairs and catches a glimpse of Lucy. He loses no time in reporting her presence there to Burrows, who feels that his "honor" has been outraged by "the dirty Chink" who has established an "unnacheral" relationship with his girl. As soon as his fight with the Limehouse Tiger is over, he sets out to "learn" them both.

Arriving at Cheng Huan's place during the Chinaman's absence, Burrows wrecks the shrine, smashing everything in it, and drags Lucy "home." Terrified, though wildly protesting that there "wasn't nothing wrong," she locks herself in a closet, but Burrows smashes in the door, drags her out, and beats her to death.

Cheng Huan, having discovered his ruined shrine, goes to Burrows's place, where he finds Lucy dead. He shoots Burrows, then carries Lucy back to his place, where he crouches beside her and stabs himself while "all the tears of the ages rush over his heart."

Lucy (Lillian Gish) on the waterfront

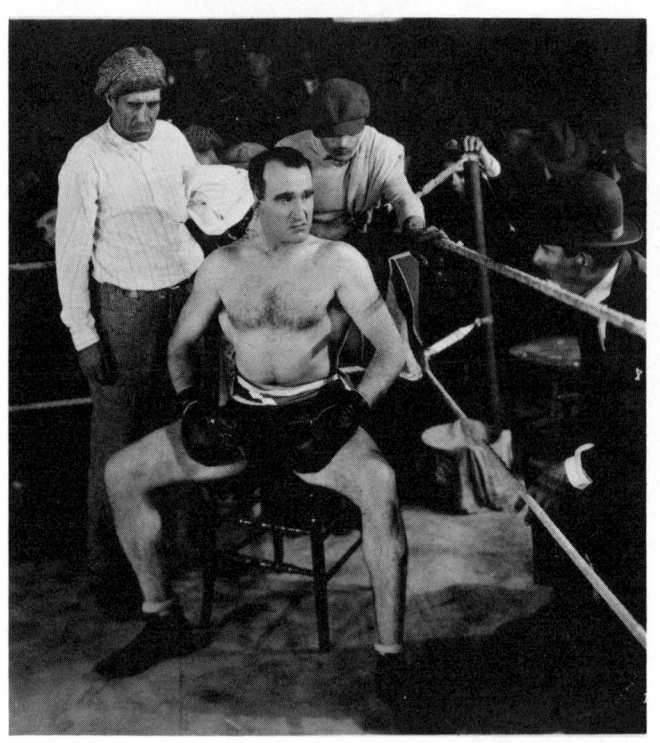

Battling Burrows (Donald Crisp)

At right and on opposite page:
Lucy in the haven prepared for her by Cheng Huan (Richard Barthelmess)

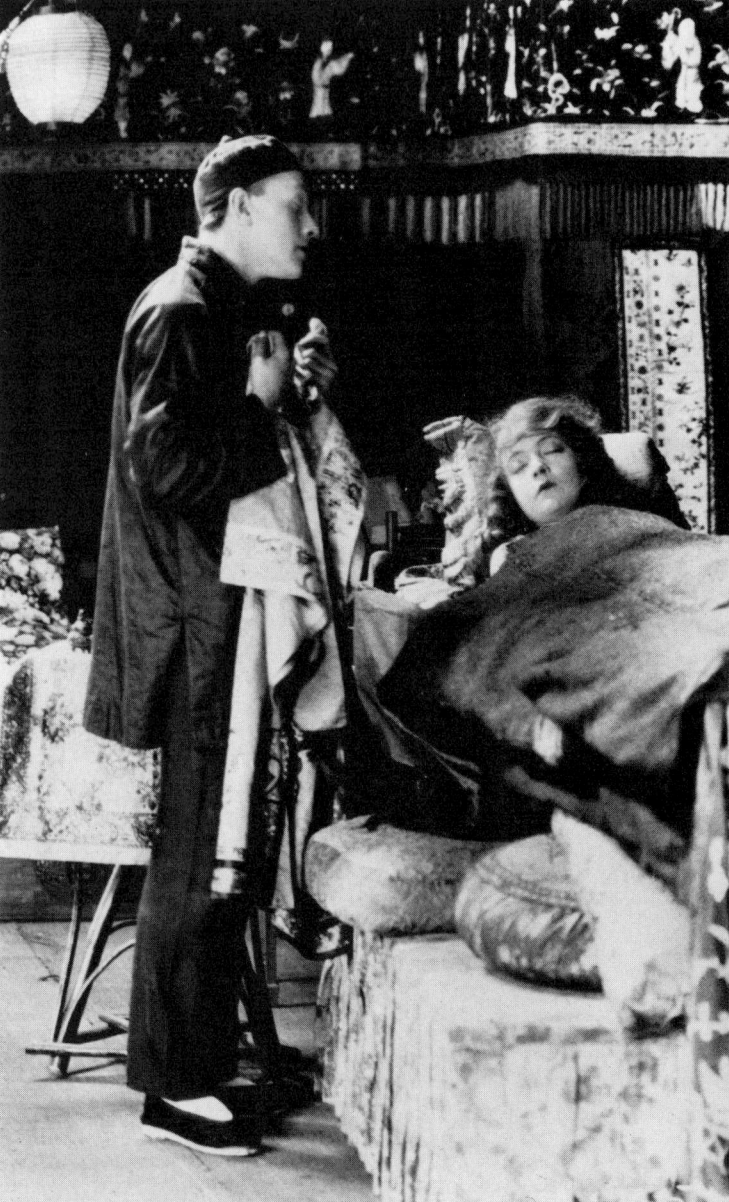

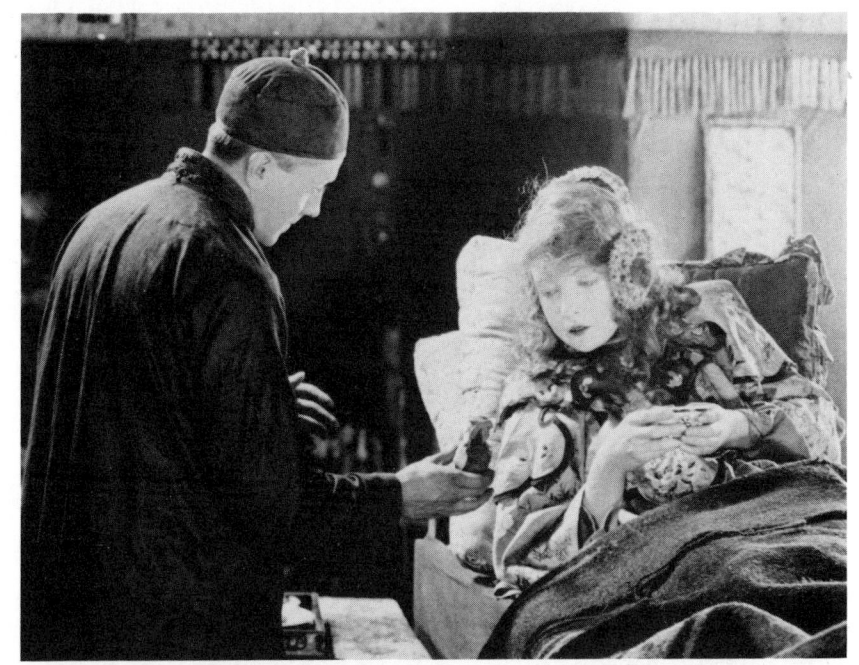

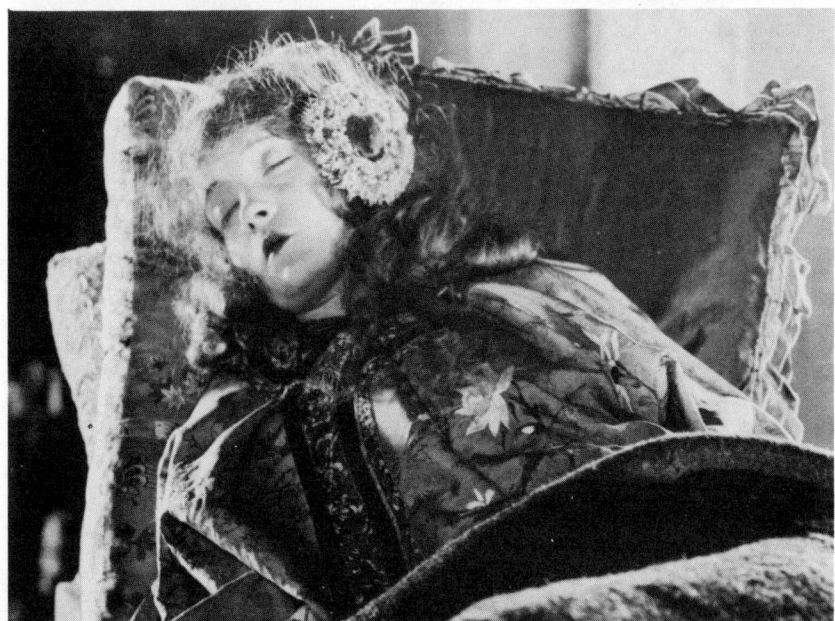

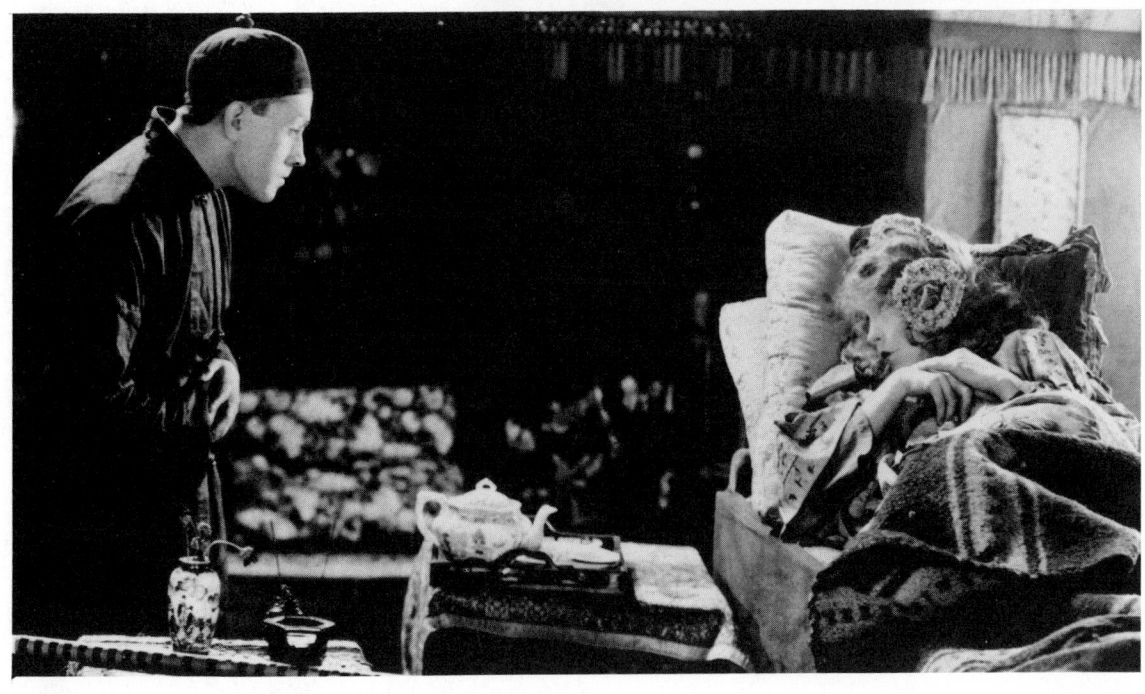

Lillian Gish in the famous closet scene

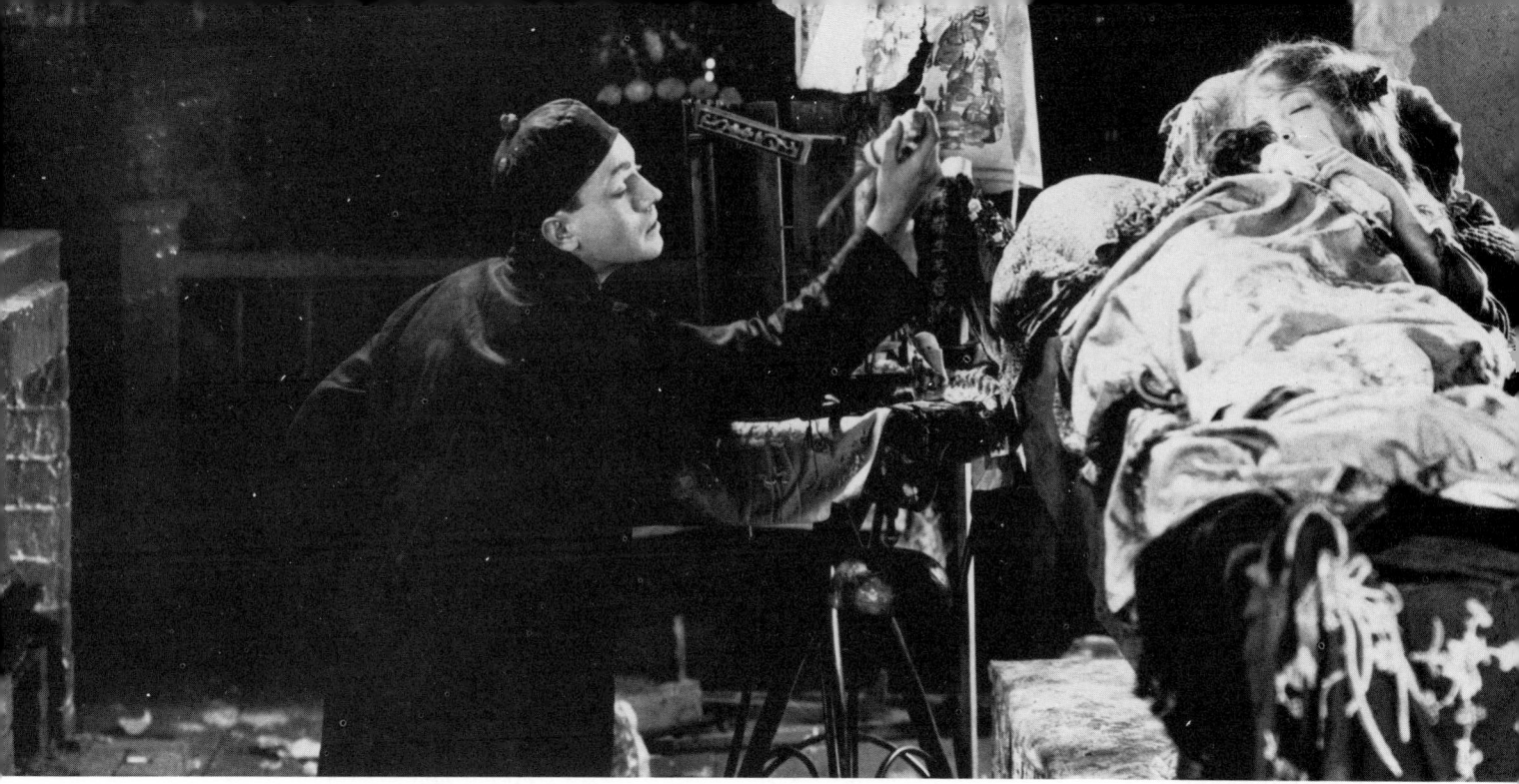

The death of Cheng Huan

CRITICISM

Broken Blossoms is based upon "The Chink and the Child," the first story in Thomas Burke's *Limehouse Nights* (1917), which had been brought to D. W. Griffith's attention by Mary Pickford. Though both Lucy and her father call Cheng Huan a "Chink," Griffith dropped the offensive title, even making his subtitle read *The Yellow Man and the Girl.* But *Broken Blossoms* was a weak and sentimental label for a film of such power and beauty as was turned out; it almost invited the contemporary wag's variation of "Busted Buds."

Griffith followed Burke's story line very closely; even the purple prose of the subtitles, which has been so much criticized, is, in large part, taken from Burke's tale, which is artfully, effectively, and almost confidentially related, achieving an odd combination of horror, poetry, and sentimentality. Even the ironical caption about Burrows hating all who were not born in the same great country as himself, which seems so thoroughly Griffithian, is from Burke.

The principal change comes at the end. In Burke, Cheng Huan kills Burrows by depositing a venomous serpent in his bed, which, when he flops down upon it, stings him to death. This, in London, is a piece of extravagant grotesquerie even in the story; in a film it would have been impossible. Griffith substitutes a more reasonable, and much more dramatic, direct confrontation between the two men. As a matter of fact, he disliked snakes so much that when working on location, he would send someone out before him to beat the bushes, lest he should inadvertently encounter one.

Cheng Huan's noble Chinese idealism and the idea of his mission to the West are original with Griffith. So is his shop; Burke does not tell us how Cheng got his living in Limehouse. Though Burke's Lucy is twelve as against Griffith's fifteen, Cheng Huan finds her in a bagnio, to which she had been taken by another girl after Burrows had locked her out of their hovel. Though she is innocent, she is rather more knowing than the girl in the film, and she returns his kisses "impetuously, gladly." Burke, like Griffith, makes Cheng's love for Lucy "a pure and holy thing," but he gives it more erotic coloring than Griffith, who permits the sexual motif to enter momentarily only once, and then only for the man, not for Lucy.

Broken Blossoms stands in the sharpest possible contrast to the great epic films that had hitherto represented Griffith's highest accomplishment. There are only three characters of any importance, and the action is simple and slow moving. It was a studio film, which had wide influence upon subsequent production, both here and abroad. When it was first shown in the spring of 1919, it was universally proclaimed that the screen had acquired new dignity and achieved a truly classical tragedy.

The synopsis may not show this, for the story itself, reduced to its bare bones, is horrible and repulsive; the judgment, nevertheless, was correct. Griffith had made slum films before, but never had the camera probed and meditated as it did here. Until the climax there is very little action. Even Lillian Gish, who, as Lucy, is the principal character, is almost passive until she reaches the great closet scene, one of the most celebrated scenes ever screened, in which she turns hysterics into beauty and fine art. Rudolph Schildkraut called it the finest acting he had ever seen.

The same alchemy operates in other respects. Atmospheric shots of ships and temple bells open and close the picture; even Burrows's den and the Limehouse slums, swathed in the cloaking river mist, are beautiful as they are lighted and photographed here. Western squalor is set over against the Chinese luxury and refinement with which the film opens and to which almost the whole first reel is devoted, and in London itself Lucy's passage from the "home" where she has known only cruelty to the Oriental refuge which Cheng Huan's loving-kindness sets up for her is a passage from hell to heaven. It should be remembered, too, that, as the film was first shown, not only was the film stock itself tinted but the screen was bathed in rich red and blue lights proceeding from the projection booth. It is difficult to believe that this magnificent film was shot in eighteen days, and that when it was finished, Griffith thought it so depressing that for some time he could not bring himself to look at it!

The Cheng Huan of Richard Barthelmess was a beautiful and sensitive characterization; already decidedly a personable screen hero, Barthelmess now proved that he was also an actor. I doubt that having him a frequenter of opium dens contributed much more to the characterization desired than did Conan Doyle's making Sherlock Holmes a cocaine addict in the early stories; in *Broken Blossoms* this aspect may best be regarded as a carry-over from Burke's tale. But it was not sufficiently prominent in the picture to cause any real trouble. I have never been able quite to make up my mind about Donald Crisp's Battling Burrows. He plays with splendid force, and his handling of the chair and the various articles of the table is masterly, but I cannot say quite the same for his "mugging"; it is hard to believe that any man would express his villainy by twisting his mouth out of shape quite so consistently as Burrows does.

Lucy was the last of the three main characters to be introduced, and at this late date it would surely be carrying coals to Newcastle to labor the point that *Broken Blossoms* was Lillian Gish's acting picture first of all. Griffith habitually allowed his players considerable freedom, though he certainly corrected and edited their performances where they went astray or failed to fit into the general design. But if this was true of his trusted players in general, it was, by this time, much more his method with Miss Gish, who had now sufficiently established her authority to have become in some sense a collaborator. Doubting her ability to play a child, she had, at the outset, not been attracted to the role that she was to make easily the high point of her career thus far. Having accepted it, she delayed production by (literally) collapsing with a very dangerous case of Spanish influenza in the deadly 1918 epidemic, and she began rehearsals wearing a medical mask. Harry Carr says she went to the hospital to study hysteria and learn how to simulate death from beating. When she finished playing the closet scene, Griffith was limp. "My God," he exclaimed, "why didn't you warn me you were going to do that?"

Nothing in a really good motion picture can be described. It must be seen, and words are valuable only to recall impressions or teach the spectator what to look for. But sometimes this seems preeminently true not of the big scenes but of the many little touches in which all really great films abound. Take, for example, the moment in passing when the now disillusioned Cheng Huan, who had himself come from China to London as a kind of missionary-in-reverse, encounters the smug cleric and the bigoted brother who is just leaving for China "to convert the heathen." "I wish him luck," says Cheng, and the brother hands the Chinaman a tract whose cover is imprinted with a single word: HELL. Take the scene in which before they have met, Lucy and Cheng look at each other through the shop window in which her childish eyes devour the pretty things displayed there: we look at what she sees, and we look at him as she sees him and at her as she appears to him. Take, again, the much more wonderful moment when, basking in his loving care of her, she raises her fingers to widen her mouth into a mechanical smile and then, as if realizing that this is no longer necessary, smiles naturally, and this time with her eyes as well as her lips. The end of the film too is handled with great subtlety. Burrows's associates find him dead and rush to the police office to report, but the officer at the desk keeps them waiting while he finishes what he is writing, and George Nicholls, as a London bobby, looks up from the war news he has been reading, and says, "Better than last week. Only 40,000 casualties." When the authorities come at last to Cheng Huan's we see them enter but we do not go in with them. We have already been there.

E. W.

17

THE GREATEST QUESTION

SCENARIO: S. E. V. Taylor, based on a story by William Hale

PHOTOGRAPHY: G. W. Bitzer

FILM EDITOR: James Smith

LENGTH: 6 reels

PRODUCTION/DISTRIBUTION: First National

NEW YORK PREMIÈRE: Strand Theater, December 28, 1919

RELEASED: November 1, 1919

LILLIAN GISH (*Nellie Jarvis, otherwise known as "Little Miss Yes'm"*)

ROBERT HARRON (*Jimmie Hilton*)

RALPH GRAVES (*John Hilton, Jr.*)

EUGENIE BESSERER (*Mrs. Hilton*)

GEORGE FAWCETT (*John Hilton, Sr.*)

TOM WILSON (*Uncle Zeke*)

GEORGE NICHOLLS (*Martin Cain*)

JOSEPHINE CROWELL (*Mrs. Cain*)

THE STORY

As a small child, Nellie Jarvis ("Little Miss Yes'm"), a peddler's daughter, accidentally sees the Martin Cains, husband and wife, murder a girl whom he has betrayed and bury her body. After the peddler's death, his wife and daughter continue their itinerant life in the peddler's wagon. We encounter them again, after ten years, in the same area of Silver Waters, where the mother dies. Nellie is succored and given a place to stay by the poor but pious and generous Hiltons, whose household consists of a partly disabled father; a saintly mother; an older son John, who is soon drafted for World War I; a younger son Jimmie, who becomes Nellie's special friend and, at the very end, is designated her husband-to-be; and Zeke, a black servant.

To help the Hiltons in their poverty, Nellie hires out, despite forebodings, as servant to the Cains, whom she does not yet recognize, in their home, the neighboring House of Darkness. Cain's motive for desiring to have her about is that he lusts after her, while Mrs. Cain apparently needs an object upon which to release her sadistic impulses and spite her husband.

John is lost at sea when his submarine suddenly sights a destroyer and is obliged to dive without giving him adequate time to get inside (a well-staged scene). Upon leaving for the war, he had told his mother that there was something between them that no bullet could kill, and she experiences a mysterious sense of his presence at the time of his death.

Nellie is kept busy dodging Cain's lascivious approaches, which she is too innocent to understand, and Mrs. Cain's sadistic and finally murderous impulses. At one point she leaves the House of Darkness to return home, but, having witnessed, through a window, how important the ten dollars wages she has sent home means to the Hiltons, she returns to her bondage.

The Hiltons grow steadily poorer, and when they find they must sell their home, the father's faith gives way. Close to despair, husband and wife go to the little graveyard where they have set up a memorial to their son, and the mother prays fervently for a sign that her faith is justified. Here the dead boy appears both to her and to his father, and both parents are convinced and comforted.

Just in time to avoid selling it to a sharper who has already made the discovery, the Hiltons find that there is oil on their land, and when Jimmie rushes off to tell Nellie, he finds her in deadly peril in the attic of the House of Darkness, menaced first by the husband's lust, then by the wife's vengeance. She has increased her peril by suddenly achieving a total recall of the scene she had witnessed long ago (of which she had experienced only faint troubling intimations before) and by suddenly accusing them. Jimmie arrives in time to knock Cain out, however, and they escape. The Cains are taken into custody, and the Hiltons celebrate their new prosperity by dining at a fashionable hotel, though without forgetting their piety, for Mrs. Hilton prays for "those who still grope in darkness."

Lillian Gish as Little Miss Yes'm

Little Miss Yes'm with Mrs. Cain (Josephine Crowell)

Little Miss Yes'm trying to prevent Martin Cain (George Nicholls) from climbing up into the loft

Mrs. Cain draws a bead on her husband and Little Miss Yes'm

Little Miss Yes'm with Jimmie (Robert Harron)

CRITICISM

Lillian Gish says that *The Greatest Question,* "A Story of the Strange Meandering of the River of Life," was filmed hastily, mainly in California, before Griffith removed to his new studio at Mamaroneck, New York, and that it, *The Idol Dancer,* and *The Love Flower* were all financial failures. When W. K. Everson ran *The Greatest Question* for her in 1964, it pleased her but she failed to recollect any of it.

In its larger aspects, the film must probably be rated an aesthetic failure also. The greatest question is as old as Job ("If a man die, might he live again?"), but, despite his title, Griffith did not succeed in making this the main concern of his film. He had always been interested in religion, and it may not be fair to say, as has been said, that the spiritualistic element was introduced into this film in order to take advantage of the interest in psychic matters which, under the influence of Sir Oliver Lodge and others, followed World War I. The ghostly manifestations in the film are not entirely unprepared for. Mrs. Hilton is obviously not without psychic sensitiveness, and there is an amusing pseudosupernatural scene when Zeke and the children are frightened by a tramp sleeping in the graveyard and whom they mistake for a ghost. But whatever one may believe about psychic matters, it can hardly be argued that the experience in the graveyard succeeds in achieving even what Coleridge called "that willing suspension of disbelief for a moment which constitutes poetic faith." And, in art, this is the final test.

The Greatest Question has other faults. The evil forces embodied in the Cains are so broadly conceived and projected as to be almost disgusting. The terrible "mugging" of Josephine Crowell (who had proved herself such a fine actress in *The Birth of a Nation*) was the only part of the film I recollected clearly from my first viewings of it when it was released, and her beating of Nellie with her long whip was a weak repetition of what Lillian Gish had just undergone at the hands of Donald Crisp as Battling Burrows in *Broken Blossoms.* The opportune discovery of oil on the Hilton land is a melodramatic trick, and the final juxtaposition of the hotel scenes with the views of the now suddenly and unconvincingly repentant Cains being carted off to jail is as glaring as the epilogue to *The Last Laugh,* and, to make it worse, there is no indication that Griffith, like Murnau, was only fooling.

In 1920, when there were so many fine films to choose from, these faults might well have been serious enough to sink *The Greatest Question;* today, when we have so few, the situation is different. A flawed work of art in the

beginning, *The Greatest Question* remains that today, but in it there is much that is worthy to be cherished.

The principal entry on the credit side of the ledger is, not surprisingly, that supplied by Miss Gish herself. No doubt it was her success in *Broken Blossoms* as a child just turning into girlhood that led to her being cast as Nellie Jarvis, but the performance she turns in here is surely sufficiently distinguished, and sufficiently lyrical, in its own right to support a very substantial reputation even if no bolstering evidence could be cited. She receives excellent support from Robert Harron, in another of the country boy roles in which he was unsurpassed, and the film gains an additional extrinsic interest from being the last they did together. Eugenie Besserer shows a lovely restraint as Mrs. Hilton and turns in about as different a performance from her masterly characterization of the coarse but warmhearted dance-hall mother in *Scarlet Days* as one could ask for. Nor is hers the only performance in which sheer goodness and deep human feeling and kindliness are unerringly projected.

All this gains notably from the idyllic rural background of the film which, if possible, is even lovelier here than in *A Romance of Happy Valley* and *True Heart Susie,* and if it be replied that Griffith did not create these backgrounds, I must reply that only he and Billy Bitzer seem to have had the eye and the heart to find them and photograph them. When, in later years, Griffith objected to modern films that they had forgotten beauty, he may not have had these pictures particularly in mind, but it would have been perfectly reasonable for him to do so. I could not agree more thoroughly with what Mr. Everson has written on this point:

I can't think of any [other] Griffith film that has used the landscape of rural America so effectively, or so extensively. *Way Down East* put that landscape to subtler and more effective dramatic use, admittedly, but with Griffith's dynamism and Lillian Gish's sensitivity, it could probably have been pulled off shot entirely within studio walls. But *The Greatest Question* breathes the outdoors, and illustrates so well what Griffith meant when he said he wanted to put his war pictures behind him, and get back to "the wind, and the sun on the corn." Scenes of the young lovers in woodland glades, or by brook or riverside, are enchanting; and there are exteriors of stunning power too, as in that overpowering and brooding long shot of Josephine Crowell running along a lane against a background of waving trees and darkening sky that, in this context, seems truly menacing.

These elements of strength are especially notable in the first half of the film before the melodrama has quite taken over. Zeke (played by Tom Wilson, the kindly policeman of *Intolerance*, in blackface), delivers the kind of racial comedy that was not yet taboo in 1920, and irony, coincidence, and suspense operate much as in Biograph days. At one point Jimmie is prevented from going to Nellie in response to his mother's prescience, because Zeke's partly feigned attack of rheumatism compels him to go bring in the cow instead. At this date nobody would deny that Griffith overworked the situation of the innocent heroine menaced by the lascivious monster, and indeed Burns Mantle attacked him severely for this while he was still in his prime. But at least this film introduces some interesting complications. Nellie climbs the ladder up to the attic and pulls it up after her, so that her pursuer must pile up a perilous mountain of boxes to reach her; then a wife even more vicious than he is arrives, armed with a pistol, to threaten both of them with death itself, until Nellie complicates the situation by her ill-timed flash of recollection and thus causes them to join forces against her.

E. W.

In *The Moving Picture World*, for January 3, 1920, First National Exhibitors Circuit ran two pages advertising *The Greatest Question*. One read as follows:

The other suggested that the exhibitor of *The Greatest Question* run the following in the local newspaper:

Griffith, the Master

reveals himself as

Griffith, the Showman

"The Greatest Question" is a Triumph of Showmanship

Not a tragedy nor a highbrow picture.

A Bang-up Melodrama

Amazing Advertising Possibilities

With it Griffith will make the world
Thrill, Laugh and Wonder

A Show Picture for Showmen

MAN OR WOMAN
(Professional Spiritualist Medium Excepted)
Wanted to sleep all night alone in Graveyard
From 10.30 P. M. to daylight on (date opening of show)

$25 Per Night to White Man
$50 Per Night to Colored Man
$75 Per Night to White Woman
$100 Per Night to Colored Woman

An easy night's rest with good pay for someone who has nerve and is not afraid of spirits. Applicant will be taken to cemetery in auto, provided with warm, comfortable bed, but must submit to being chained and locked to bed, which is to be placed right amongst graves. Representative of (name of newspaper) will unlock the person at dawn and take his or her experiences with spirits during the night and publish the story in the newspaper.
The person must spend the night absolutely alone without even a dog for company, but may provide himself with gun or pistol to drive away any human disturbers.

This is a bonafide offer
Made in the interest of science
Apply to **"The Greatest Question" Editor**
(Name of Newspaper)
or to **Manager, LYRIC THEATRE**

18

THE IDOL DANCER

SCENARIO: S. E. V. Taylor, from a story, "Blood of the Covenanters," by Gordon Ray Young

PHOTOGRAPHY: G. W. Bitzer

FILM EDITOR: James Smith

LENGTH: 7 reels (75 minutes)

PRODUCTION/DISTRIBUTION: First National

NEW YORK PREMIÈRE: Strand Theater, March 21, 1920

RELEASED: March 22, 1920

RICHARD BARTHELMESS (*Dan McGuire, the Beachcomber*)

CLARINE SEYMOUR (*Mary, otherwise known as White Almond Flower*)

CREIGHTON HALE (*Walter Kincaid*)

GEORGE MAC QUARRIE (*Rev. Franklin Blythe*)

KATE BRUCE (*Mrs. Blythe*)

PORTER STRONG (*Peter, a native minister*)

ANDERS RANDOLF (*the Blackbirder*)

WALTER JAMES (*Chief Wando*)

THOMAS CARR (*Donald Blythe*)

HERBERT SUTCH (*Old Thomas*)

ADOLPHE LESTINA (*the black slave*)

BEN GRAUER (*the native boy*)

WALTER KOLOMOKU (*the native musician*)

FLORENCE SHORT (*Pansy*)

THE STORY

At Rainbow Beach, "a Romance Island under the Southern Cross," dwell the Reverend Franklin Blythe, missionary, and his wife; a trader known as Old Thomas, with an adopted daughter, Mary, or White Almond Flower, of mingled "blood of vivacious France, inscrutable Java, and languorous Samoa," "a curious little creature, of boldness, yet timidity," whose ancestors sold ivory and peacocks to the Phoenicians when Solomon was building his temple; and Dan McGuire, beachcomber, drunkard, and derelict, remorseful over the way he is wasting his life. The missionary does not seem to be making much impression upon the natives. His first convert and assistant, Peter, sees Christianity largely in terms of a frock coat and spectacles without any lenses in them, and his servant Pansy accepts missionary clothes but no other conventions.

The missionary's invalid nephew, Walter Kincaid, comes from New England to stay with him and, despite his intense puritanism, is at once captivated by White Almond Flower, who loves Dan but is repelled by his dissipation. She enjoys Walter's attentions and is intensely sympathetic toward his sufferings; in a measure she plays

him off against Dan. Walter's Christianism is pitted against Dan's paganism and cynicism also, and the beachcomber becomes very jealous and hostile.

Other complications begin when a brutal and unscrupulous adventurer known as the Blackbirder is attracted to the missionary village by the report that a store of pearls is concealed there. Allied with a native chief, Wando, the Blackbirder uses gin and brutality to hold together a following of cannibals and headhunters from the Solomon Islands. At one point he and Wando try to abduct White Almond Flower as she is dancing before her idol in a grove, but are prevented by Dan and Walter, who are also watching her.

Walter quarrels with his uncle over the young man's association with a "loose girl," and the excitement brings on an attack which prostrates Walter. The missionary's prejudices conquered by affection, he begs the girl to come to Walter's bedside, which she does. To Dan's amazement, he also invites him. Believing that White Almond Flower loves Walter, Dan is deeply moved by the sweet spirit which the invalid shows toward him and the utter absence of all assumptions of superiority on his part, resolves to lead a better life, and asks Old Thomas for work. White Almond Flower, similarly impressed, throws her idol into the sea and decides to trust Walter's God for his recovery. As an outward manifestation of her change of heart, she now consents to wear missionary clothes.

The Blackbirder's excuse to loot the village comes when a native whom he has beaten for insubordination flees to the missionary for protection. The missionary's house is besieged. Old Thomas, Dan, and the other men of the village have just left on a fishing expedition, but Walter draws upon his final reserves of strength to sound the ancient war drum, more recently used to call the natives to church, for the purpose of bringing them back. They turn their boat about and furiously row toward Rainbow Beach, arriving as the Blackbirder and his crew have broken into the room where the women are cowering. The Blackbirder is just carrying off White Almond Flower when Dan shoots him. Walter Kincaid, fatally injured in the fighting, dies in the arms of Dan and the girl.

Still unaware of the true state of White Almond Flower's feelings, but determined to rebuild his life, Dan prepares to leave the island, but she intercepts him. "Foolish one—I have loved you all the time." Fully dressed and in their right minds, the couple are married by Mr. Blythe.

This beautiful photograph of Clarine Seymour was made by the White Studio shortly before her death.

The central figure in this picture—Clarine Seymour dancing as White Almond Blossom— was almost a trademark for the film as it was first shown.

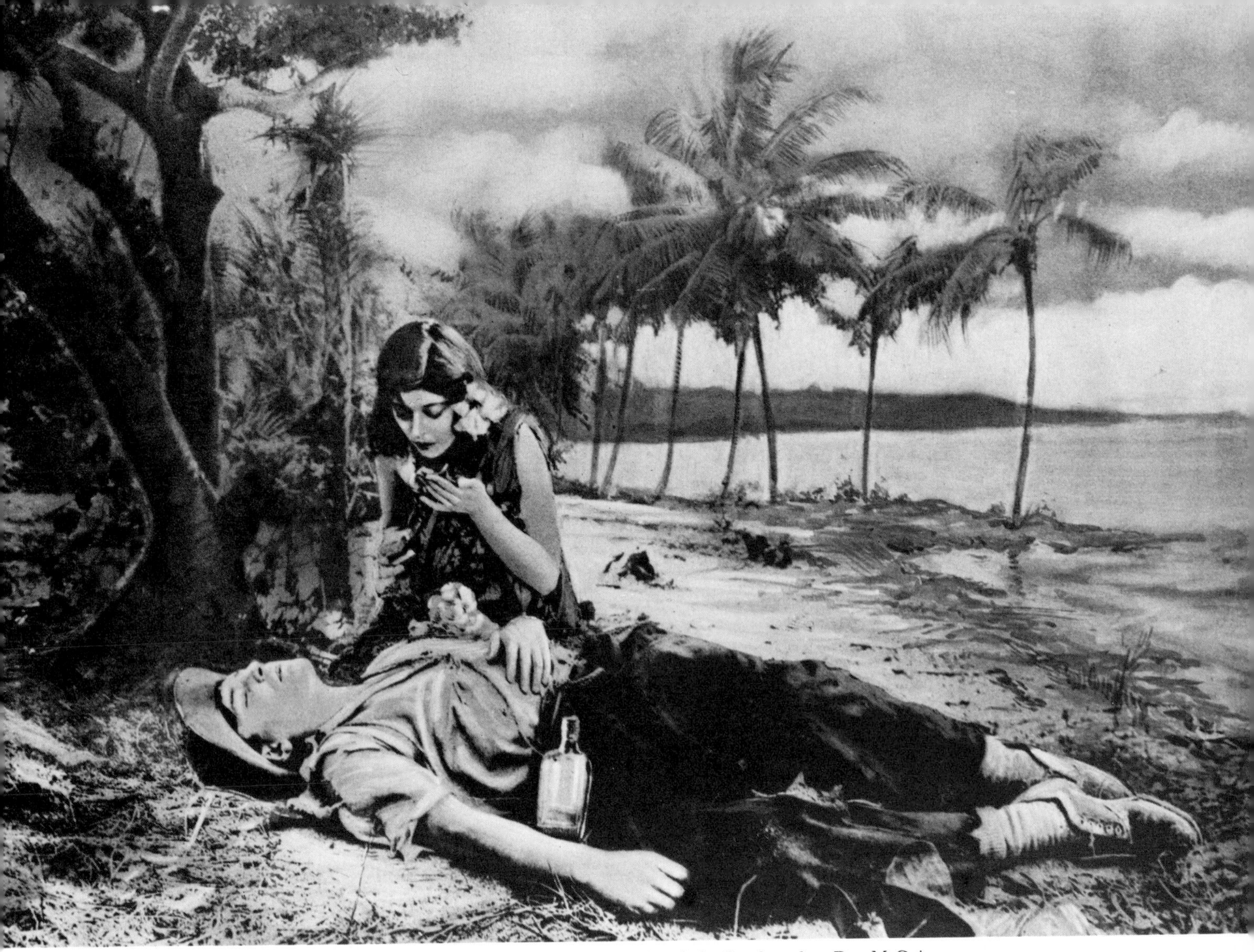

White Almond Blossom (Clarine Seymour) and the Beachcomber, Dan McGuire
(Richard Barthelmess)

White Almond Blossom with her admirers, Walter Kincaid (Creighton Hale) and the Beachcomber

140

White Almond Blossom is enraged by the deliberate discord the Beachcomber has created during her dancing.

The wooing of Pansy (Walter James and Florence Short)

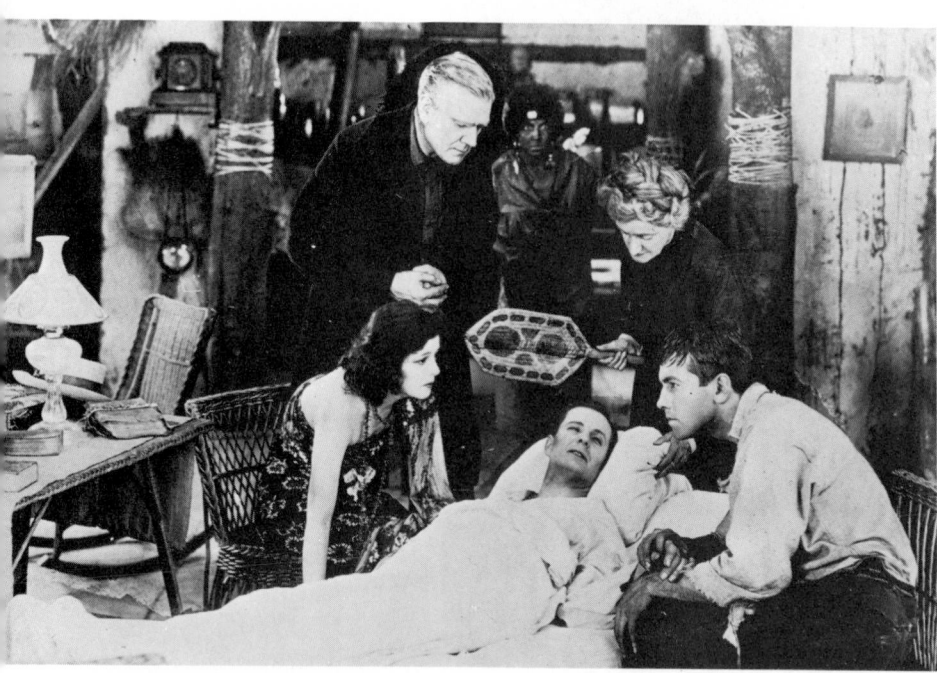

The missionary (George MacQuarrie) invites White Almond Blossom and the Beachcomber into his home duirng Walter Kincaid's illness. Kate Bruce as Mrs. MacQuarrie

During the attack on the mission

The Beachcomber defends the mission.

White Almond Blossom and Dan McGuire are wed.

CRITICISM

The exteriors for both *The Idol Dancer* and *The Love Flower* were made in the Fort Lauderdale area in Florida and in the Bahamas. Griffith sailed for Nassau with a party on December 10, 1919, in a yacht called *The Grey Duck;* the trip was supposed to take twelve hours, but because of a tropical storm the boat was unreported for three days. This created a newspaper sensation, and when it was afterward learned that they had very sensibly put into a safe harbor at an early stage, suspicion arose that the incident had been manipulated for publicity purposes. The allegation, however, seems never to have been proved.

Except toward the end, *The Idol Dancer* seems to lack the "flow" characteristic of his best work, and some of his admirers dislike it so much that they cannot bear to believe that he directed it personally! Elmer Clifton, who is known to have been on the scene during the filming, is the favorite rival candidate. Both the skepticism and the disparagement seem to me somewhat overdone. Richard Barthelmess ascribed the film to Griffith both publicly and in private; he repeated the ascription for my benefit, when I was working on *The Movies in the Age of Innocence.* I never met Clarine Seymour, but I was acquainted, after her death, with her father, Albert V

Seymour, and though he was almost crushed by his loss, we talked at length about Clarine, Griffith, and other members of the Griffith company. Mr. Seymour gave me no reason whatever to suppose that Griffith had not personally directed his daughter's most important film.

She had already played for Griffith in *The Girl Who Stayed at Home* (in which she gave what Mr. Slide regards as her best performance), *True Heart Susie*, and *Scarlet Days*, but she had never before been "featured" as she is featured here, and she made the most anybody could have made of her opportunity. She was still living when the picture opened at the Strand in New York, on March 21, 1920, but she died, at the age of twenty-one, in New Rochelle, New York, at nine o'clock on Sunday evening, April 25, after an operation for strangulation of the intestines, and most of the country did not see her in *The Idol Dancer* until after her death. It was an experience of mingled anguish and delight, unparalleled in many years of movie-viewing. If she had lived, she would undoubtedly have been an important star. Though she was a girl of character, integrity, and refinement (Lillian Gish cannot speak of her to this day without a warm expression of regard), she was far from being the characteristic Griffith heroine in her physical type. She would have suited the screen in the twenties, and her presence could not have failed to elevate it. I know of no other film actress whose career was so cruelly aborted who has also been so affectionately remembered more than half a century after her death.

Richard Barthelmess turns in an excellent characterization in a very uncharacteristic role. Whatever may be said of the respective merits of *The Idol Dancer* and *The Love Flower* as films, Barthelmess is much better here. *The Love Flower* only gives him an opportunity to be charming and heroic; here, as in *Broken Blossoms*, he offers a characterization. The redemption of a derelict is as difficult to make seem credible in art as it all too often is in life, but to my mind Barthelmess is entirely convincing in *The Idol Dancer*. Almost from his first appearance, he makes us understand that he is a sensitive man who has somehow taken the wrong turning and lost his grip upon himself and that he is suffering agony because of this. For such a man the only choice in the end is between suicide and conversion.

It will be clear by now, I think, that *The Idol Dancer* is Griffithian in its spirit and point of view, whatever its technical limitations may be, and indeed this appears not only in its strength but in its weaknesses. The cannibals are pretty much out of *The Katzenjammer Kids*, and the comedy supplied by Peter and Pansy is as "corny" as anything Griffith ever achieved elsewhere. The persistent efforts of Donald Blythe, the only white boy on the island to get a pair of pants on a native boy (Donald has no other function in the film) is somewhat better, but his success is regrettable, for the native boy looks much better without them. Clarine Seymour too looks better in her pagan grass skirt than in her Christian missionary clothes (long ago Mr. Dooley remarked that the white man's idea of an uncivilized nation was one that did not wear uncomfortable clothes). It is amusing now to reread the comments made in 1920 on Miss Seymour's native attire; though it was probably not authentically South Seas, she wore as much as girls now wear on the street.

There are a few examples of the interest in outlandish customs and ceremonies characteristic of Griffith's films. The most successful is the use of the ancient war drum, to which we are introduced casually, as a detail interesting in itself, all unaware of the almost determinative part it will play in the climax. Pansy's wooing and "marriage" to Wando, a footnote assures us, depicts "actual custom" in the etiquette of tribal matrimony; the essential thing seems to be that the groom must knock out the bride's teeth. It is easy to be amused by the opening title: "If in all this there is a moral, it is that good example is the best preachment." Actually, however, this is less deliberate moral-hunting than it seems. The moral is there in the action of the story, and the "if" might just as well have been omitted.

E. W.

19

THE LOVE FLOWER·

SCENARIO: D. W. Griffith, based on the story, "The Black Beach," by Ralph Stock

PHOTOGRAPHY: G. W. Bitzer

FILM EDITOR: James Smith

LENGTH: 7 reels

PRODUCTION: D. W. Griffith, Inc.

DISTRIBUTION: United Artists

NEW YORK PREVIEW (under title *Black Beach*): Rivoli Theater, April 21, 1920

NEW YORK PREMIÈRE: Strand Theater, August 22, 1920

RELEASED: August, 1920

CAROL DEMPSTER (*Stella Bevan*)

RICHARD BARTHELMESS (*Jerry Trevethon*)

GEORGE MAC QUARRIE (*Thomas Bevan, Stella's father*)

ANDERS RANDOLF (*Matthew Crane*)

FLORENCE SHORT (*Mrs. Bevan*)

CRAUFURD KENT (*Mrs. Bevan's lover*)

ADOLPHE LESTINA (*Bevan's old servant*)

WILLIAM JAMES and JACK MANNING (*Crane's assistants*)

THE STORY

Thomas Bevan, a West Indian trader, with a devoted daughter by a previous marriage and a smoldering wife who hates the West Indies and cares nothing for him, surprises the woman with a lover, who defies him when he is ordered out of the house and pulls a gun when Bevan attacks him. In the ensuing scuffle, the gun goes off and the lover is killed, and when Crane, a detective who has been watching Bevan for a long time because of one false step in the past, arrives, Mrs. Bevan accuses her husband. Bevan escapes with his daughter and reaches a secluded island, Monaki, in the South Seas, where the two live happy in each other. But Crane has sworn "I'll get you if you are at the end of the world," and a global manhunt is activated.

Ironically, Crane is finally brought to Monaki in the sailboat of a romantic young adventurer Jerry Trevethon, who is following Stevenson's trail, and who has no idea what Crane is after. Jerry met Stella Bevan, when he accidentally landed on Monaki for water, and they were instantly attracted to each other, but she now believes him to be an informer and bitterly upbraids him. To prevent Crane from taking her father away in Jerry's boat, Stella chops a hole in its bottom and sinks it, after which all three persons are obliged to settle down to wait, while Crane sends up smoke signals. Meanwhile other officers of the law start a search for the missing Crane.

Horrified by a vision of her father mounting the gallows, Stella attempts to kill Crane, first by dropping a rock on him from a cliff, then by trying to drown him by swimming under him to pull him down while he is bathing. When the tide washes up Jerry's boat, she tells him she sank it, and he convinces her of his honesty and wins her confidence and love by himself finishing the job.

With the arrival of Crane's brother officers imminent, Stella makes her third attempt to kill Crane by weakening the supports of the rope bridge that spans a neighboring chasm and then luring him out on it with her, though she knows this will mean her death also. They are interrupted at the last possible moment by Jerry, who does not know what she is doing.

Immediately afterward Jerry himself tries to take the situation in hand by barricading Crane in a cabin while he

plans to take Stella and her father up the river in a canoe. Crane is liberated by a native, but when he attempts to apprehend Bevan, the latter flatly refuses to go with him. There is a desperate struggle on a cliff, from which both men tumble into the sea. Crane emerges, believing Bevan to have been drowned. Stella and Jerry, sharing this belief, have already arranged to leave on the police boat when they reencounter Bevan, whose underwater prowess has saved him. To cover for him, they carry out the plans they have made, but we are given to understand that their honeymoon journey will be made to deliver Bevan, who has meanwhile been marked dead in the police files of the world.

Stella (Carol Dempster) and her father (George MacQuarrie), fleeing after the death of Mrs. Bevan's lover, encounter the detective Matthew Crane (Anders Randolf), who does not yet know that the shooting has occurred.

Stella and her father in their island retreat

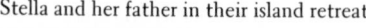

Richard Barthelmess as Jerry Trevethon

Stella on the bridge

Stella after sinking Jerry's boat

148

Stella and Jerry encounter her father, whom they have supposed drowned.

CRITICISM

The Love Flower ponders the paradox of reprehensible deeds, committed by "the fair hand of woman," for the sake of love. Its heroine commits sabotage and thrice attempts murder to save the life of a beloved father. Griffith had shown his interest in ethical paradoxes of this kind as far back as Biograph days, and whatever else may be said of this element in his work, its presence does show that his moral stance was less simplistic than it is often thought to have been.

It would be easy to pick holes in *The Love Flower*. Ignoring such trifling questions as that of where Stella obtained her pretty bathing suit, one might still ask whether Crane had nothing to do but roam over the earth in search of one fugitive. And surely Stella must have known that Crane's death would bring little comfort to her father if she must go to the bottom of the chasm with him, leaving Bevan all alone on the island. But to raise such objections is to treat *The Love Flower* as if it were a serious realistic novel and to submit it to evaluation by standards which light romantic literature was never meant to be subjected to. On its own terms, the film hangs together fairly successfully as a good South Sea melodrama; if its development is more consistent than logical, it still holds the interest throughout.

The lyrical element so characteristic of Griffith is for-tunately much better expressed photographically than in the purple prose of some of the captions. The many shots of tropical vegetation are richly atmospheric, and the rope bridge is a novel, interesting, and slightly terrifying property. The action involving Stella's kitten and pet goat is developed at greater length than even Griffith customarily accorded such material. Less characteristic of the director but well done and brilliantly photographed are the spectacular underwater swimming scenes, and both these and Bevan's escape at the end have been well prepared for by what we have already learned of his swimming prowess and the way he has trained his daughter.

Carol Dempster is handicapped, especially in the early scenes, by Griffith's apparent determination to have her behave as a much younger girl than the one she is supposed to be portraying, and it is not her fault that one is tempted for a moment to sympathize with her wicked and unsympathetic stepmother when she bids her to stop running about like an idiot. Griffith's "fluttering" heroines have already been commented upon, both in this book and in practically everything that has been written about him; in this film there are even moments when one fears that he may be directing Richard Barthelmess in much the same style.

E.W.

149

20

WAY DOWN EAST

SCENARIO: Anthony Paul Kelly, elaborated by D. W. Griffith, from the stage play by Lottie Blair Parker and Joseph R. Grismer

PHOTOGRAPHY: G. W. Bitzer and Hendrik Sartov

ASSOCIATE DIRECTOR: Elmer Clifton

FILM EDITORS: James and Rose Smith

ART DIRECTORS: Charles O. Seessel and Clifford Pember

TECHNICAL DIRECTOR: Frank Wortman

MUSIC COMPOSED AND SELECTED BY: Louis Silvers and William F. Peters

DECORATIVE TITLES: Victor Georg

PRODUCTION ASSISTANT: Leight Smith

GOWNS IN PROLOGUE: Lady Duff Gordon (Lucile)

FURS IN PROLOGUE: Otto Kahn, Inc.

GOWNS WORN BY MISS GISH IN PROLOGUE: O'Kane Cromwell

LENGTH: 13 reels

PRODUCTION: D. W. Griffith, Inc.

DISTRIBUTION: Initially released on a road-show basis, and subsequently by United Artists

NEW YORK PREMIÈRE: 44th Street Theatre, September 3, 1920

LILLIAN GISH (Anna Moore)

MRS. DAVID LANDAU (her mother)

JOSEPHINE BERNARD (Mrs. Tremont)

MRS. MORGAN BELMONT (Diana Tremont)

PATRICIA FRUEN (her sister)

FLORENCE SHORT (the eccentric aunt)

LOWELL SHERMAN (Lennox Sanderson)

BURR McINTOSH (Squire Bartlett)

KATE BRUCE (Mrs. Bartlett)

RICHARD BARTHELMESS (David Bartlett)

VIVIA OGDEN (Martha Perkins)

PORTER STRONG (Seth Holcomb)

GEORGE NEVILLE (Reuben Whipple)

EDGAR NELSON (Hi Holler)

MARY HAY (Kate Brewster)

CREIGHTON HALE (Professor Sterling)

EMILY FITZROY (Maria Poole)

"The fiddler and many of the merrymakers in country dance scenes are from White River Junction, Vermont."

(In 1914 the Solax Company had released a film titled *Way Down East*, and in the same year the Photodrama Company released *The Folks from Way Down East*. Neither production used the story of the Parker-Grismer play. The Griffith production was reissued in 1931, with a musical sound track, in a slightly shorter version, and in 1935 Twentieth Century–Fox did *Way Down East* as a "talkie," under Henry King's direction, with Rochelle Hudson and Henry Fonda in the leading roles.)

THE STORY

Anna Moore lives alone with her mother in a New England village. When they get into financial difficulties, the girl goes, at her mother's request, to seek aid from their rich and fashionable Boston relatives, the Tremonts. Mrs. Tremont and her snobbish daughters treat her coldly, but at a Tremont party, she captivates an unscrupulous playboy and rotter, one Lennox Sanderson, who traps her into a mock marriage, which he persuades her to keep secret on the ground that the revelation would anger his father from whom he derives his support. Anna obeys until she becomes pregnant; when she tries to bring pressure upon Sanderson, he tells her the truth and deserts her.

After her mother's death, Anna takes refuge in a rooming house in Belden, where her baby is born and dies. Turned out by a cold and unsympathetic landlady, who suspects that she has no husband, she finds work as a hired girl on the Bartlett farm, near Bartlett Village. Here she endears herself to both the kindly Mrs. Bartlett and her husband, the Squire, who had at first been suspicious of her, and their son David falls in love with her. The Squire had intended David for his cousin Kate Brewster, but David and Kate, though good friends, are indifferent to each other, amorously speaking, and Kate soon falls in love with an eccentric entomologist, Professor Sterling, who is summering near the Bartlett farm. But Lennox Sanderson, whose family owns a country estate nearby, and who is now pursuing Kate, keeps pestering Anna to leave, and though she returns David's love, she feels that her "past" makes it impossible for her to accept him.

The crisis in Anna's affairs occurs when Maria Poole, the Belden landlady, visiting Bartlett Village, sees Anna and whispers her story to Martha Perkins, the village gossip, who, on the night of the big barn dance, passes it on to the Squire. Having journeyed to Belden to interview Maria Poole, the Squire returns home at suppertime and orders Anna out of the house. Before she leaves, she denounces Lennox Sanderson, a guest at the Squire's table, as her betrayer. Sanderson is thereupon attacked by David Bartlett and shown the door. The hysterical and grief-stricken Anna is caught in a terrific storm and stumbles out onto the frozen river, where she faints. But the river is just beginning to break up in the spring thaw, and Anna is carried downstream on an ice cake toward the falls. She has nearly reached the brink when she is saved by David.

The Squire begs forgiveness of Anna, which is granted, and Sanderson offers to marry her but is scornfully refused. The film ends with a triple wedding in the Bartlett parlor—David and Anna, Kate and the Professor, and Martha Perkins and Seth Holcomb, who has been following her about for twenty years.

Anna Moore (Lillian Gish) arrives at the residence of her wealthy and unsympathetic Boston relatives.

Anna attracts the attention of the playboy Lennox Sanderson (Lowell Sherman).

Anna, fashionably attired for the ball by the eccentric Tremont aunt, further captivates Sanderson.

Sanderson proposes.

After the mock wedding

Her baby dead, Anna searches for a place of refuge.

Mrs. Bartlett (Kate Bruce) welcomes Anna to the Bartlett farm.

Anna at the village store

Squire Bartlett, apprised of Anna's past, orders her out of the house. *Left to right:*
Bruce McIntosh, Kate Bruce, Vivia Ogden, Lowell Sherman, Lillian Gish, Mary Hay,
Creighton Hale, George Neville, Richard Barthelmess, Edgar Nelson.

David Bartlett (Richard Barthelmess) saves Anna from the ice floe.

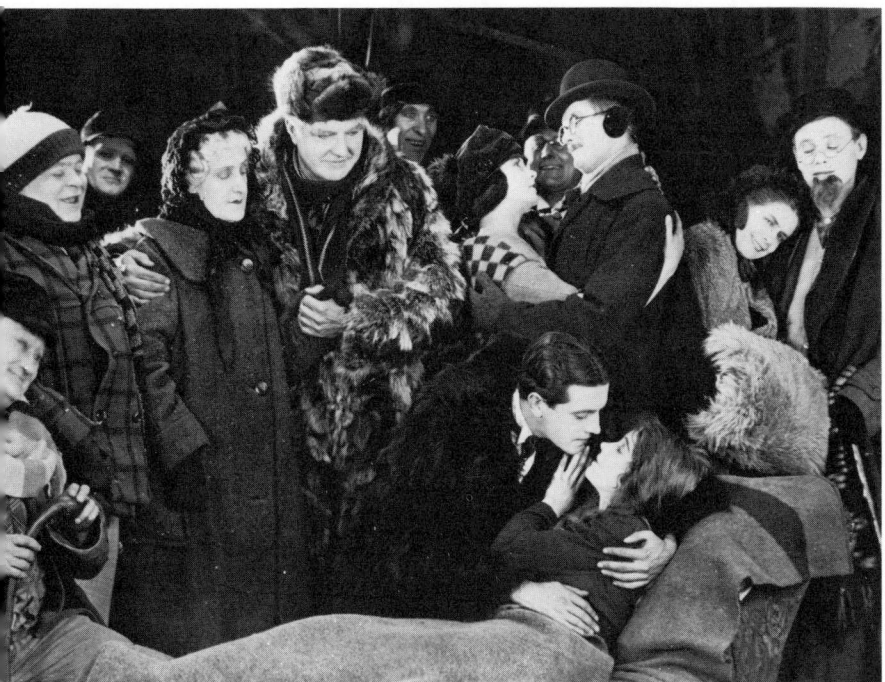

After the rescue and reconciliation. Porter Strong as Seth Holcomb at extreme right

"The one man for the one woman, life's cleanest and sweetest."

CRITICISM

Though *Way Down East* is a "spectacular" only in the thrilling ice scenes of the last reel, it has always been rated one of D. W. Griffith's "big" pictures, and there are many more cogent reasons for this than the fact that it made more money than any other picture of his after *The Birth of a Nation*. Though his three supremely great pictures were already behind him when it was made, his fame was at its height. On the opening night, best seats cost ten dollars plus tax, not only in New York but also in Chicago, where the *Tribune* attacked Griffith editorially for alleged megalomania!

The play, written in the 1890s by Lottie Blair Parker and revised by Joseph R. Grismer, had been a William A. Brady stage success for many years; like *The Round-Up* and *In Old Kentucky*, it became a perennial on the "road." Since it was already regarded as old-fashioned when Griffith allegedly paid $175,000 for the right to film it, Lillian Gish and many others feared he had lost his good judgment. For once, however, he had guessed right. Like *Little Women* and Currier and Ives prints, the play was in the American bloodstream, and nostalgia alone became a powerful element in Griffith's success. As to its alleged "outmoded" morality, it must be admitted that the preachy subtitles at the beginning of the film about woman's innate monogamy and the "male animal's" unwillingness or inability to rise to her level are pretty hard to take, but any sophisticate of the "roaring twenties" who imagined mock marriages to exist only in Griffith's imagination must have been far more naïve than the innocents who wept unashamedly over the story. Squire Bartlett's behavior *is* a problem, but the difficulty here did not originate with the twentieth century. Though the Squire makes handsome amends after he learns that Anna is blameless, the notion that though it would be outrageous to turn a "good" girl out into the winter night to perish in the storm, this would be perfectly all right, or even praiseworthy, with a "bad" girl finds no sanction in either common sense or the code of ethics sanctioned by Christianity or any other respectable religion. The Squire seems nevertheless to make this assumption, and nobody, not even his gentle wife, explicitly challenges it. No wonder the kindly Burr McIntosh went about apologizing to Miss Gish for the terrible way the film had required him to treat her.

The elements of strength in *Way Down East* are many. For all its lack of subtlety, it deals, like all good melodrama, with vital matters and people for whom the audience cares. This, above all others, is the film in which D. W. Griffith glorifies the home.

After I had seen Lillian Gish in *Broken Blossoms*, I told her I did not see how she could ever equal her work in this film. In *Way Down East*, however, she offers a much fuller, varying, developing, and complex characterization, rising to grandeur in the scene where Sanderson tells her the truth and even more when she baptizes her dying child, alone in her lonely room, in the silence of the night, because her horrible landlady had told her that if he died without being baptized, he must be damned. No wonder the father of the baby used in this scene fainted while it was being filmed and Griffith himself wept. Nor is it the least of Miss Gish's virtues that she dared, at the outset, to be honest enough to infuse a certain cloying quality into Anna's affection, which, the spectator cannot fail to understand, must have been stifling to a man of Sanderson's temperament even if he had been less a villain than he was. And if the elaborate scene at the supper table, before she runs out into the night, is less completely effective than her other high moments, the fault is neither hers nor Griffith's; the "punch" here is Anna's denunciation of Sanderson, and the material is just not ideally adapted to the visual methods of the silent screen. This is the one point in the film where we miss sound.

Though David Bartlett gave Richard Barthelmess no such opportunity as Anna Moore afforded Lillian Gish, he was at the height of his youthful charm when the film was made, and it was one of the pictures that established him as the great favorite he became. Mrs. Bartlett was the quintessence of all the innumerable mother roles that Kate Bruce played for Griffith, and Burr McIntosh seemed to have been born Squire Bartlett, though there are scenes in which we are reminded that he was also an old-time actor. The role of Kate Brewster was originally assigned to Clarine Seymour, who died while *Way Down East* was being filmed. It is difficult to see anything in the role that would have enabled her to make it a worthy successor to her White Almond Flower in *The Idol Dancer*, but Mary Hay (who married Barthelmess) was winning in her combined appreciation of her eccentric suitor's genuine worth and her amused tolerance of his hilarious idiosyncrasies. Lowell Sherman as the seducer was so convincing as to be more than faintly disturbing, more convincing, perhaps, in the first half, where he was still occasionally visited by qualms of conscience, than later on, when he was so consistently cruel and evil.

The comic characters are another story. Vivia Ogden, who had spent years on the stage playing such characters as Martha Perkins and Miss Hazy in *Mrs. Wiggs of the Cabbage Patch,* has left us in this film a brilliant and faultlessly timed record of how stage tradition handled such characters. If her work is inharmonious with the more naturalistic style of the leads, it deserves praise on its own terms; no gesture is wasted, no nuance misplaced. Unfortunately the same thing cannot be said for the male comics, who are certainly the weakest element in the picture. As for Maria Poole, whom that remarkable character actress Emily Fitzroy (whose great triumph on the screen was as the mountain mother in Charles Brabin's *Driven*) managed to make both a menace and a zombie, she is less a comic character than an evil one. For that matter, Martha Perkins too has her evil side; she gloats over what she thinks of as the revelation of Anna's sin, and the shot of her crouched grimly, like a brooding vulture, during the barn dance, waiting for the chance to tell Squire Bartlett her story, is unforgettable.

Griffith had always been at his best when dealing with beautiful nature backgrounds, but this time he does not confine himself to admiring their beauty. Nature becomes an actor in the drama, and the modified "chase" over the ice in the last reel pits a man's will not against that of another man but against natural forces themselves. Yet when all is said and done, it seems to me that charm predominates in *Way Down East,* more than in any of Griffith's other frontline films. The winter sleighing scenes and the barn dance are full of good cheer. The scenes at the Bartlett well and by the river are richly idyllic, and charm mingles with drama in the interchange between Anna and David in the Bartlett parlor as the climax draws near. The Bartlett kitchen, with its abundant food and good fellowship, and the village store are places where we should all like to linger. Nobody ever forgets the little white kitten that falls asleep with the other village sleepyheads while we watch it, nor the fine long shot of Anna on the lonely road before she comes to the Bartlett farm, nor yet the touching moment when, still grieving for her own child, she pauses on her way to the store to caress a baby who is being pulled on a little sled through the snow. Such scenes have more to give than many whole films can offer.

Griffith's famous intercutting and use of parallel action are in evidence mainly in the second half, where the barn dance is going on while other more vital matters are under consideration in the Bartlett parlor and Martha Perkins waits impatiently to tell her evil tale. The Squire's journey to Belden to check on Martha's story is intercut with what goes on at the farm while he is absent; when he arrives back home, David is in the barn with the cattle, and we are on tenterhooks wondering whether he will come in before Anna is thrown out. Once Anna is on the ice, however, we intercut only between her and her rescuer; the tension is now too great to admit of our being willing to be deflected even momentarily to other scenes. Yet the intercutting in the first half of the picture, though sparse, is very effective. Griffith begins introducing us to the Bartlett Village characters at the beginning of Reel 2, which is some time before their story becomes intermingled with Anna's. It was enough of an inspiration to have David Bartlett awakened from an evil dream at the time of the mock marriage so that we can overlook and even forgive the consideration that he probably would not be sleeping in the daytime; later he seems to "feel" her approach before she walks into the Bartlett yard. But the most masterly cut of all occurs when we shift abruptly from Anna, in her poverty and loneliness, with her dead baby, to the graceless Sanderson, in his haughtiest mood, in luxury on the family estate.

Not all of the technical detail in *Way Down East* is flawless, however. The subtitles do not always agree with the corresponding action, and the background of the close-ups is often obviously not that of the scenes out of which they are taken. It is almost incredible that a director of Griffith's talent could have passed such a crude scene as that in which the hen's egg drops upon Hi Holler's head in the barn; this could have been done quite as smoothly in 1903. The blizzard was filmed in March 1920 at Orienta Point (the company had waited all winter for it) and the bulk of the ice scenes at White River Junction, Vermont, in zero weather, but the scene at the brink of the falls was made in summer at Farmington, Connecticut, and here the ice cakes were painted blocks of wood attached to piano wires. The actual falls here were about fifteen feet high, but the falls shown briefly on the screen are Niagara. As we see the ice scenes, therefore, they are patched together out of materials shot at different times, and in places they show it. With the technical resources now available, these scenes might well be filmed today with less risk and agony than in 1920. Though Allan Law and Elmer Clifton doubled for Miss Gish in some of the long shots, what she went through is not to be underestimated. She herself has said that for three weeks she was on a slab of ice twenty times a day. Her hair froze and the hand she foolishly trailed in the freezing water in the interest of realism still troubles her today, more than half a century later. In the storm scenes, her eyelashes became icicles and she had difficulty closing her eyes. No director has the right to ask of his players what Griffith asked in *Way Down East,* and no film can be worth such risk and suffering.

E. W.

Our party dashed wildly across the beach at Atlantic City last Saturday afternoon, scrambling and sprawling and diving and dropping into the water in an effort to forget the heat, when a girl's voice arose above the sound of voices and the breaking waves:

"What does this remind you of?" came the query.

"Almost nothing—" I began. "What does it suggest to you?"

"Remember that night last February, up at Mamaroneck, in a blinding snowstorm, with the wind howling across the Sound, and Lillian Gish staggering up the little path, facing a small battery of cameras, with 'D. W.' shouting directions every which way to make himself heard, and Clarine Seymour—"

Of course, I remembered. And also I remembered that this was a story that I had planned to "save up," for a hot summer day, and try to recount some of the details over a lemonade, in the cool of the evening, with music to charm the narrative.

So we splashed about in the surf until the lights in the Traymore glimmered and we scampered into our clothes.

And on the veranda we ordered our lemonade.

February was more than half gone, and the series of blizzards of the preceding month left their impress everywhere about the spacious grounds of the Griffith studio in Mamaroneck. The lure of the place took our party back to Orienta Point time and again, and about the time the four o'clock 'bus for the station rolled up, we were prepared to say "good-bye" to Mr. Griffith and the boys and girls, when "D. W." extended a personal invitation to remain over for the evening, and see some night work, which meant that we would get a very late train back to New York. We agreed, and to keep warm we clung close to the studio restaurant, where hot coffee was the order of the day.

Way Down East was in the making, and the players were in splendid spirit for the unleashing of the cameras. Here and there about the studio, and outside in the blizzardy weather, flitted G. W. ("Billy") Bitzer, Griffith's cameraman, and in his wake we detected Sartov (Sartov! the *great* Sartov—wonderful photographer of beautiful women, and now a Griffith cameraman!), and everybody was muffled up to their necks in heavy coats, or "sweaters" and fur caps and heavy overshoes.

Richard Barthelmess, Creighton Hale, Burr McIntosh, Kate Bruce and the long array of Griffith players had spent the afternoon "on location" some distance from the studio, but on the grounds, however, and as 9 o'clock approached, the electricians outside the administration building lighted up all the lights (thousands of them, it seemed), and the night was turned into day. Two great, powerful lights swept the Sound and penetrated the blinding snow, only to be shot back over the specially selected "location" where Lillian Gish was to go through one of the most touching scenes in the photodrama—little Anna Moore staggering about in the night! The frail little heroine of the play, wholly at the mercy of the elements! And what a night! Could any director ask for more? A high wind sweeping northwest across the Sound; snow falling in great masses, and intermingled with the snow came rain—snow, rain, wind, a howling gale!

"I shall have to *insist* that you put on a pair of heavy overshoes," Mr. Griffith said, in his low voice. "Mr. Sutch will supply them."

I was completing the operation of buckling on overshoes—a breathless task for a squat, fat man, when Miss Gish came downstairs.

"Mamma and Dorothy are returning tonight from the South," Lillian said, "and I am as excited as any kid."

"But what about 'working' out in a night like this?" I asked.

"Oh, I'm sure I shall not mind it a bit," Lillian responded. "How is it outdoors?"

And as Dick Barthelmess opened the door to go out, a great gust of snow swept in. This was Lillian's answer.

Miss Gish wore a plain, dark dress, halfway to her shoe tops—an old pair of wornout shoes, I thought, and she carried a little shawl over her arm. Her throat was bare, and her hair carefully disarranged.

From outside came voices, relaying in until we heard:

"Miss Gish is wanted."

"Let's go," Lillian suggested, and we went outdoors. I felt absurdly ungallant, offering Lillian my heavy coat.

"But I shall not need it, immediately. And besides, there *is* a big coat out here somewhere, I think."

"This way, Miss Gish," came from the Griffith megaphone, and Lillian was blown away from my side and away two hundred yards to where Mr. Griffith stood.

Nothing remained for me to do but to find a spot back of the cameras where Bitzer and Sartov huddled under a great umbrella. In another few seconds Mr. Griffith came up the little path and turned about. No voice could be heard above the howling wind, so Mr. Griffith and Miss Gish used a series of signals.

From our somewhat protected positions in the shelter

of the great administration building matters were not so bad. But out there! Never was a storm better employed, said I.

"D. W." signaled for the lights, and the place was lighted.

"Cameras," came the big voice.

Then came the signal, an uplifted hand, and through the blinding snow Lillian Gish, attired precisely as I had seen her indoors, staggered up the path. Little Anne was weak. She was homeless and deserted. In her short walk we saw depicted in the face of the young girl all the misery of a cruel world. She struggled against the wind, and moved forward a few more steps, when the gale caught her and carried her sheer out of the path and she fell in the snow (out of the range of the cameras, however).

Came a voice at my elbow, as a diminutive figure snuggled up close:

"I have a favor to ask," said dainty little, beautiful little Clarine Seymour. "Won't you take charge of this coat for Miss Gish, and when she comes up, be sure that she is wrapped up in it?"

And I promised, and Clarine walked over to Mr. Griffith's side.

"Now, we shall do that over again, Miss Gish," Mr. Griffith said, and Miss Seymour and Mr. Barthelmess stepped back.

Away off, down the path ran Lillian, and turning about, faced the cameras again. The wind was increasing in fury and the snow seemed worse than before, and "Billy" Bitzer was singing "You'd Be Surprised," and "D. W." was singing "Every Morn I Bring Thee Violets—" (or something like that), when suddenly the singing ceased, and the signals went forth for lights, cameras, action.

"Here she comes," whispered Clarine.

Barthelmess, Hale and I peered through the snow, and surely enough, Lillian was again staggering up the path toward us—but also toward the cameras which were registering her every move, her every gesture, her every change of face. On, on, on she came, until in the grasp of a wind that blew round the corner of the great building with the ferocity of a cyclone, she could go no further. This was the precise effect Griffith wanted! Lillian fell in the snow, and we ran out to pick her up. I threw the big coat about her and grasped her arm, and she laughed, and we started for the door.

"How do you feel, Miss Gish?" came the soft, low voice of Mr. Griffith through the megaphone.

"Fine," came the answer.

"Will you do it *once more?*" asked Mr. Griffith.

"Certainly," came the cheery response, and she handed me the big overcoat, and more than a hundred of us watched her as she scampered out into the blast.

That *once more* sounded to me like an invitation to a severe chill or an attack of the "flu," or pneumonia, or sudden death, or something, and I couldn't tell just what it meant!

Ten minutes later, when Lillian was standing beside the great furnace in the studio basement, separating ice particles from her hair, she said:

"But all this is quite nothing, compared to that November night, more than a year ago, out on the Coast, when we were taking the fog scenes in Limehouse, for *Broken Blossoms*. It was a cold night, and I was dressed just as you saw me in the picture, and *what* a night that was. Tonight it is just *awfully* cold, and *awfully* blustery, but *that* night—"

And Lillian shuddered, remembering Los Angeles!

And we ordered coffee, and more coffee, until Mr. Griffith and the crowd came in.

But on the veranda at the Traymore, we ordered lemonade, for it was a beastly *hot* night!

—From *Exhibitor's Trade Review*, July 10, 1920.

21

DREAM STREET

SCENARIO: Roy Sinclair (i.e., D. W. Griffith), based on two stories, "Gina of the Chinatown" and "The Sign of the Lamp," in *Limehouse Nights*, by Thomas Burke

PHOTOGRAPHY: Hendrik Sartov

ART DIRECTOR: C. Blythe Sherwood

SET DESIGNER: Charles M. Kirk

FILM EDITORS: James and Rose Smith

MUSIC ARRANGER: Louis Silvers

TECHNICAL SUPERVISOR: Frank Wortman

LENGTH: 11,000 feet

PRODUCTION: D. W. Griffith, Inc.

DISTRIBUTION: United Artists

NEW YORK PREMIÈRE: Central Theatre, April 12, 1921
RELEASED: April 25, 1921

CAROL DEMPSTER (*Gypsy Fair*)

RALPH GRAVES (*James "Spike" McFadden*)

CHARLES EMMETT MACK (*Billy McFadden*)

EDWARD PEIL (*Sway Wan*)

W. J. FERGUSON (*Gypsy's father*)

PORTER STRONG (*Samuel Jones*)

GEORGE NEVILLE (*Tom Chudder*)

CHARLES SLATTERY (*the Police Inspector*)

TYRONE POWER, SR. (*a preacher of the streets*)

MORGAN WALLACE (*the Masked Violinist*)

THE STORY

Gypsy Fair, a Limehouse girl, is the daughter of a former dancing master who has declined to the position of a "stool pigeon" under the Inspector of Police. One night, a fire breaks out in the music hall where Gypsy supports herself and her father by dancing, and she prevents a panic by continuing her performance.

In the audience that night are James (Spike) McFadden, a handsome young swaggerer, and his weakling brother, Billy, both in love with Gypsy; also the Chinaman, Sway Wan, who catches her garter when she throws it into the air.

Sway Wan lives in a room just across the court from Gypsy's own and is in the habit of watching her through the window. When he makes advances to her, it occurs to her to use his infatuation for her father's benefit. She bargains with the Police Inspector to betray the whereabouts of the gambling establishment to which Sway Wan has invited her in return for her father's exemption from further obligations. Thus she incurs the enmity of Sway Wan.

After the death of Gypsy's father, Spike enters her room one night and attempts to force his attentions upon her. Billy overhears the struggle, draws his revolver, and prepares to keep the oath he has sworn to kill anybody who endangers Gypsy. But at the latest possible moment,

he hears the Voice of Good (personified in this film by a street preacher) and repents. The brothers have always been very close to each other, and although Spike, returning home, is at first tempted to crush Billy, their old love triumphs and they are reconciled. Later Gypsy and Spike reach an understanding also, and she accepts him as her lover.

A few nights later, Billy finds a thief in his room, stealing his savings. A struggle follows and the thief is killed. When Spike returns and finds Billy hysterical, he takes the blame for the shooting upon himself.

Intricate complications follow. Spike escapes. The Police Inspector forces Gypsy to promise to raise the shade on a lamp in the window if Spike returns. She has no intention of keeping this promise, but Sway Wan, who has overheard, gives the signal, and Spike believes that Gypsy has betrayed him.

At the inquest, Spike refuses to incriminate his brother, but after a terrible struggle with his conscience, Billy sufficiently conquers his cowardice to be able to come and tell the whole story. Ultimately his plea of self-defense is accepted.

Spike and Gypsy are married and establish a happy family. Both are successful in the music halls, and Billy becomes a successful composer.

The Good Influence: Tyrone Power, Sr., as the Street Preacher

The Evil Influence: Morgan Wallace as the Masked Violinist

Carol Dempster as Gypsy Fair in the theater scene

The brothers: James "Spike" McFadden (Ralph Graves) and
Billy McFadden (Charles Emmett Mack)

CRITICISM

In 1919, Griffith decided to go independent, left the West Coast, built studios in Mamaroneck, New York, and shortly after embarked on *Way Down East*, which had its première in September, 1920. And thus another period in his life began.

If Griffith had followed his usual procedure, he would have begun on another film while editing *Way Down East* during the late summer of 1920. But Griffith was tired, having hurried out one feature after another for the past couple of years. However, he was not idle: he was overseeing the roadshowing of *Way Down East* and also reevaluating the function of D. W. Griffith, Inc. Because of Bobby Harron's death and the departure of Richard Barthelmess and Dorothy Gish to other companies, his studio lay barren, while technicians and players under contract continued to draw their weekly checks. This was a problem he would never cure, and, in fact, was the major cause of the company's eventual demise. Under Griffith's new policy of making only two films a year, each picture had to carry an immense amount of overhead if the company were to remain solvent. If he had directed three pictures a year or if he at least could have produced some others, his nemesis, the wolf of poverty, would have been kept at bay.

Finally, during the fall of 1920, Griffith began planning his next production. Because he was strapped for money —the box-office response to *Way Down East* was excellent, but cash was not immediately coming in—he decided to do a smaller film. But what? As usual, Griffith searched over his previous successes. *Broken Blossoms* had won all kinds of praise and . . . it had done reasonably well at the box office. If he could make a similar kind of story, give it a happy ending, and get it out cheaply, he would have a success. He read over Thomas Burke's stories and decided to blend two of them—"Gina of the Chinatown" and "The Sign of the Lamp." He hoped the result would be more profound, more philosophical, more full of message, and even more artistic than *Broken Blossoms*. Out of a sense of modesty, or perhaps caution, he attributed the screenplay to Roy Sinclair (a pseudonym). Griffith thought that by using the same author (Burke), the same Limehouse district, and even the same Oriental villain (Edward Peil), he would have the same success. But he did not consider the absence of Lillian Gish and the presence of Carol Dempster, nor did he realize the limitations of Roy Sinclair.

Griffith titled his new film *Dream Street*: "Our people are dream people," an introductory title says, "who look from wistful windows or walk with visions on the Street of Dreams." There are good dreams and bad dreams, and *Dream Street* unfortunately turned out to be one of the latter. Griffith intended to capture the poetry of *Broken Blossoms*, and to add to it some larger philosophical import. He wanted to examine the concepts of good and evil and also to express himself at some length upon the beauty of love. Unfortunately, the result is one of Griffith's least successful efforts. Its main problem is that it stems heavily from the poetic thinker side of Griffith. As a showman, as a master of melodrama, as a creator of great battle scenes, and as an observer of the little things of life, Griffith could be superb; but when he tried to be intellectual and cultured, to preach and be profound, he was in dangerous waters. And when he didn't have a Lillian Gish or a Mae Marsh or a Clarine Seymour, but a heroine as limited as Carol Dempster, the sympathy which audiences felt—and which made them forgive Griffith some of his excesses—disappeared, and the bare bones of his visionary equipment stood out too starkly. Griffith was no great thinker. His "higher" thoughts were often inseparable from the popular ladies' fiction of the time. When he made homey philosophical observations, great charm and loveliness often resulted; but when he decided to tackle big subjects like the principles of Good and Evil, he seemed sophomoric. Of course, Griffith's ideas were more sophisticated than the script for *Dream Street* suggests (his play, *The Treadmill*, shows that), but when he tried to reduce his already clichéd theories to his audiences' level, he somehow lost the poetry and naïveté and kept only the didacticism. He ended up being not only wooden but absurd. In fact, of all his feature films, *Dream Street* probably comes off the worst with modern audiences.

The film presents the two poles of humanity: good and evil. Good is symbolized by Tyrone Power (the elder) as a street preacher with harmonium, accompanist, and a shock of white hair worthy of a holy man of the best Protestant persuasion. Evil is represented by a masked violinist who appears at the precise improper moment to urge his listeners on to commit evil. Under his mask of a handsome-looking man (behind, therefore, the attractiveness of sin) lurks a face resembling John Barrymore's makeup for Mr. Hyde (in his film of a few months before) including a pointed head, loathsome face, a coiffure crying out for some hair creme, and a set of snaggle teeth that would be an orthodontist's dream of retirement. Not only does this walking symbol of evil look like hell, we are also given some scenes from that warm locale, with a dragon-dinosaur moving in the background and an energetic devil with a pitchfork prodding a few souls. In contrast, a scene of Christ on the Cross before a painted backdrop supports the idea of good. These symbolic scenes are not new to Griffith: he presented similar ones in some of his Biographs and in *The Avenging Conscience*, *Home Sweet Home*, *The Birth of a Nation*, and *Intolerance*, and later in the prologue of *The Sorrows of Satan*. These theatrical *tableaux vivants* were a nineteenth-century fashion and perhaps reminded Griffith of the Doré illustrations he had known as a boy, but, whatever the case, he was inordinately fond of them. To him, these allegorical inserts were not only culture, but symbolism besides. They were obviously attempts to transcend mere realism into a larger, grander realm. Such scenes also are found in other films such as Ince's *Civilization* (1916), Tourneur's *Woman* (1918), Ingram's *The Four Horsemen of the Apocalypse* (1921), Stroheim's *Merry-Go-Round* (1923), and *Greed* (1924), a few of the pompous forays of C. B. DeMille, and many other pictures as well. Such scenes, at least in Griffith's films, were not always savored by his public, and in fact seemed rather absurd at the time; most have not aged well in the intervening years.

Unlike *The Birth of a Nation* and *Intolerance*, which had grand visions at the end as a kind of cosmic conclusion, *Dream Street* has its symbolism and allegory interwoven within the plot. Good and evil, like the opposing angels in Marlowe's *Dr. Faustus*, do not enter directly into the plot but appear every once in a while to personify the moral struggle of the characters. Although this method seems primitive and embarrassingly blatant, it was Griffith's attempt to move beyond mere surface action.

But there was yet a third force: love, as represented by the "eternal star." If Griffith had trouble with good and evil, he got really bogged down with love, for the scenes between hero and heroine, although intended to be poetic, high-minded, lyric and, of course, charming, are slow, mawkish, and in some instances ridiculous. Unfortunately, eternal close-ups characterize the effects of the "eternal star."

Dream Street is more sophisticated visually and technically than Griffith's most famous films. Its pools of light, deep shadows, and somewhat stylized sets are far more imaginative than the simple and comparatively artless interiors of his previous films, even *Broken Blossoms*. This stylistic breakthrough stemmed from a number of factors. Griffith had more time to spend on his film; he drew upon more expert photographers than Billy Bitzer (who had been in the habit of lighting a set flatly).

In fact, the film has an almost "Germanic" look about it. This new look did not stem from the influence of imported expressionistic films but from the fact that the film by necessity had to be made entirely within the studio (one consequence of winter shooting at Mamaroneck) and that Griffith was also trying to be more consciously artistic. He and his technicians were going to use all that new electrical equipment.

There was one other factor as well—his leading lady. The question was not whether Griffith wanted to see Miss Dempster's face at length on the screen, but whether the paying customers did. And often they didn't. True, Griffith at least recognized the changes in postwar society by abandoning for the moment the fragile Gish type and making his heroine more bouncy and spirited. She is rather like the Mountain Girl in *Intolerance* and the Little Disturber in *Hearts of the World*. She reflects her name, Gypsy Fair (an appellation ludicrous in postwar America). A rough, sharp and tough city kid, essentially a gamin, she is a far cry from Gish's rural heroines, and far harder than that other victim of urban environment (Mae Marsh in *Intolerance*) who, after all, was a small-town girl transformed to the city. But this more modern heroine of Miss Dempster's is not terribly appealing. She doesn't have the zip and charm of the Mountain Girl, the humor of the Little Disturber, nor the plaintiveness of the young mother in *Intolerance*. Her actions, in short, are not redeemed by her acting or screen charm, nor are they enhanced by the creakings of Griffith's plot. Miss Dempster was miscast. . . .

In the course of her misadventures, Gypsy meets two brothers. Spike (Ralph Graves) is a tough, cocky fighter who is rather dashing, connected with the underworld, and a budding singer. The other brother, Billy (Charles Emmett Mack), who writes his brother's songs, can best be defined in the vernacular: he's a "creep." Thin, bent over, with a homely, cringing face, he is the opposite of Spike. Both brothers, however, love the girl and eventually fight over her. The "creep" threatens to shoot and the other threatens to beat him up, but they are reconciled. Later, the "creep" kills an attacker in self-defense. The man's face in close-up goes out of focus as he dies, an interesting use of the camera by Griffith. The murderer escapes and allows his brother to "take the rap." Spike evades arrest and, while the police look for him in atmospheric fog (Griffith has some stunning shots here), he hides out at a Chinaman's place and then at his girl's quarters. Caught and brought to trial, he is about to be sentenced when his brother confesses and Spike is freed.

This scene is followed by one of Griffith's happy endings. A title says that "sometimes dreams do come true," for now the hero and heroine are rich and sign a contract for their skills of singing and dancing. The brother is freed ("after an atonement—the King's pardon") and now a successful composer, he apparently settles down with them in their comfortable apartment. The "creep" sits on a chair smiling at Spike and Gypsy and their child, no longer bothered by his love for the girl and presumably letting his frustrations out in songwriting. The last shot shows the star of love shining brightly over London.

Griffith presents a curious set of characters. His hero and heroine are not unblemished paragons of virtue, but rather unpleasant in some ways. The girl is a tease, a tattletale, a bigot; Spike, a braggart and a would-be rapist; the other brother, a loser—more mouse than man. In this sense the film has realistic aspects, but Griffith's titles, such as "While above all earth's shadows there's the Star of Eternal Love," and the didactic intrusion of both good (the preacher) and evil (the violinist) who hover nearby while significant action takes place—and both right on schedule, too—betray a heavy-handedness that is not only oppressive but embarrassing. This fault stems from his sincere effort to convey a message. He wanted to do more than just film a story; he wanted to speak from his heart by means of certain scenes and by means of his titles.

Dream Street contains one of those epiphanies of comradeship and brotherhood that so affected him. It occurs at the end of the police inquest: the brother (after going through a Soul Struggle—violinist and preacher alternating) runs into the room, and with a "greater love hath no man" title accompanying him, confesses to the crime. The two brothers kiss, almost on the mouth, and members of the jury cry. Griffith had a similar scene in *The Birth of a Nation* when the two young soldiers die on the battlefield embracing each other, and again in *Intolerance* when Belshazzar and the Mighty Man kiss just prior to their deaths. Griffith also included such scenes in some of his war films. These moments were to him actually of religious intensity. Indeed, the brother runs in with a beatific look on his face, an expression just preceded by a shot of Christ on the Cross. The sincerity of Griffith is not to be questioned here; he certainly didn't insert this scene just for box office, but unfortunately the sequence does not work. The concepts of brotherhood, self-sacrifice, and crucifixion cannot by the exigencies of the plot be accommodated to the embrace of a crook and a "creep." Such material, in short, cannot support the allegorical and symbolic meanings that Griffith wanted to express.

The opening of the film is slow and the exposition not particularly fascinating. Whereas Griffith formerly would play a scene in medium shot and then cut to some other location, he now breaks the scene into various shots, giving it greater visual variety, but unfortunately taking twice as long to get through the same action. The result is dragging. Admittedly, the last two reels are packed with excitement, but they can't quite redeem the previous eight reels. The film has too many incidents, it rambles, and obviously shows that Griffith did not have enough content to fill a ten-reel film without padding. He would have done better to have made an inexpensive short film than to puff this piece up to larger-than-normal length. When Griffith made it a full evening's entertainment, there was little entertainment left. In fact, the film slows down so much in the middle that it almost stops. Occasionally a comic touch lightens it, but generally the film plods from scene to scene. Carol smiles and pouts in various long-dwelling close-ups as if her face alone were sufficient.

The effect of *Dream Street* is almost completely at variance with the gentle attitudes expressed in *Broken Blossoms*. Whereas in that film Griffith showed the delicate love of a Chinaman for a white girl, in this film he makes the Chinaman the villain, one who peeks through a window into the girl's bedroom and watches her undress. When he makes a pass at her at another point, he gets a little roughed up and she tells him that that should teach him to leave white girls alone. Still later, he tries to rape the girl. So Griffith, who made such an impassioned plea for the brotherhood of white and yellow races in his earlier film, now switches his ground; the Oriental once again becomes the stock "heavy." Griffith probably saw no inconsistency in this change. It was a different story and that was that. This time he was interested in showing the comradeship of the two brothers and not of the yellow and white races.

Arthur Lennig

—Excerpted by permission from a much longer discussion of *Dream Street* in *The Silent Picture*, No. 17.

22

ORPHANS OF THE STORM

SCENARIO: Gaston de Tolignac (i.e., D. W. Griffith), based on *The Two Orphans* by Adolphe Dennery and Eugène Cormon

PHOTOGRAPHY: Hendrik Sartov, Paul Allen, and G. W. Bitzer

ASSISTANT CAMERAMAN: Herbert Sutch

ART DIRECTOR: Charles M. Kirk

SET DESIGNER: Edward Scholl

FILM EDITORS: James and Rose Smith

MUSIC ARRANGED BY: Louis F. Gottschalk and William F. Peters

TECHNICAL DIRECTOR: Frank "Huck" Wortman

LENGTH: 13,500 feet, cut to 12,000 feet for general release

PRODUCTION: D. W. Griffith, Inc.

DISTRIBUTION: United Artists

BOSTON PREMIÈRE: Tremont Theater, December 28, 1921

NEW YORK PREMIÈRE: Apollo Theatre, January 2, 1922

RELEASED: April 30, 1922

LILLIAN GISH (*Henriette Girard*)
DOROTHY GISH (*Louise*)
JOSEPH SCHILDKRAUT (*Chevalier de Vaudrey*)
FRANK LOSEE (*Count de Linières*)
CATHERINE EMMETT (*Countess de Linières*)
MORGAN WALLACE (*Marquis de Praille*)
LUCILLE LA VERNE (*Mother Frochard*)
SHELDON LEWIS (*Jacques Frochard*)
FRANK PUGLIA (*Pierre Frochard*)
CREIGHTON HALE (*Picard*)
LESLIE KING (*Jacques-Forget-Not*)
MONTE BLUE (*Danton*)
SIDNEY HERBERT (*Robespierre*)
LEE KOHLMAR (*King Louis XVI*)
MARCIA HARRIS (*Henriette's landlady*)
ADOLPHE LESTINA (*a doctor*)
KATE BRUCE (*Sister Geneviève*)
FLORA FINCH (*a starving peasant*)
LOUIS WOLHEIM (*the Executioner*)
KENNY DELMAR (*the Chevalier, as a boy*)
HERBERT SUTCH (*a meat-carver at the fete*)
JAMES AND ROSE SMITH (*dancers*)

(*The Two Orphans* had been filmed three times previously, under that title, in 1907 in one reel and in 1911 in three, both by the Selig Company, and in 1915 by Fox.)

THE STORY

*O*rphans of the Storm opens as abruptly as did ever a Biograph of them all with the slaying by her kinsmen of the commoner whom a daughter of the great de Vaudrey family has, from their point of view injudiciously, married. Her baby daughter they take from her and expose before Notre Dame, but not before her mother has placed a rich purse inside her wrappings, with the message "Her name is Louise. Save her."

When a poverty-stricken member of the proletariat, one Girard, brings his own baby Henriette to the cathe-dral steps, because he and his wife lack the means to feed her, he finds Louise there and cannot bring himself to expose Henriette to what seems to him her probable fate. "With the usual inconsistency of mankind, he returns home with both babies."

The treasure found with Louise saves the Girards from their poverty, and the two little girls grow up happily in a northern province. But while they are still in their teens the plague comes, kills both parents, and blinds Louise. (This calamity is told in retrospect.)

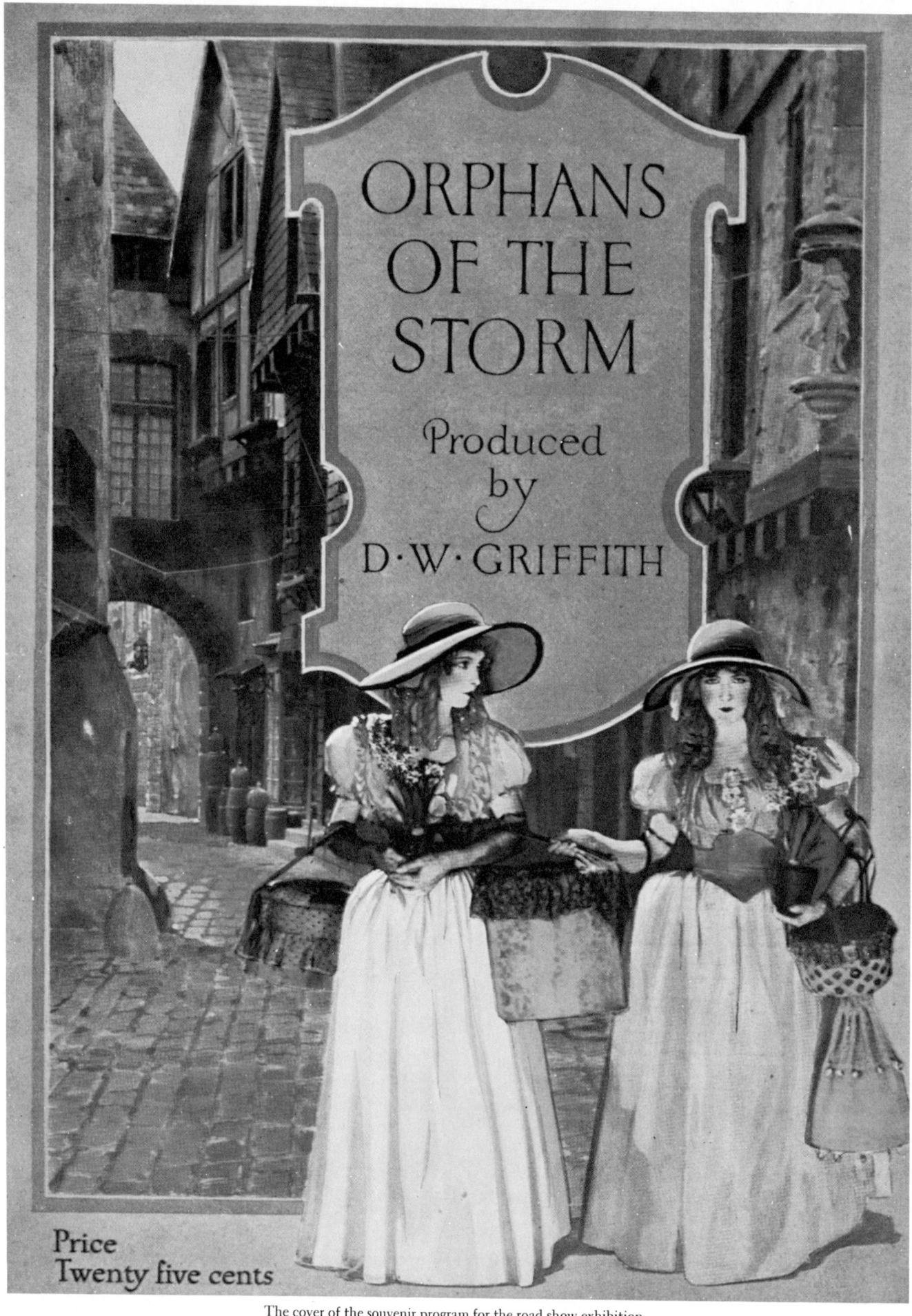

ORPHANS
OF THE
STORM

Produced
by
D·W·GRIFFITH

Price
Twenty five cents

The cover of the souvenir program for the road show exhibition

The story proper begins when Henriette takes Louise to Paris in the hope of finding a doctor who can restore her sight. On the way they attract the attention of a dissolute nobleman, the Marquis de Praille, at whose instigation Henriette is kidnaped upon the arrival of the two orphans in Paris and brought to a fete that the Marquis is giving that night at his great estate. The blind and helpless Louise, left alone, is saved from falling into the Seine by Pierre, a knife grinder, the crippled younger son of an old hag La Frochard, who is abused not only by his mother but also by her adored criminal older son Jacques. When she sees that Louise is pretty and learns that she is blind, La Frochard takes her home with a view to having her sing and beg in the streets.

At the de Praille fete is the young Chevalier de Vaudrey, an aristocrat with a heart and radical sympathies. He is the nephew of Louise's mother, now the wife of the Count de Linières, Prefect of the Paris Police, to whom she has never confessed her past. Insulted and abused by the dissolute aristocrats, Henriette cries out for one man of honor to save her, and de Vaudrey accepts the challenge, though he is obliged to draw his sword upon de Praille and wound him before he and Henriette can escape from the fete.

Angered by the scandal, the Prefect refuses de Vaudrey's request for police aid in searching for Louise, his whole interest now being centered on furthering an arranged marriage between de Vaudrey and a lady of high rank. The Countess, however, is sympathetic, and agrees, at her nephew's request, to visit his sweetheart at her lodgings. Henriette has also attracted the friendly interest of Danton, though without knowing his identity, and incurred the suspicion and mistrust of the woman-hating Robespierre, with his abnormal fetish of "purity."

Louise, meanwhile, menaced by the cruelty of La Frochard and the lust of Jacques, has been enabled to survive

The Two Orphans: Lillian Gish as Henriette; Dorothy Gish as Louise.

Henriette tells Louise that she has been blinded by the plague.

The Orphans at home

in their underground hovel only by the sympathy and kindness of Pierre. Though she had at first refused to sing in the streets, they had finally brought her to terms by confining her in a rat-infested cellar. While conferring with the Countess de Linières, Henriette hears Louise singing outside and rushes to the balcony to call her, but before she can reach the street, the Prefect arrives and places her under arrest for confinement in La Salpêtrière. La Frochard drags Louise back into slavery, and de Vaudrey still proving recalcitrant, de Linières has him confined in a fortress away from Paris.

Meanwhile the Revolution breaks out. The Bastille is stormed, and Henriette is released from prison. She makes her way through mobs wildly dancing the carmagnole to La Frochard's hovel, where she recognizes her sister's shawl round the old woman's neck but is told that Louise has died. De Vaudrey escapes from his fortress and makes his way back to Paris, but is recognized by Jacques-Forget-Not, a revolutionary leader who has an old score to settle with the de Vaudreys and all associated with them. He is arrested in Henriette's room and she along with him for having sheltered an aristocrat. Pierre, long the underdog, rouses himself and fights a duel with knives against his brother, during which he wounds Jacques sufficiently to make it possible for both himself and Louise to escape. They are present in the revolutionary courtroom, presided over by Jacques-Forget-Not, when de Vaudrey and Henriette are sentenced to the guillotine. During the proceedings, Henriette has recognized Louise but has not been permitted to join her.

Danton, who has become the moderating influence among the revolutionists, arrives just as de Vaudrey and Henriette are taken out of the courtroom. Outraged, he demands the right to be heard and delivers an oration which is not only a plea for the lives of the two young people but an indictment of the whole bloodthirsty revolutionary trend, ultimately winning the crowd over to such an extent that the judges are compelled to yield. Meanwhile, however, both Henriette and de Vaudrey have started to the guillotine, and Danton and his followers must undertake a wild ride after them through the streets of Paris. When they arrive, Henriette is already on the scaffold and would have been decapitated had not Pierre, at the last moment, rushed impulsively up the steps and stabbed one of the executioners in the back.

The Countess de Linières has by this time told her husband about Louise and he has proved understanding. The good doctor at La Force restores Louise's sight, Henriette accepts de Vaudrey, and the Countess rewards Pierre for protecting her daughter by taking him under her care.

Preparing for the trip to Paris

Louise

Henriette vows not to marry until Louise has regained her sight.

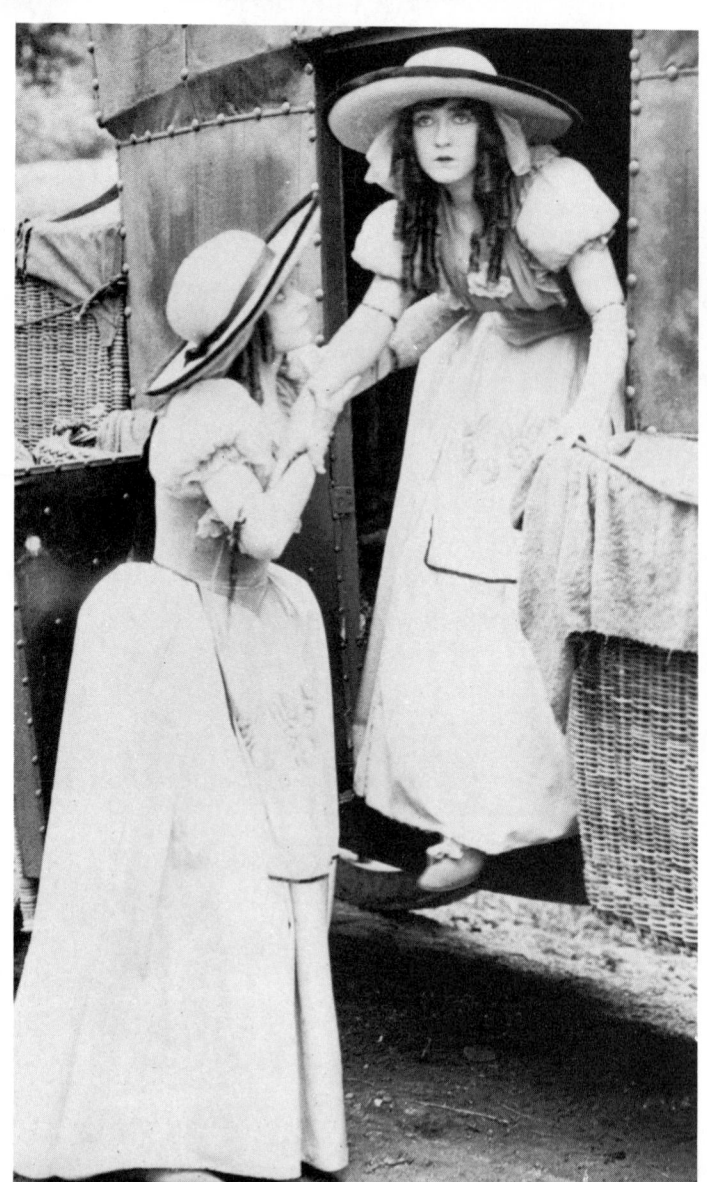

Louise, left alone when Henriette is abducted by orders of the Marquis de Praille, is saved by Pierre Frochard (Frank Puglia).

On the way to Paris

Henriette befriended at the fete by the Chevalier de Vaudrey (Joseph Schildkraut)

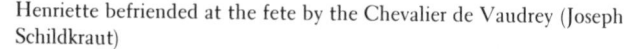

The Chevalier assists in the search for Louise.

Louise, in the clutches of La Frochard, is menaced by the old woman and her evil elder son and befriended by Pierre. *Left to right*: Frank Pugia, Lucille La Verne, Dorothy Gish, Sheldon Lewis

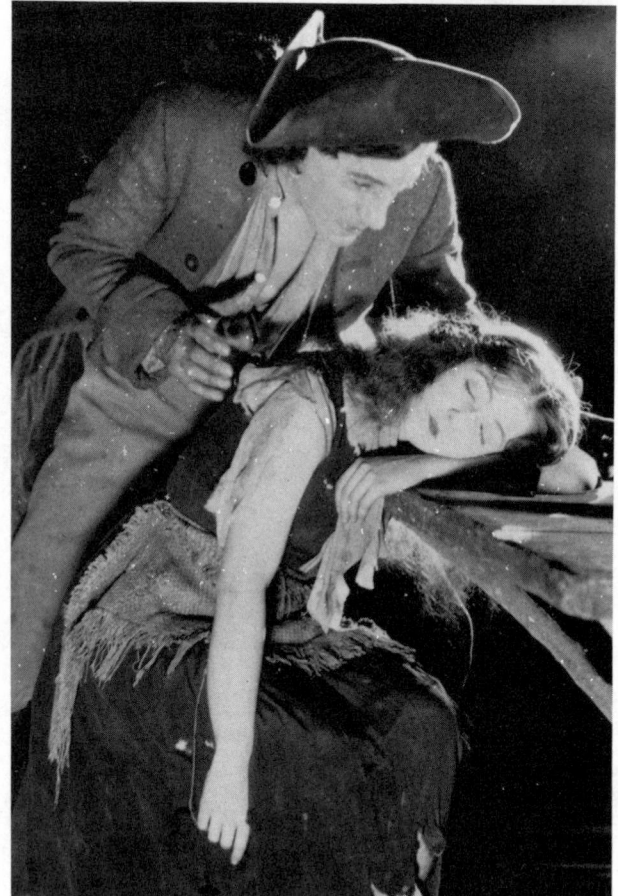

Henriette in her lodging house

Henriette befriended by Danton (Monte Blue) and suspected by Robespierre (Sidney Herbert)

Henriette dragged to the prison for fallen women

Henriette recognizes her sister's shawl on La Frochard.

Henriette before the Revolutionary tribunal

Henriette and the Chevalier de Vaudrey at the guillotine

Griffith directing the guillotine scene

The two orphans safe again after the Revolution and
with Louise's sight restored

CRITICISM

It was something of a paradox that Lillian Gish, who, at the outset, had doubted the wisdom of filming *Way Down East,* should have been the one who persuaded Griffith to base his next big picture on another old chestnut, *The Two Orphans.* ("You only want me to make the story because there's a part in it for Dorothy.") An Italian company was playing *The Two Orphans* in New York while the Griffith production was under consideration, and Lillian took Griffith to see it. There they found Frank Puglia playing Pierre and later invited him to do the same role in the film.

Orphans of the Storm did make money, though much of it was lost through mismanagement of the road tour. Griffith also had to buy a contemporary German film on the same subject to keep it off the American market and to pay $85,000 to William Fox, who had bought foreign rights to the play, in order to be allowed to show his picture in Europe, where, even so, it competed with a recent Italian film. In Paris its unfriendly picture of the *ancien régime* sparked a hostile demonstration by unreconstructed royalists. Incidentally it was to distinguish his product from the Italian competitor that Griffith finally adopted the rather silly title *Orphans of the Storm,* later borrowed by Irene Castle for the name of an animal refuge in Chicago.

Though it came late in the history of French classical melodrama, Adolphe Dennery's *Les Deux Orphelines* (1874) enjoyed a world vogue and was one of the most successful works of its kind ever produced. Though it is quite without literary quality, at least in its English version, its theatrical power is unquestionable; Daniel Frohman called it the perfect play. The first American production was at A. M. Palmer's Union Square Theater, New York, on December 21, 1874. It ran until June 15, 1875, and Kate Claxton, who played Louise, later bought the rights and toured with the play for twenty years. Its innumerable productions include two important New York "all-star" revivals in 1904 and 1926; in the former, Clara Morris played her farewell to the stage as Sister Geneviève. Selig's three-reeler of 1911, with Kathlyn Williams, was elaborate, but crowded and confused. The Herbert Brenon production of 1915 had Theda Bara, of all people, as Henriette, Jean Sothern as Louise, and himself as Pierre. In 1933 there was a French talking film by Maurice Tourneur, with no less a personage than Yvette Guilbert as La Frochard.

Through its first half, Griffith's film keeps close to the play; even some of the subtitles echo the play's language.

In Part II, however, he proceeds to graft the French Revolution onto the old melodrama, with particular reliance upon Dickens and Carlyle. Like Dickens, Griffith condemns both the aristocrats and the extremists among the revolutionaries. Only the incident of the child destroyed by de Praille's coach is taken directly from *A Tale of Two Cities,* however; though de Vaudrey is a Charles Darnay sort of aristocrat, this is suggested in the Dennery play. Griffith's principal departure from the play is his dropping of the character Marianne, a girl who has been led into evil ways by Jacques Frochard. In Act I of the play Henriette saves her from suicide and shows such true womanly goodness and compassion toward her that Marianne mends her way of life. Later they meet again in prison, and when Henriette is about to be deported, Marianne attests the reality of her redemption by taking her place, so that Henriette can remain in Paris and continue to search for Louise. The most unfortunate result of the omission of this material from the film is that it reduces to almost nothing the role of Sister Geneviève, played by Kate Bruce, who tells her first lie (the Doctor tells her it will be recorded to her credit in heaven) to support the deception. In *Orphans of the Storm,* Sister Geneviève still swears, but nobody watching the picture has any idea what she is swearing to. De Vaudrey's valet Picard has a more important, and less completely comic, role in the play than in the film. In the play, the orphans meet again in La Frochard's hovel, and de Vaudrey himself breaks in to rescue them there.

Orphans of the Storm does not have the vitality or the "significance" of either *The Birth of a Nation* or *Intolerance.* Griffith tried hard to give the film contemporary relevance by sermonizing in subtitles about "Anarchism and Bolshevism" (Robespierre seems to be identified with both, and both he and the king are branded intolerants because they condemned everybody who did not think like themselves); this sometimes drew applause when the film was first shown, but it certainly is no help today. The picture is not quite a "spectacular" in the *Intolerance* sense either, but it certainly has its spectacular elements. Fourteen acres of Paris were built at Griffith's Mamaroneck studio, with replicas of historic buildings; it was even claimed that the coach in which the girls come to Paris was an accurate reproduction of the Normandy coach in use at the time and that Lafayette's sword from the American Congress, shown for an instant, was an accurate reproduction of the original. De Praille's Bel-Air fete was easily the best of Griffith's filmed orgies, and it was marvelously photographed in the original tinted prints. But of course it was the revolutionary mobs—storming the Bastille, fighting the king's troops, dragging aristocrats out of their carriages and hanging them, and dancing the carmagnole through the streets—which, along with the guillotine scenes at the close and Danton's furious ride to save de Vaudrey and Henriette that gave Griffith his best opportunities for spectacle. And the finest thing about all this was not the material itself but the truly imaginative and cinematically sophisticated way in which everything was presented. Many of the finest scenes were photographed from a distance or through a window. Often part of the screen was blocked off, and there were some effective lunettes.

In *Orphans of the Storm*, Lillian and Dorothy Gish appeared together in a film for the first time since *Hearts of the World* and for the last time ever; it was also the last film either was to make for Griffith. I think it was Julian Johnson who once called Dorothy "the female Chaplin," but though the screen has known no finer comedienne, she was not limited to the comic muse. When the *Orphans* was first announced, many assumed that Griffith would cast Lillian in the more pathetic role, but he did not do so, and Dorothy rewarded him with a beautiful and sensitive performance. She would not wholly agree, I know, but she was an intensely self-critical artist; she once told me that though she thought she had done good work in a few plays, she liked none of her films!

As to whether the *Orphans* gave Lillian an opportunity equal to that afforded by the closet scene in *Broken Blossoms* or the baptism of the baby in *Way Down East*, there may well be more than one opinion. That she did have excellent opportunities is beyond dispute. Perhaps the best of all was at the end of Part I, where she sees and hears Louise from her balcony but is blocked in her attempt to go down to her and carted off to prison instead. Griffith afterward told her that she had played this scene so intensely that the climax of the picture was flat in comparison. She has other moments of great intensity: her encounter with La Frochard; when she and de Vaudrey are arrested; when she sees Louise during her trial; and of course at the guillotine. But acting is not primarily furniture breaking, and it would be a mistake to overstress the importance of these moments at the expense of such things as the exquisite charm of her love scenes with de Vaudrey or the beautifully finished roundness of Henriette's portrait as a whole. *Orphans of the Storm* is, of course, a considerably more "stylish" production than *Way Down East*, and all the advantages on the score of picturesqueness are on its side. The costumes and the settings provide a continual feast for the eye. As to the latter, the scene is of course the late eighteenth century,

but many of the old buildings shown are medieval in style.

I think it also worth noting, and I do not recall ever having seen it pointed out, that in this film, more than anywhere else in her serious portrayals, Lillian Gish has made a comparatively free use of the relief of humor. She gives Henriette a whole series of endearingly quaint, almost awkward, little touches. When she empties her wastebasket in the corridor, she sticks her head into the container after it. She labors earnestly to help the wounded Danton when he takes refuge from his enemies in her room, but since she is not strong enough to lift his arm from where it has fallen across her body, she must crawl out from under it. When his enemies come to the door and he makes himself ready to strike should they break through, she stands ready beside him with her poised umbrella.

It is not necessary to comment here in detail on all the players. When Lucille La Verne was on tour with her greatest success, Lula Vollmer's *Sunup*, she developed a taste for lecturing at schools and colleges, and I twice heard her identify herself by saying, "Most of you have seen me in *Orphans of the Storm*; I was the hag." She was indeed a hag to end all hags, what Mrs. Malaprop might well call "the very pineapple" of hagdom, and she played the role to the hilt, though perhaps she reveled too obviously at times in being just as "terrible" as she could possibly be. The Count de Linières was entirely too kind in Part II for one who had been so cruel in Part I, but this was neither Frank Losee's fault nor Griffith's; the contradiction had been written into the character by Dennery himself. The New York *Times* reviewer may well have been right in finding Monte Blue's Danton and Sidney Herbert's Robespierre less praiseworthy than the characterizations offered by Emil Jannings and Werner Krauss in Dimitri Buchowetzki's *All For a Woman*, but when he complained of *Orphans of the Storm* that "the historic characters become figures of the story rather than men of their times," he forgot that that is exactly what they should be in a film or in any work of fiction; otherwise they remain unassimilated and had better be left out altogether. Finally, I wish to pay tribute to one until now quite uncelebrated artist in *Orphans of the Storm*: Marcia Harris, who played Henriette's landlady. Griffith did not even put her name in the cast, yet she accomplishes a minor miracle. She makes only a few fleeting appearances and has practically no material to work with, yet she creates a whole character; we know exactly what sort of woman she is and should recognize her anywhere.

More than fifty years after it was made, *Orphans of the Storm* remains a practically perfect film; in a day when the motion picture has nearly committed suicide, it remains as a prime example of how good a film can be. Griffith made greater films, but except for *Broken Blossoms*, I think there is none with so few loose ends. True, there are a few awkward footnoted titles, like the one in which Danton is called "the Abraham Lincoln of France," and some of the comedy is poor, though less so than in *Way Down East*. The scene showing the child run over by the de Praille coach is crudely staged, and the head carried on a pike by the revolutionists is obviously plaster. Beyond that there is nothing, or nothing worth mentioning. Speaking for myself, I cannot but remember that it was during one of my own early viewings of *Orphans of the Storm*, half a century ago, that I first realized fully that the difference between Griffith and nearly all other directors except Maurice Tourneur was that with him every scene was "composed" as a painter understands composition, and I think it significant that this hit me with the greatest force not while I was watching any scene of splendor but when I was with Louise in La Frochard's underground den. For if the film is crammed with scenes one delights to recall for their beauty alone, there are also hundreds of touches that linger in the memory for other reasons. Item: the close-up of the drum beating for the Revolution, which moves alone into an empty scene that thereafter gradually fills up with armed revolutionaries who seem almost literally to be dropping out of the woodwork. Item: the degenerate de Praille's elegant little muff, which so amuses the blind Louise when Henriette tells her about it on the way to Paris. Item: the scene in the pouring rain, where Henriette runs after a girl she has for a moment mistaken for Louise. Consider the man who sits in court admiring Robespierre and the expectorating horseman who rides with Danton. I once wondered whether the girl who shouts revolutionary defiance with the frightful tirelessness of a machine at the foot of the guillotine might not be overdone, but she is not, for I saw (and this time, alas, also heard) her exact replica on television at the beginning of the Six-Day War.

This, finally, raises again the question of sound versus silence. In my notes on *Way Down East*, even such a confirmed devotee of the silent film as I am was forced to admit that the scene in which Anna is driven out into the storm would have been better with sound. Would I say the same thing about Danton's oration here? Not, I think, with anything like the same force. Partly, perhaps, because we *wish* to hear Sanderson denounced while most of us are more than willing to accept the *report* of an oration, but much more because Danton's oration is continually being broken in upon by other scenes, while in *Way Down East* we were right there in the Bartlett kitchen all the time, and there was no action to compensate for what the silent film lacks. As for the scene at the end of Part I, where Henriette hears Louise singing in the street, undoubtedly we do miss sound here when we project the film in silence in our homes, but we must remember that Griffith conceived all such scenes with suitable musical accompaniment in mind. As the film was originally shown, the orchestra that accompanied it raised its emotional temperature here far more effectively than speech alone could have done it.

E. W.

23

ONE EXCITING NIGHT

SCENARIO: D. W. Griffith, based on an original story, "The Haunted Grange," by Irene Sinclair (i.e., D. W. Griffith)

PHOTOGRAPHY: Hendrik Sartov

ADDITIONAL PHOTOGRAPHY: Irving B. Ruby

SPECIAL EFFECTS: Edward Scholl

SET DESIGNER: Charles M. Kirk

MUSIC ARRANGER: Albert Pesce

LENGTH: 11,500 feet

PRODUCTION: D. W. Griffith, Inc.

DISTRIBUTION: United Artists

NEW YORK PREMIÈRE: Apollo Theater, October 23, 1922

RELEASED: December 24, 1922

CAROL DEMPSTER (*Agnes Harrington*)

HENRY HULL (*John Fairfax*)

PORTER STRONG (*Romeo Washington*)

MORGAN WALLACE (*J. Wilson Rockmaine*)

C. H. CROCKER-KING (*the neighbor*)

MARGARET DALE (*Mrs. Harrington*)

FRANK SHERIDAN (*the detective*)

FRANK WUNDERLEE (*Samuel Jones*)

GRACE GRISWOLD (*Auntie Fairfax*)

IRMA HARRISON (*the black maid*)

HERBERT SUTCH (*Clary Johnson*)

PERCY CARR (*the butler*)

CHARLES EMMETT MACK (*a guest*)

THE STORY

A group of white hunters are traveling through Africa when one of the wives in the party dies in childbirth. The baby girl is adopted by Mrs. Harrington and brought to the States, where she is treated none too kindly by her "new" mother.

Grown up, she is sought in marriage by a wealthy man, J. Wilson Rockmaine, much older than herself, whom she intensely dislikes, but because he has a hold over her adopted mother, whom he threatens with disgrace, she agrees to marry him.

At this point, a wealthy and desirable young man, John Fairfax, returns from Europe, and he and Agnes Harrington fall in love. Fairfax gives a party at his country house, which is attended by the Harringtons and all the people in their set. Without Fairfax's knowledge, a gang of boot-leggers have been using the house during his absence, and the chief of the band, Clary Johnson, trying to escape with his loot, has been shot and killed shortly before the beginning of the party.

Suspicion is cast upon Fairfax; mysterious figures appear; terrifying sounds are heard. Eventually Fairfax, Agnes, the Negro maid, and her sweetheart, Romeo Washington, who supplies the comic relief in this film, are all locked in the house while detectives search for the slayer. When everything seems about as tense as it could be, new pressure is applied by the breaking of a terrific storm. At the height of the storm, Agnes discovers that Rockmaine is the guilty party. She also discovers her true parentage, inherits a fortune, and marries John.

Agnes Harrington (Carol Dempster) with John Fairfax (Henry Hull)

Agnes with Mrs. Harrington (Margaret Dale)

Agnes with J. Wilson Rockmaine (Morgan Wallace)

Romeo Washington (Porter Strong) and the Black Maid (Irma Harrison)

Agnes encounters the mysterious masked man.

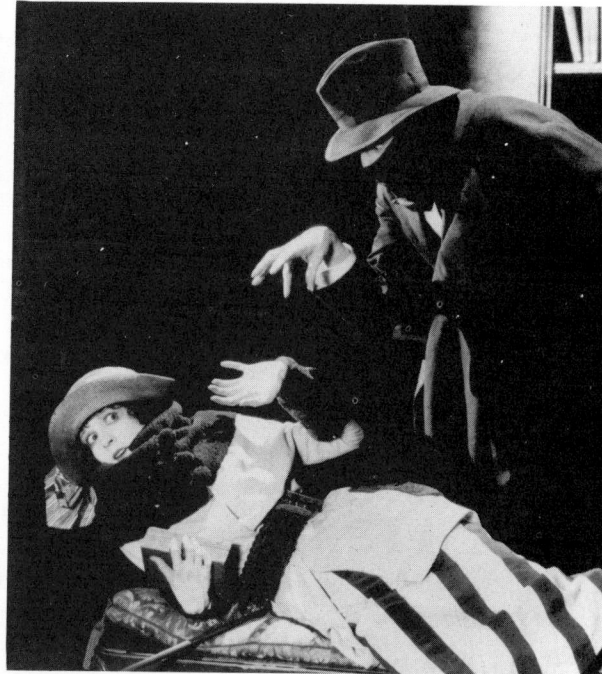

CRITICISM

On July 29, 1922, a Helen Sinclair copyrighted with the Library of Congress a short story in the form of a film scenario titled "The Haunted Grange." The author was, in reality, D. W. Griffith, and "The Haunted Grange" was the basis for his film *One Exciting Night*.

After the magnificence of *Orphans of the Storm*, *One Exciting Night* is a bitter disappointment. Indeed, it is probably not unfair to describe it as Griffith's poorest production. Certainly, it should never be screened by itself as an example of the work of D. W. Griffith, but rather considered within the context of the director's entire output.

One Exciting Night is subtitled "A Comedy Drama of Mystery" and opens with a number of lengthy titles instructing the viewer to pay close attention to the plot, and asking "please do not divulge the solution of the plot to anyone!" The latter request is really superfluous, as it is doubtful that any audience enduring the production would wish to remember it, let alone reveal the denouement to anyone else.

After a prologue, set in Africa, some sixteen years or so before the main story begins, the film's locale is moved to Louisville, which, being not far from Griffith's birthplace, must have given the director a feeling of security. Quite obviously, Griffith was feeling nervous about having made a film such as this. He found it necessary to tell a reporter from the *New York Tribune* (November 12, 1922):

Perhaps this picture appears like a hastily made work. It is the exact opposite. There is no more difficult thing than to put suspense and mystery on the screen. . . . I like *One Exciting Night*. I like its comedy. I like several things about it. I like it because I feel that it will take many people out of themselves during the minutes they are seeing it. And anything that does that, is worth liking.

Following the prologue, the remaining ten-and-a-half reels are concerned with uncovering the identity of the heroine, Carol Dempster, saving her from a forced marriage, unmasking the leader of a gang of bootleggers, and recovering a box containing the bootleggers' loot. Griffith is very careful to make sure that his audience does not forget the existence of such a box by inserting endless close-ups of it. It is a tie as to whether Carol Dempster or the box of money receives the larger number of close-ups in *One Exciting Night*. Also popping up throughout the film are references to "the mystery of greed" and "the mystery of fear."

The whole ghastly mystery is solved during a climactic storm sequence, apparently partly shot during a real storm in the Westchester Hills on the night of June 11, 1922. Since it is unlikely that cardboard trees grow in the Westchester Hills, it is not difficult to tell which portions of the storm sequence were shot in the studio.

One particularly large cardboard tree threatens to fall upon a trapped Carol Dempster, but, in the nick of time, the hero (Henry Hull) arrives. This entire scene lacks any suspense, because of the eternity it seems to take the tree to collapse. In *Way Down East* one really cares what happens to Lillian Gish in the ice-floe sequence; here one does not greatly care about Carol, who is an intrepid heroine. One caption informs us that her class motto is "Conquer or Die." Unfortunately, in this film, she conquers only the elements.

The most interesting aspect of *One Exciting Night*, at least from a modern point of view, is Griffith's use of blacks—or, to be more precise, white actors in blackface—for comedy effect. It has often been written that Griffith produced *Intolerance* to atone for the intolerance toward the black race that he displayed in *The Birth of a Nation*. *One Exciting Night* should prove quite conclusively that Griffith felt he had nothing for which to atone. He depicted blacks in his films as he himself saw them and knew them. Not that he should in any way be condemned for his viewpoint—it was, after all, the viewpoint not only of D. W. Griffith but of his generation. Griffith could see nothing wrong in subtitles referring to "Black Sam, the dark terror of the bootleggers' gang," as a "nigger."

The Negroes in *One Exciting Night* are depicted as lazy and stupid. Their behavior involves much eye-rolling and quaking in terror. In a mystery such as this, the Negro is the ideal comic relief. Sadly, such humor is crude and vulgar, and might seem more suited to an Al Christie comedy than to the work of a master director. It can even be cruel, as when, for example, in one of the closing scenes of the film, Porter Strong's house is blown away in a storm.

Porter Strong was the quintessential Griffith Negro. A stage actor of many years' standing, he appeared in six Griffith features: *A Romance of Happy Valley*, *The Idol Dancer*, *Way Down East*, *Dream Street*, *One Exciting Night*, and *The White Rose*. In the last three, in blackface, he portrayed Negroes. He was found dead in New York on June 11, 1923.

To me, he is the El Brendel of the silent era. Just as all El Brendel comedies should be heaped in one gigantic pile and burned, so should all Porter Strong performances be edited out of silent features and destroyed. However, apparently contemporary audiences felt differently. The most famous blackface of all time, Al Jolson, was quoted in the New York *American* (November 21, 1922): "Something entirely new and masterly in the films is *One Exciting Night*. It is poetry. If the picture were twenty reels long, I couldn't get enough of it, particularly the comedy of Mr. Porter Strong."

Playing opposite Porter Strong, also in blackface, was Irma Harrison. She likewise was much appreciated. "Irma Harrison . . . walks away with the hit of the film despite the footage given Carol Dempster," commented *Photoplay* (January, 1923).

It is interesting to note that Charles Emmett Mack, after a leading role in *Dream Street*, here plays a small part as a houseguest. His acting shows no improvement, and, thankfully, he is stabbed to death early in the film. Perhaps Griffith saw something of Robert Harron in Mack. Certainly his role in *Dream Street* seems to hark back to some of Harron's, of almost a decade previous, as in *Bobby the Coward* and *The Misunderstood Boy*. Like Porter Strong's, Charles Emmett Mack's life ended in sudden death, in an automobile accident on March 17, 1927.

As a melodramatic stage farce, something along the lines of Agatha Christie's *Ten Little Indians* or Arnold Ridley's *The Ghost Train*, *One Exciting Night* might have been entertaining. As a film it is a disaster.

Surprisingly, at the time, the film was fairly well received, though most critics realized that Griffith could—and should—have done much better. Laurence Reid, in *Motion Picture Classic* (January, 1923), wrote: "The picture may be called a success from the standpoint that it serves in furnishing an evening of excitement. But we expect bigger things from the man who gave us *Broken Blossoms*, *Way Down East*, *Intolerance*, and *The Birth of a Nation*." Similarly, the distinguished critic Robert E. Sherwood explained, in the New York *Herald* (October 24, 1922): "Mr. Griffith often has to devote his attention to pictures like this, because it is an open secret that some of his more ambitious offerings have not been quite as profitable as they might be. . . . Let us trust, then, that *One Exciting Night* will make enough money to pay for another *Broken Blossoms*."

But *One Exciting Night* did not make money, at least not for Griffith. It did pave the way for further filmed mystery melodramas, in particular *The Bat* (1926), *The Cat and the Canary* (1927), and *Seven Footprints to Satan* (1929). As usual, it was Griffith who led the way, and others who profited by his action.

A. S.

24

THE WHITE ROSE

SCREENPLAY: Irene Sinclair (i.e., D. W. Griffith)

PHOTOGRAPHY: G. W. Bitzer, Hendrik Sartov, and Hal Sintzenich

SET DESIGNER: Charles M. Kirk

SPECIAL EFFECTS: Edward Scholl

MUSIC: Joseph Carl Breil

ASSISTANT DIRECTOR: Herbert Sutch

LENGTH: 12,000 feet, cut, upon release, to 9,800 feet

PRODUCTION: D. W. Griffith, Inc.

DISTRIBUTION: United Artists

NEW YORK PREMIÈRE: Lyric Theater, May 21, 1923

RELEASED: August 19, 1923

MAE MARSH (*Bessie "Teazie" Williams*)

CAROL DEMPSTER (*Marie Carrington*)

IVOR NOVELLO (*Joseph Beaugarde*)

NEIL HAMILTON (*John White*)

LUCILLE LA VERNE (*"Auntie" Easter*)

PORTER STRONG (*Apollo*)

JANE THOMAS (*cigar stand girl*)

KATE BRUCE (*an aunt*)

ERVILLE ALDERSON (*a man of the world*)

HERBERT SUTCH (*the bishop*)

JOSEPH BURKE (*the landlord*)

MARY FOY (*the landlady*)

CHARLES EMMETT MACK (*a guest at the inn*)

THE STORY

Joseph Beaugarde, a handsome, wealthy, young Southern aristocrat, preparing for the ministry, is informally engaged to Marie Carrington, whose background matches his own. His rival is a grocer's clerk, John White, whom Marie does not take seriously.

After graduating from the seminary (and attending a masked ball given by the Carringtons), Joseph sets out on an excursion of his own, believing that, for professional reasons, he ought to learn more about "the world" before he begins to minister to it. At an inn near New Orleans, he meets a poor orphan girl named Bessie Williams, generally known as Teazie. Teazie, who is innocent but uncultivated, is doing her best to behave like a "flapper" because her friends have advised her that this is the time she must make the best of her opportunities.

Joseph is attracted to Teazie in spite of himself, and sexual contact follows. Thereafter, Joseph's conscience torments him, and he flees from the girl.

As pastor of his first church, Beaugarde, like Arthur Dimmesdale in *The Scarlet Letter*, preaches anguished sermons, reflecting his own consciousness of sin. John White, now convinced that his pursuit of Marie is hopeless, goes out into the world to make his way. Teazie, pregnant and desolate, is befriended by a Negro family.

A marriage is arranged between Beaugarde and Marie Carrington, but their plans are set aside when Teazie and her baby appear in the parish and Beaugarde realizes that the claims of conscience and the dictates of his heart coincide. John White returns, a successful businessman, and Marie discovers that she loves him after all.

Opposite:
Top row: D. W. Griffith, with Lucille La Verne, holding baby. *Middle row:* Ivor Novello, Neil Hamilton. *Bottom row:* Mae Marsh and Carol Dempster, with unidentified man between them

Far left:
Ivor Novello

Left:
Marie Carrington (Carol Dempster) with Joseph
Beaugarde (Ivor Novello)

Marie with John White (Neil Hamilton)

Teazie (Mae Marsh) with Joseph Beaugarde

CRITICISM

"I shed more tears at your latest film, *The White Rose*, than it rains drops in *Rain*. . . . I think *The White Rose* carries a wonderful message of *hope* to those passing through their share of suffering." So wrote the great, tragic actress Jeanne Eagels to D. W. Griffith of a production which many consider to have been the director's last great film, a film which reunited him with the actress whom I consider the silent screen's finest, Mae Marsh.

For *The White Rose*, Griffith went on location to the Bayou Teche area of Louisiana, and along the New River, above Fort Lauderdale, Florida. For the Beaugarde mansion of the film, Griffith chose "The Shadows," the old Weeks House, built in 1830, in New Iberia, Louisiana. On these locations he created a production which all those lucky enough to have seen it in an original tinted and toned nitrate print regard as one of his most visually beautiful. Sadly, much of that beauty is missing from the dull, lifeless copies extant in the film collection of the Museum of Modern Art.

The White Rose was in many ways an old-fashioned picture; in its simple, sentimental outlook on life, it belonged to an earlier decade. The dance hall sequence, with its "wallflowers" and "queens," shows how out of touch Griffith was with the twenties. The lengthy introductory titles are far too wordy and heavy handed, and must have been dull and boring to an audience that demanded fun, not an English lesson. Its theme of a helpless girl's fight for herself and for her illegitimate baby against an unsympathetic world would have had little meaning to, and could expect little understanding from, a typical cinema audience of the jazz-mad twenties.

It is Mae Marsh's performance that makes *The White Rose* such a fine film. In the first half of the production, nothing much is demanded of her, but after the birth of the child, she is given every opportunity to display her capabilities as an emotional actress. As a result, the film improves considerably, and it is almost as if Griffith were back in his stride again as the screen's greatest director.

"A little worn, outcast girl lights the room, like an altar lamp, with the terrible mystery of woman's unselfish love" reads one title, and a little, wonderful actress, Mae Marsh, lights up the screen. There is no terrible mystery as to why; it is the sheer genius of her playing. It was her farewell performance for D. W. Griffith, and, as such, the last great role she was to portray on the screen. The director could have expected nothing better from her, and, certainly, Mae could have given nothing better.

For his leading man, Griffith chose the Welsh actor-composer, Ivor Novello, a popular matinee idol on the British stage, and the man responsible for such popular songs as "We'll Gather Lilacs," "Rose of England," and "Keep the Home Fires Burning." As a stage actor, he was severely limited, being little more than a pretty face; in *The White Rose* he shows himself no better suited to film acting. His wooden acting makes the character of Joseph Beaugarde come across not only as a hypocrite but also as a very stupid man. When he asks Mae Marsh,

"Have you ever read the story of Jezebel?" he is nothing more than a pompous ass.

Negroes again play an important part in *The White Rose*, but, in spite of the presence of Porter Strong, they are not used merely for comic effect. In *The White Rose*, it is the blacks who are the pure in heart. They hear no fancy preaching, unlike the whites in the film who listen to the sermons of the hypocrite Joseph Beaugarde, but rather sing "a hymn of faith" to a gentle Saviour. It is the two kindly black folk—Porter Strong and Lucille La Verne in blackface—who take in Mae Marsh and her child. They are shown as the true exponents of Christian charity.

Despite his sympathetic treatment of the Negro in *The White Rose*, Griffith would seem to have clung off screen to the old Southern attitude, regarding blacks as children to be humored. A press release explained the director's handling of the Negroes in his film:

It took lots of patience the first day, but in ensuing days the colored people were on hand early and eager to work. "Dat man sure can handle us folks, and he treats us right," said one lanky negro who registered quite comically in the film. Being a Southerner and having been reared among numbers of negroes, Mr. Griffith knows the little tricks of cajolery and patient thoughtfulness necessary to keep the negro in good humor and responsive to calls upon his intelligence.

When Mae attempts to get work as a waitress after the birth of her child, a title tells us: "Like many others, her only recommendation is of the past." The same statement might be applied to Griffith and his star. They had only past achievements to recommend them, and the reminder of past successes after which to strive. With *The White Rose*, neither Griffith nor Mae Marsh let themselves or their reputations down.

A. S.

Teazie sheltered in her extremity by a Negro family. Lucille La Verne at the right

25

AMERICA

SCENARIO: John Pell, based on an original story by Robert W. Chambers

PHOTOGRAPHY: Hendrik Sartov, G. W. Bitzer, Marcel Le Picard, and H. S. Sintzenich

ART DIRECTOR: Charles M. Kirk

FILM EDITORS: James and Rose Smith

MUSIC ARRANGER: Joseph Carl Breil

ASSISTANT DIRECTOR: Herbert Sutch

DIRECTOR OF CONSTRUCTION: William J. Bantel

ARTIST DESIGNER: Warren A. Newcombe

SCENIC ARTIST: Charles E. Boss

STILL PHOTOGRAPHER: Frank J. Diem

LENGTH: Copyrighted as 14 reels, subsequently cut to 12,600 feet and then to 11,000 feet

DISTRIBUTOR: United Artists

NEW YORK PREMIÈRE: 44th Street Theater, February 21, 1924

RELEASED: August 15, 1924

NEIL HAMILTON (*Nathan Holden*)

ERVILLE ALDERSON (*Justice Montague*)

CAROL DEMPSTER (*Nancy Montague*)

CHARLES EMMETT MACK (*Charles Philip Edward Montague*)

LEE BEGGS (*Samuel Adams*)

JOHN DUNTON (*John Hancock*)

ARTHUR DONALDSON (*King George III*)

CHARLES BENNETT (*William Pitt*)

DOWNING CLARKE (*Lord Chamberlain*)

FRANK WALSH (*Thomas Jefferson*)

FRANK MC GLYNN, JR. (*Patrick Henry*)

ARTHUR DEWEY (*George Washington*)

P. R. SCAMMON (*Richard Henry Lee*)

LIONEL BARRYMORE (*Captain Walter Butler*)

SYDNEY DEANE (*Sir Ashley Montague*)

W. W. JONES (*General Gage*)

E. ROSEMAN (*Captain Montour*)

HARRY SEMELS (*Hikatoo*)

HARRY O'NEILL (*Paul Revere*)

HENRY VAN BOUSEN (*John Parker, Captain of the Minute Men*)

HUGH BAIRD (*Major Pitcairn*)

JAMES MILAIDY (*Jonas Parker*)

H. KOSER (*Colonel Prescott*)

MICHAEL DONOVAN (*Major General Warren*)

LOUIS WOLHEIM (*Captain Hare*)

RILEY HATCH (*Joseph Brant, Chief of Mohawks*)

H. PAUL DOUCET (*Marquis de Lafayette*)

W. RISING (*Edmund Burke*)

DANIEL CARNEY (*Miss Montague's personal servant*)

E. SCANLON (*household servant at Ashley Court*)

EMIL HOCH (*Lord North*)

LUCILLE LA VERNE (*a refugee mother*)

EDWIN HOLLAND (*Major Strong*)

MILTON NOBLE (*an old patriot*)

THE STORY

At the beginning of the Revolution, Nathan Holden, a Minute Man, Son of Liberty, express rider, and comrade of Paul Revere, is a farmer living near Lexington. On a visit to Virginia, he had met Nancy Montague, "a famous belle" and "far above his station," who lives with her father and brother Charles on a great estate on the James River. Despite the differences between them, Nathan fell hopelessly in love with Nancy and knew that for him she was the only girl. After the Port of Boston is closed in retaliation for pre-Revolutionary disturbances, Nathan meets Nancy again when he is sent by the Boston Committee of Public Safety with despatches to the House of Burgesses in Williamsburg, and this time Nancy admits having enjoyed the verses he sent her, even though they were "exceedingly bold." The Burgesses send messages of sympathy and support to Boston over the protest of Justice Montague and other Tories. In taking leave of the son of his old friend, George Washington embraces him and tells him to do his duty *as he sees it*.

Montague's brother, Sir Ashley Montague, lives on an estate in northern New York. Montague goes there to confer with General Gage and the Governor of Canada, while Captain Walter Butler, representing the King's Superintendent for Indian Affairs, is soliciting the aid of the Six Nations in the coming conflict. Secretly Butler is disloyal even to the King, hoping to carve out an empire for himself in the New World. He also meets and is attracted by Nancy.

John Hancock and Samuel Adams flee to Lexington upon learning that a warrant is out for their arrest. The Montagues arrive at the tavern there on the eve of the battle, and Holden is part of the muster. When the British move upon Lexington and Concord and the military supplies stored there, Paul Revere rides out from Charlestown to warn and arouse the countryside.

Holden woos Nancy standing on his horse's back under her window at the inn, and when his horse moves out from under him, he is left hanging on her windowsill, half in and half out of the window. Her father sees him there and accuses him of breaking into Nancy's room, and her brother Charles challenges him to a duel with pistols. The duel is just about to take place at the inn when it is interrupted by Revere's arrival in Lexington.

The Montagues watch the battle from the inn, but Charles, his sympathies strangely stirred, steals out without his father's knowledge and joins the colonials. When

Neil Hamilton as Nathan Holden

Nancy Montague (Carol Dempster), her brother Charles (Charles Emmett Mack), and her father (Erville Alderson)

Nathan sent from Boston to carry the news of the city's plight to the Virginia burgesses.

the fire-eating Montague goes out to denounce the rebels, a soldier jogs Holden's arm and Montague is accidentally shot and crippled. Even Nancy now believes that Holden has deliberately shot her father and turns against him. Charles goes from the Lexington fight to Bunker Hill, where he behaves with great heroism and is fatally wounded. After his death in the hospital, his body is brought to his father's bedside for leave-taking, but Nancy drapes the casket in the Union Jack so that the old Tory may be spared the agony of knowing that his son died for the wrong cause.

The action now shifts to the Mohawk Valley, where Butler and his Indian allies are attempting to split the colonies. The Montagues are again at Ashley Court, where Nancy's father, as yet unaware of Butler's true character, promises him his daughter's hand.

From Valley Forge Washington sends Holden north against Butler with Morgan's Rangers. When he stops at Ashley Court, Nancy learns that a military court has exonerated him in the shooting. Holden insists on seeing Montague and trying to tell him the truth about Butler, but he makes no impression.

A year later Butler's troops raid Ashley Court; Sir Ashley is killed and Butler sets up a council of war. Holden and Major Strong are sent as spies to Ashley Court to try to find out the exact striking point Butler has in mind so that the inadequate American forces can be concentrated there. Montague, now estranged from Butler by the Cherry Valley Massacre and other atrocities, orders him out, but Butler accuses him of having turned traitor and places him under arrest. Holden and Strong, however, fortunately overhear him giving the order to destroy Fort Esperance (Fort Sacrifice) and kill all rebels there including the children.

An Indian on guard at Ashley Court sees Holden and Strong and succeeds in stabbing Strong, but is himself killed by Holden. Meanwhile Butler, dropping all pretenses, has Nancy brought in to him at a drunken feast, just as Holden is forced to leave in order to ride off and carry the warning of imminent attack to the inhabitants of the valley. Butler is just carrying the girl upstairs when his Mohawk ally Joseph Brant interrupts him with a demand that they proceed at once to the warpath: "My Mohawks say now or not at all." Nancy and her father escape to the fort, where people on both sides of the conflict have now taken refuge. Holden and Morgan's Rangers ride to the rescue, on the way encountering Butler's troops, and Butler is killed. News of the end of the war comes upon the heels of the fort's deliverance, and the film closes with Washington's inauguration, watched with delight by Nancy, Holden, and her father, who now see all things eye to eye.

Paul Revere rouses the countryside.

The Boston patriots take refuge in Lexington.

Nancy and Holden meet again at Lexington.

War begins.

Charles Montague challenges Nathan.

Bunker Hill

Washington at Valley Forge

Walter Butler (Lionel Barrymore) sets his sights on Nancy.

War in the valley

Washington inaugurated President

CRITICISM

Nobody knows why Civil War films tend to be much more popular than films about the American Revolution, but the fact is undeniable, and *America*, generally rated D. W. Griffith's last front-rank silent film, was no exception. The production began with a letter sent by the Daughters of the American Revolution to Will Hays, then the "czar" of the motion picture industry, lamenting the lack of a big Revolutionary War film and urging that one should be undertaken. The picture was made in New England, in upper New York State, and in Virginia, but more of it, including the Battle of Lexington, at the Griffith studio in Mamaroneck, New York. Assistance was received from the War Department and various libraries and learned societies. Infantrymen had to have special training in the use of Revolutionary weapons and in tactics. The first sequence filmed was Paul Revere's ride, which took two weeks. The Valley Forge sequence was filmed last, after the date for the February 22 première had already been set, because the snow was late in coming that winter.

Photographically *America* was an unqualified triumph.

Scene after scene of breathtaking beauty crossed the screen: a weeping willow silhouetted against the sky at dusk, a body of Redcoats traveling along the brow of a hill under a bloodshot sun, the Old North Church, with its signal lights gleaming across the moonswept waters of Charlestown Bay, Bunker Hill seen through the masts and rigging of a British man-of-war. Some of these were glass shots, giving the unbelievable effect of quaint old prints, marvelously impregnated with light. They and dozens of others had no fault except that they came and went so quickly; one longed to take them off the screen and hang them on the wall, where they might hold their beauty forever. It was a pity that this could not be done, for their loveliness has considerably faded in the prints of *America* now available, though enough survives to give the intelligent spectator an idea of what once was there. In the original prints they were perfect.

Scarcely less deserving of praise are the historical sequences. The comparatively lengthy reconstructions of Lexington, Concord, and Bunker Hill leave nothing to be desired, and even that which comes and goes in moments is memorable. The spectator sees Patrick Henry ringing out his defiance before the Virginia burgesses; he is with Burke when he pleads in Parliament against the employment of savages in the American war; he stands in Independence Hall when the Declaration of Independence is signed; he accompanies Paul Revere on a more thrilling ride than he can have had in actuality; he is present when Washington receives the sword of Cornwallis and when he takes his oath as President. Washington's crossing the Delaware was omitted, however, at the request of William Randolph Hearst, in order not to compete with its presentation in the film version of Paul Leicester Ford's *Janice Meredith*, starring Marion Davies.

In spite of these virtues, *America* does not grip and hold to the extent of some other Griffith films, and it is rather difficult to determine why. It is true that the second half, dealing with Walter Butler's depredations and the war in Mohawk Valley, seems almost to belong to a different film from what we have seen in Part I, but the difference here is no more striking than that between the Civil War portion of *The Birth of a Nation* and the Reconstruction portion. The beginning of Part II almost sinks under the history lessons that are thrown at us in long subtitles, yet the story itself is more interesting than it is often said to have been. Some of the material is perhaps a little too highly colored: Louis Wolheim, for example, as a sadistic and degenerate soldier who strips himself to the waist and covers his face with Indian war paint so that he may feel freer to commit atrocities. Lionel Barrymore is excellent, however, as a thoroughly evil Walter Butler, who may have been as bad in life as he is in the film but can hardly have been quite so important; in the second half of *America*, the colonials almost seem to be fighting not England but Captain Butler.

One of Griffith's idiosyncrasies as a director had always been his heavy emphasis on scenes staged in halls and corridors. Among the features, there are striking examples in *Intolerance*, *Hearts of the World*, and *Orphans of the Storm*, and the same tendency appears in many Biographs. Some of the best of his corridor scenes are in *America*, where Holden and Strong are shown spying at Ashley Court.

The film ends with the most elaborate depiction of wilderness fighting Griffith ever achieved, in which he makes good use of everything relevant he had learned, going clear back to Biograph days.

A greater difficulty in *America* than the shift from Part I to Part II is the weakness of the love story. It seems strange that a pair of lovers who encounter so many difficulties as Nancy Montague and Nathan Holden should rouse such tepid interest as they do. It has become the fashion to blame Carol Dempster for this, but the real difficulty lies elsewhere. *America* has no powerful, unbroken line of personal interest, and all the characters stand in imminent danger of being overwhelmed by history. Griffith moves them about from place to place, like pieces on a checkerboard, as the exigencies of the war or the story seem to require. Just as we are beginning to be interested in their affairs, the film takes off to depict historical events, and in these we become so absorbed that when the focus shifts again we have half forgotten the characters. The lovers have very little opportunity to get acquainted with each other (love, surely, has seldom thrived upon such insubstantial food), and we, consequently, have even less opportunity to get acquainted with them or to care greatly what becomes of them. The scene in which Carol Dempster drapes her brother's casket with the Union Jack is poignant and powerful indeed as to situation, but she is given very little to do in it, and for the hero of an action film, Neil Hamilton too is kept remarkably quiet and passive.

There is, to be sure, a very intense moment in the Ashley Court sequence toward the close of the film, where Holden seems to face a horrible dilemma. Shall he start off to warn the valley, as duty clearly commands, or shall he stay to deliver Nancy from Butler's lascivious clutches? Actually, however, this is a kind of fake dilemma. Holden has no chance to save the girl. If he were to enter the room where Butler is holding her, he would be cut down at once, and this would do neither her nor the valley any good. Indeed the most powerful scene in *America* goes to neither the hero nor the heroine but to Charles Emmett Mack as Charles, squirming in his death agony as he rolls the powder keg he had given his life to capture into the trench at Bunker Hill. Here the spectator squirms with him as the scene approaches the confines of the bearable.

Though Robert Sherwood overplayed this point in his review of *America* in the old *Life*, it is true that Griffith's attitude toward the Revolution is about what one would expect in a film that had been sponsored by the D.A.R. Naturally this bias does not lessen the dramatic power of the film; nobody has ever supposed that the force of *The Birth of a Nation* proceeded from the rightness of its attitude toward Reconstruction and the Ku Klux Klan! It is interesting, however, that before *America* was shown in England, under the title *Love and Sacrifice*, it was subjected to a judicious editing process whose purpose was to tone down criticism of the English, and it seems amusingly ironical that this should be the version now available in the United States through the Museum of Modern Art's Film Library and Blackhawk Films.

E. W.

26

ISN'T LIFE WONDERFUL

SCENARIO: D. W. Griffith, based on the short story by Major Geoffrey Moss in his book *Defeat*

PHOTOGRAPHY: Hendrik Sartov and Hal Sintzenich

MUSIC ARRANGED BY: Louis Silvers and Caesare Sudero

LENGTH: 8,600 feet

PRODUCTION: D. W. Griffith, Inc.

DISTRIBUTION: United Artists

RELEASED: December 1, 1924

NEW YORK PREMIÈRE: Town Hall, December 4, 1924

CAROL DEMPSTER (*Inga*)

NEIL HAMILTON (*Paul*)

HELEN LOWELL (*the grandmother*)

ERVILLE ALDERSON (*the professor*)

FRANK PUGLIA (*Theodor*)

MARCIA HARRIS (*the aunt*)

LUPINO LANE (*Rudolph*)

HANS VON SCHLETTOW (*the leader of the hungry workers*)

PAUL REHKOPF and ROBERT SCHOLZ (*the hungry workers*)

WALTER PLIMMER, JR. (*the American*)

(In 1925, Hal Roach produced a two-reel skit, titled *Isn't Life Terrible*, featuring Charlie Chase and Oliver Hardy.)

THE STORY

Isn't Life Wonderful centers on a family of Polish refugees in and about a suburb of Berlin, following the Armistice of 1918. The family comprises the professor; two sons—Theodor, a university student, and Paul, who returns from forced service in the army and nearly dies from the effects of poison gas; their grandmother; an aunt; and Inga, an orphan who has been brought up by the family and who loves Paul. The professor corrects examination papers at a local school; Theodor works as a waiter in a nightclub, patronized largely by foreigners; Paul, after having recovered his health, goes to work in a shipyard; and Inga clerks in a store and works overtime in a secondhand shop, where she is paid by being allowed to take home an occasional piece of secondhand furniture, which she saves against her eventual marriage to Paul. The food available, at first limited to potatoes, later deteriorates to horse turnips, which everybody hates and which make Grandmother sick.

Paul is assigned a plot of ground where he may grow vegetables and builds a small house for Inga and himself

out of ammunition boxes, but economic conditions being what they are, the family takes a dim view of plans for an early marriage. The situation begins to change for the better when Paul brings home his first crop of potatoes, followed by the assurance that there are enough in the ground to last all winter, Theodor delivers a whole liverwurst given to him by a rich American at the café, and the hens which a departing neighbor had left with Inga begin laying. The grandmother makes over her own wedding dress as a surprise for Inga.

Their problems, however, are not over. When Paul and Inga go out with a cart to gather the harvest upon which both their marriage plans and the family's winter food supply depend, they are attacked by starving men who have at first taken them for food hoarders and profiteers, slugged, and robbed. Paul is crushed, believing that nothing is of any use, but Inga is so happy when she finds that he has not been killed and that they still have each other that she helps him to rally his spirits, and we are given to understand that the marriage has not been cancelled but only postponed.

The family. *Left to right:* Theodor (Frank Puglia); the professor (Erville Alderson); Paul (Neil Hamilton); the aunt (Marcia Harris); Inga (Carol Dempster); the grandmother (Helen Lowell)

The wedding dress

The grandmother objects to Paul and Inga marrying without resources.

The house Paul built for Inga

Two shots of the food queue scene, one showing D. W. Griffith directing it

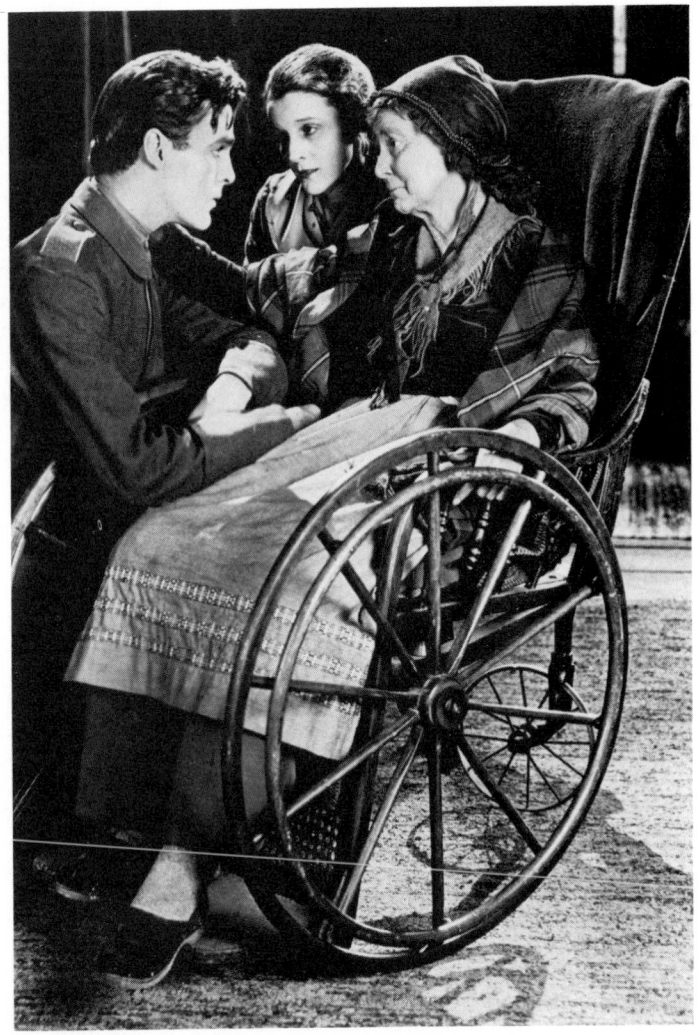

CRITICISM

Isn't Life Wonderful, shot in Germany in the summer of 1924, is devoted to depicting the conditions which existed there after the armistice concluding World War I (displacement of persons, hunger, breadlines, riots, runaway inflation, etc.). It begins with war footage left over from Griffith's *Hearts of the World* period, which is followed by the familiar Griffith assertion that war is glorious only to autocratic rulers and by shots showing refugees and cripples. Griffith uses real-life material much in the manner of the early Russian directors, and his film is as much a document as those made by Pabst and other German directors. By all means the simplest, most deliberately subdued and underplayed of all Griffith's major films, *Isn't Life Wonderful* is also one of the most touching and sincere, and, within its limitations, one of the best. It expresses the compassionate side of the director, which was the deepest aspect of his nature; when he made war propaganda films, he was more successful in expressing the warped passions and convictions of the society in which he lived than his own.

Isn't Life Wonderful was a daring film to make at the time, and it is no wonder that it was not a great "success." Apparently even Griffith did not dare to go the whole way and make a suffering German family appeal to our sympathies; indeed he tells us at the outset that his scene was laid in Germany because conditions were best there for showing the triumph of love over hardship. Inga and her people are Polish refugees, and early in the film the grandmother tears up a picture of the Kaiser and stamps on it. There is even an uncomfortable suggestion of the anti-Russian feeling that was rising just as hatred of the Germans began to subside in the presence in the film of the surly and potentially murderous Russ with whom Rudolph is required to room (there are always villains in the melodrama which is being played on the international stage, but the ethnic complexions of the cast change bewilderingly from time to time). Nevertheless Griffith makes it abundantly clear that the Germans themselves are sharing in the agonizing hardships with which the picture deals.

Nothing could be more touching than the first four reels, through which we explore the privations of the little family, the courage with which they stand up to them, and the expedients to which they are driven in their attempt to conquer them. Thereafter it runs a little long for a film with so little variety to it, and there is certainly a touch of sentimentality at the close. That the human spirit is undefeatable, that life has its compensations even under intolerable conditions, and that love can accomplish miracles—these ideas not only have validity but are the basic affirmations of the film. Nevertheless the "isn't life wonderful" note is forced at the end, where Inga's instant rally from the loss of the potatoes whose theft not only postpones her marriage but raises grave neglected questions about what the family is to live on through the winter is hard to believe.

Griffith was well aware of the differences between *Isn't Life Wonderful* and most of his films, for he makes a point at the outset about eschewing melodrama and sensation. Some may feel that he violates this intent by depending for his climax on the theft of the potatoes, which even involves a chase through the forest, but this criticism can hardly be held valid. What is at stake is very different from what we have dealt with in the chase sequences of other Griffith films, and conditions being what they were in Germany at the time, the theft was almost inevitable. Moreover the thieves, formidable as they appear, are not really "villains" but simply desperate, hungry men. They begin their pursuit of Paul and Inga under the impression that they are hoarders or food profiteers (who would richly deserve to be pursued), and when they learn the truth (one can hardly imagine the beleaguered heroine of any other Griffith film arguing with her menace as Inga does here!), they almost relent; it is only the leader's remembrance of his starving wife that stifles the impulse toward mercy and decency. Paul is not killed; neither is Inga raped; moreover their marriage is not prevented but only postponed. On the whole, it would be a mistake to leave the impression that the second half of *Isn't Life Wonderful* is inferior to the first; nobody who sees the film ever forgets the nerve-racking scene depicting the queue outside the butcher shop. Every time the new prices are posted, Inga anxiously counts her money again, to assure herself that she still has enough to make the necessary purchase, until at last the meat offered soars out of her reach, her face droops in utter discouragement, and she steps out of the line.

Here and throughout the film, Carol Dempster's performance is out of the top drawer—simple, restrained, deeply felt, and austerely indifferent to all considerations of glamour. (My colleague Anthony Slide thinks she was even better in *The Sorrows of Satan*, and he may well be right, but I have not had a chance to see this film for so many years that I cannot judge.) Possibly the scene in which she puts cotton into her cheeks to show her ailing lover that she is getting fat, so that he will consume some of her potatoes, is a little too reminiscent of Lillian Gish's forced smile in *Broken Blossoms*, but if so this is a minor point. She is supported by an excellent cast, in which the standouts are Helen Lowell as the grandmother and Marcia Harris as the aunt. Lupino Lane, as a musician and acrobatic dancer who has been allowed to attach himself to the family, apparently for the purpose of bringing some comic relief to the film, though excellent in what he does, is given few opportunities.

E. W.

27

SALLY OF THE SAWDUST

SCENARIO: Forrest Halsey, based on the play *Poppy*, by Dorothy Donnelly

PHOTOGRAPHY: Harry Fischbeck and Hal Sintzenich

FILM EDITOR: James Smith

ART DIRECTOR: Charles M. Kirk

LENGTH: 9,500 feet

PRODUCTION: D. W. Griffith, Inc.

DISTRIBUTION: United Artists

NEW YORK PREMIÈRE: Strand Theater, August 2, 1925

RELEASED: August 2, 1925

CAROL DEMPSTER (*Sally*)

W. C. FIELDS (*Professor Eustace McGargle*)

ALFRED LUNT (*Peyton Lennox*)

ERVILLE ALDERSON (*Judge Foster*)

EFFIE SHANNON (*Mrs. Foster*)

CHARLES HAMMOND (*Mr. Lennox, Sr.*)

ROY APPLEGATE (*the detective*)

FLORENCE FAIR (*Miss Vinton*)

MARIE SHOTWELL (*a society woman*)

(*Sally of the Sawdust* was remade by Paramount in 1936 under the original stage-play title of *Poppy* with W. C. Fields and Rochelle Hudson.)

THE STORY

Sally, whose dead mother was disowned by her parents when she married a circus man, has been brought up by "Professor" Eustace McGargle, a juggler and sideshow entertainer with a small circus. Sally acts as his assistant and contributes some dancing and acrobatics.

When "Pop" realizes that his little girl is growing up, he makes up his mind to try to find her grandparents, Judge and Mrs. Henry L. Foster. But by this time the circus has gone broke, and though the Professor has secured work in a carnival, he has no money for transportation; consequently he and Sally must walk. When they can go no farther, they steal a ride on the "blind baggage," from which they are washed off by a water-tank spout at a way station, which fortunately happens to be at the town where the carnival which the Professor has joined is playing. It is also the residence of the Fosters.

Peyton Lennox, son of a close friend of the Fosters, falls in love with Sally, but is opposed by his father, who shares Judge Foster's opinion of circus people. Sally makes a great impression when Peyton persuades her to appear masked, in a beautiful gown, at a society function, but when unmasking time comes, Judge Foster orders her out of the house.

McGargle is arrested because of complications growing out of a three-card monte game, which is one of his

Carol Dempster as Sally

specialties, and Sally falls into the clutches of the law as his accomplice. Each party tries, through harrowing experiences, to come to the aid of the other. Finally McGargle, rushing into the courtroom where Judge Foster is sitting in judgment over Sally, reveals her identity.

The case is dismissed, and the opposition to Peyton's suit withers. McGargle sadly prepares to remove himself from her life, but she rushes after him, and he finds himself accepted with her and established in the real estate business.

Sally with Professor Eustace McGargle (W. C. Fields)

Sally and McGargle in their act

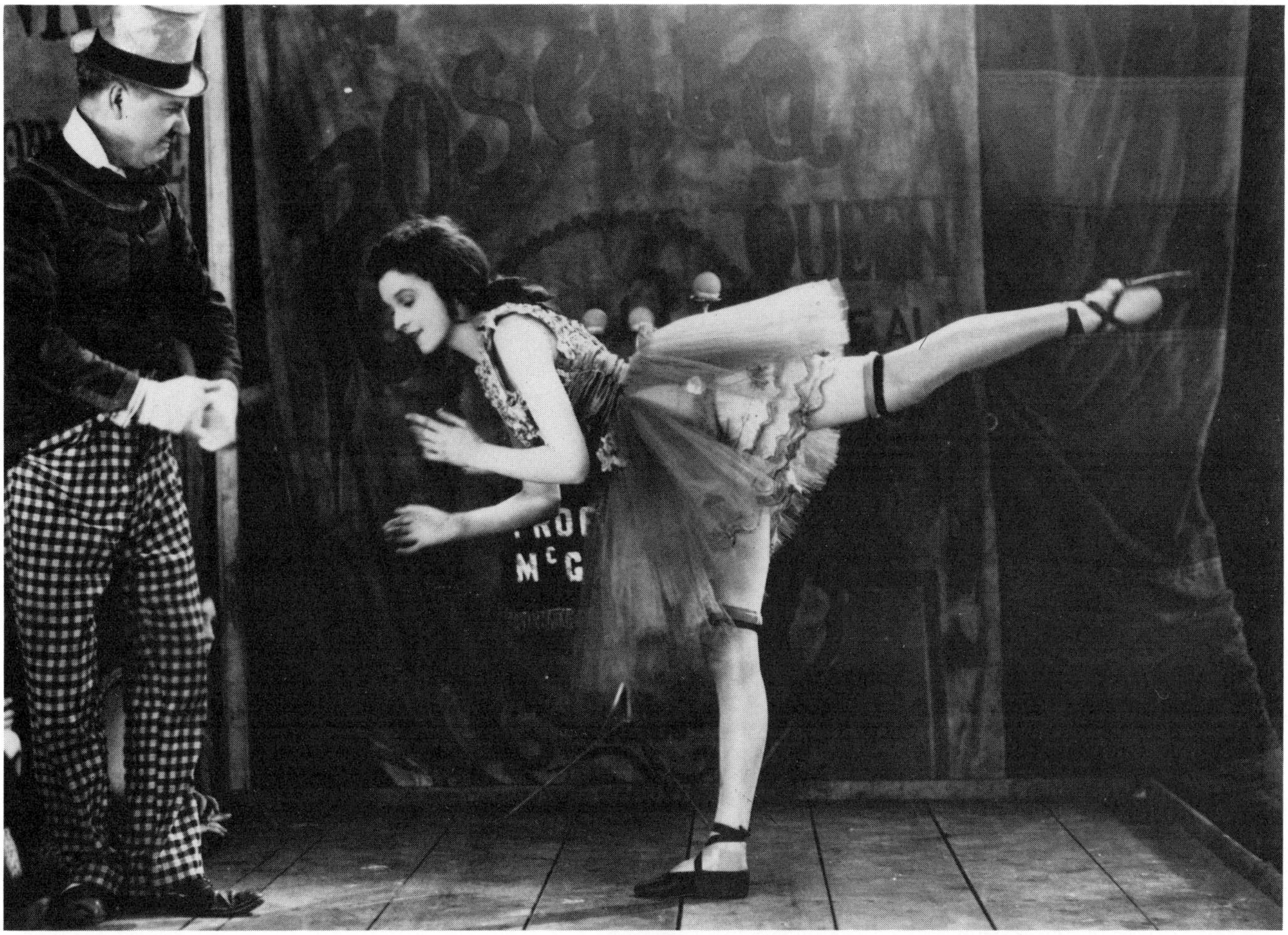

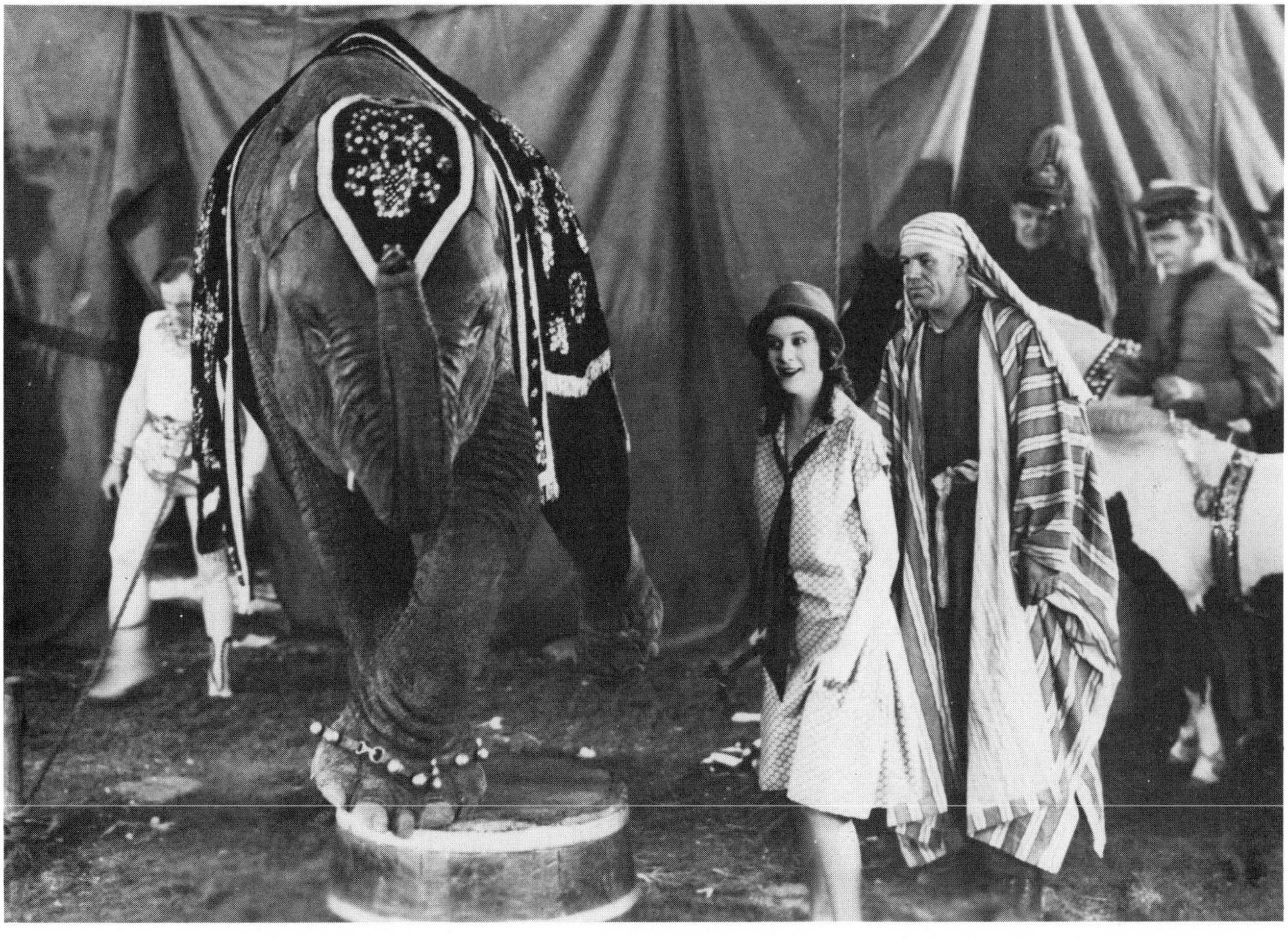

Sally becomes a fine lady at the Foster party.

Sally in court, with Mrs. Foster (Effie Shannon) and Peyton Lennox (Alfred Lunt)

CRITICISM

Sally of the Sawdust, from a business point of view, was a curious production. It was the first film produced by Griffith under a contract with Paramount, but, after its completion, Griffith took it away from that company, and released it through United Artists.

The subject was of Griffith's choosing, and the film was hailed—by *Motion Picture News* (August 15, 1925)—as "a big commercial and artistic success." Viewing *Sally of the Sawdust* today is a depressing experience; it is hard to understand the onetime popularity of this crude and too lengthy comedy-drama.

The highlight of the production is undoubtedly W. C. Fields, making his second screen appearance; his first was as a drunken British soldier in the Marion Davies vehicle *Janice Meredith*. Many of the dialogue subtitles read like the W. C. Fields most moviegoers remember from the thirties. A typical subtitle has him describe one character thus: "Got a face that looks like it's worn out four bodies." The comedian is also allowed to demonstrate his skills as a juggler, despite Carol Dempster's constantly trying to draw the audience's attention, rather as a female no-talent member of a vaudeville team might behave. Fields also presents his version of the old army game—"your eye against mine."

A number of the sight gags involving the comedian are still mildly amusing. Carol Dempster, as Sally, is about to hurl a stone at Judge Foster's residence; Fields, as Professor McGargle, admonishes her and forces her to drop the stone, after which he hands her a brick to throw. In another scene, Fields converts his peanut vendor's cart into a bar, complete with rail and sawdust on the ground.

Aside from Fields's moments of originality, much of the comedy is crude and vulgar, and would be better suited to the films of Mack Sennett than to the production of a master director. One particularly crude scene has Carol Dempster steal two bread rolls and hide them inside her blouse, thus accentuating her breasts. When Fields sees her, he does a double take, and comments, "Sally, you *are* growing up!"

The scenes leading up to the incident in which Dempster and Fields crawl into a baker's oven to warm themselves have an interesting origin. According to the version of Griffith's autobiography published as *The Man Who Invented Hollywood*, the director himself used this method of keeping warm when he was struggling to earn a living, long before the films, or even the stage, had beckoned.

Alfred Lunt as the hero, Peyton Lennox, makes no impression whatever, and appears totally lacking in personality. In one of his first scenes, Griffith manages to get him to act like one of his leading ladies, nervously giggling behind his straw hat.

Carol Dempster looks exceedingly drab throughout most of the film. She also manages to act in a most unseemly and ungainly fashion; in one of her first scenes, she swings from a trapeze by her feet, and gives one the impression that she was the circus clown rather than the "strange, whimsical creature" that Griffith describes.

She does, however, have one opportunity to look elegant, and that is when she takes part in a tableau at the society ball, and, probably for the only time in any of her films, wears a low-cut evening dress. The "new" Carol Dempster is quite a revelation. From this one sequence alone, I cannot but speculate that she had been miscast all along; perhaps she should have been starred in some of the society dramas which Norma Talmadge and Corinne Griffith had made all their own.

Sally of the Sawdust brightens up toward the close with Carol Dempster's escaping from court and being chased around town—scenes in which she displays surprising agility—while Fields drives recklessly to the rescue with news of her ancestry. In these scenes, which, in fact, last practically a full reel, Griffith shows some of his old sparkle, albeit the sparkle of many years previous. There is also one title—"A rich young man—a homeless waif—the eternal bond of youth"—which has the true Griffith ring to it. Nothing else in *Sally of the Sawdust* is worthy of the Griffith name and tradition.

A. S.

28

"THAT ROYLE GIRL"

SCREENPLAY: Paul Schofield, based on the novel by Edwin Balmer

PHOTOGRAPHY: Harry Fischbeck and Hal Sintzenich

ART DIRECTOR: Charles M. Kirk

FILM EDITOR: James Smith

LENGTH: 10,253 feet

PRODUCERS: Adolph Zukor and Jesse L. Lasky

PRODUCTION: Famous Players-Lasky

DISTRIBUTION: Paramount

NEW YORK PREMIÈRE: Strand Theater, January 10, 1926

RELEASE: December 7, 1925

CAROL DEMPSTER (*Joan Daisy Royle*)

W. C. FIELDS (*her father*)

JAMES KIRKWOOD (*Deputy District Attorney Calvin Clarke*)

HARRISON FORD (*Fred Ketlar, the King of Jazz*)

MARIE CHAMBERS (*Adele Ketlar*)

PAUL EVERTON (*George Baretta*)

GEORGE RIGAS (*his henchman*)

FLORENCE AUER (*Baretta's girl friend*)

IDA WATERMAN (*Mrs. Clarke*)

ALICE LAIDLEY (*Clarke's fiancée*)

DOROTHEA LOVE (*Lola Neeson*)

DORE DAVIDSON (*Elman*)

FRANK ALLWORTH (*Oliver*)

BOBBY WATSON (*Hofer*)

THE STORY

Joan Daisy Royle, a Chicago modiste's mannequin, of slum origin and somewhat soiled background, but an idealist at heart to whom Saint-Gaudens's statue of Lincoln in Lincoln Park is a kind of shrine, believes herself in love with the leader of a dance orchestra, Fred Ketlar, with an estranged wife who has become the mistress of George Baretta, a gangster and bootlegger.

When Adele Ketlar is murdered, suspicion points to Ketlar, and a sensational trial follows. Though attracted to Joan Daisy, the distict attorney, Calvin Clarke, handles her very severely when she appears for the defense, and Ketlar is convicted.

Suspecting that the real murderer is Baretta, Joan Daisy disguises herself and attends a party given by the gangster in a disreputable roadhouse known as the Boar's Head Inn. Here she succeeds in confirming her suspicions, but her presence is discovered, and she finds herself in great peril. Just as she has escaped, a terrible storm (suggested by the Illinois cyclone of 1919) breaks over the city. The inn is destroyed, and all the gangsters perish.

Joined by Clarke, Joan reaches the governor by phone just in time to stay the execution of Ketlar. But she now realizes that her interest in him was only infatuation. Ultimately Ketlar chooses a chorus girl as his second wife, and Joan is left to Clarke.

W. C. Fields as Joan Daisy's father

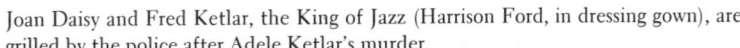

Joan Daisy Royle (Carol Dempster) communes with the spirit of her hero Lincoln at the Saint-Gaudens statue in Chicago's Lincoln Park.

Joan Daisy and Fred Ketlar, the King of Jazz (Harrison Ford, in dressing gown), are grilled by the police after Adele Ketlar's murder.

Joan Daisy with the district attorney (James Kirkwood)

The district attorney and his mother (Ida Waterman)

CRITICISM

D. W. Griffith began shooting on his second Paramount production, *"That Royle Girl,"* on July 6, 1925. The choice of subject was not his; the story had already been turned down by several other contract Paramount directors. Indeed, after the film's release, Griffith wrote a ten-page letter to Adolph Zukor, in which he noted: "I begged Mr. Lasky to let me get out of doing this picture as I did not think I could make the right kind of a picture out of it." It is perhaps indicative of Griffith's standing at Paramount that he had no alternative but to direct the picture.

Certainly this story of "ultra-modern jazz life," with its "all-spirit of jazz," as one publicist described it, does not sound the sort of a film that was meant to be handled by Griffith. As *"That Royle Girl,"* perhaps mercifully, is a lost film, we shall never know if it amounted to anything unusual. Even if the subject matter was not to his liking, one would imagine that Griffith was at ease with some of the location shooting in Chicago—at Lincoln Park, Edgewater Beach, and on the Lake Shore Drive.

Carol Dempster was on hand in the title role, described by *The Moving Picture World* as "a mixture of hoydenish tomboyishness and wistfulness, innocent of the world's evils and finding inspiration and solace in confiding her sorrows to the statue of her ideal, Lincoln." The description of hoydenish tomboyishness and wistfulness sounds all too suspiciously like what Griffith demanded of Carol Dempster in her role of Gypsy Fair in *Dream Street*. Griffith's infatuation with Miss Dempster was showing itself, as it had in *The Love Flower*, by an overindulgence in close-ups of the actress. Albert Grey, the director's business manager, was forced to write a memo, dated October 15, 1925, to Griffith: "Speaking of close-ups, I think there are too many of Miss Dempster. While each and every one is very beautiful, and as I said before, she does wonderful work, the best of her career, at the same time too many close-ups are going to harm her and also hold up the story."

"That Royle Girl" would seem to owe much to earlier Griffith productions. It bears more than a passing similarity to *One Exciting Night*. Just as the latter film tried to compensate for a disastrous plot-line with a spectacular storm sequence, so does *"That Royle Girl"* attempt to apologize for its melodramatic story with a cyclone. The cyclone did not help; nothing could help *"That Royle Girl,"* not even W. C. Fields, who tried to equal his comic father portrayal of *Sally of the Sawdust*.

When the film was released, some of the press were not too unkind. Wrote the Los Angeles *Evening Herald* (January 20, 1926): "Taking the picture as melodrama, and that is all anyone could take it to be, it is good entertainment for those who like to hiss the villain, cheer the hero and weep for the heroine."

Others were not so polite. The *New Yorker* (January 16, 1926) commented: "With 'That Royle Girl,' now decorating the front mural of the Strand, Mr. David Wark Griffith, saintly showman, established himself beyond all shadow of doubt as the magnified Samuel Shipman of the cinema. He is indisputably the grand master of moralistic-melodramatic balderdash. He has the corner of treacle, mush and trash and automatically is out of our set." The *New Yorker* was even ruder concerning Fields: "If Mr. W. C. Fields . . . sticks to Mr. Griffith he will surely be fired by Mr. Ziegfeld as being no comedian."

D. W. Griffith was obviously very affected by the response to *"That Royle Girl."* "I was forced to do the best I could with a very lame idea," he apologized to Adolph Zukor. In an interview with the Toronto *Daily Star*, the director sadly tried to explain his reasons for making the film. "He [the director] may indulge his art visions and his creative dreams and his vistas of the golden glow of humanity if he wants to—as I did once in *Broken Blossoms*, the most artistic picture I ever produced. But he has to square up at the box office on his batting average now and again." Griffith could not bring himself to admit that he was no longer a free spirit, but a hired helper in a mighty organization—Paramount—which had no time or room for art or compassion.

A. S.

29

THE SORROWS OF SATAN

SCREENPLAY: Forrest Halsey, based on the novel by Marie Corelli

ADAPTATION: John Russell and George Hull

TITLES: Julian Johnson

PHOTOGRAPHY: Harry Fischbeck

ART DIRECTOR: Charles Kirk

MINIATURES: Fred Waller

LENGTH: 8,691 feet

PRODUCERS: Adolph Zukor and Jesse L. Lasky

PRODUCTION: Famous Players–Lasky

DISTRIBUTION: Paramount

NEW YORK PREMIÈRE: George M. Cohan Theater, October 12, 1926

RELEASED: February 5, 1927

ADOLPHE MENJOU (*Prince Lucio de Rimanez*)

RICARDO CORTEZ (*Geoffrey Tempest*)

LYA DE PUTTI (*Princess Olga*)

CAROL DEMPSTER (*Mavis Claire*)

IVAN LEBEDEFF (*Amiel*)

MARCIA HARRIS (*the landlady*)

LAWRENCE D'ORSAY (*Lord Elton*)

NELLIE SAVAGE (*a dancing girl*)

DOROTHY HUGHES (*Mavis's chum*)

JOSEPHINE DUNN, DOROTHY NOURSE, JEANNE MORGAN

(*The Sorrows of Satan* had previously been filmed in Britain, in 1917, by G. B. Samuelson Productions, with Gladys Cooper and Owen Nares.)

THE STORY

Lucifer doubts God's wisdom in creating man, and God says: "Since you have said Man must be destroyed, destroy him if you can. You are no longer Lucifer the archangel, but shall be called Satan." Satan begs for mercy and receives this much: the promise that for every soul that resists him, he shall have a moment's peace at the Gates of Paradise, and that when all mankind have rejected him, he shall no longer be Satan but may resume his old place as Archangel of the Morn.

The story concerns Lucifer's attempt, in pursuance of his doom, to tempt Geoffrey Tempest, a struggling young writer, in love with Mavis Claire, who pursues the same ambition in the same boardinghouse. Satan comes to Geoffrey as Prince Lucio de Rimanez, the very epitome of a cultured, suave, fabulously wealthy, world-weary gentleman, in the moment when, more than ordinarily desperate for money that he may marry Mavis, Geoffrey loses his faith and curses God.

The Prince tells Geoffrey that he has inherited a vast fortune, but that in order to enjoy it to the utmost he must put himself under Lucio's guidance. Lucio introduces Geoffrey to English society and especially to the Earl of Elton and his niece, Princess Olga, a member of the Russian nobility, whom the Prince has designated as Geoffrey's bride. Though his heart is still drawn to Mavis, Geoffrey blindly acquiesces in the Tempter's plans.

Geoffrey soon discovers that Olga has married him for his money and in order to be near Prince Lucio, by whom she is fascinated. But that personage spurns her, and when Geoffrey learns the truth and breaks with her, she kills herself. Geoffrey again blasphemes and Lucio now reveals his true identity.

The now terror-stricken Geoffrey returns at last to Mavis, whose faith in God drives the devil away, and the reunited and now reconciled lovers are left together to find happiness and fulfillment in each other.

The War in Heaven

Geoffrey Tempest (Ricardo Cortez) and Mavis Claire
(Carol Dempster)

Geoffrey weds Princess Olga (Lya de Putti); Adolphe Menjou as Prince Lucio (Satan), at the left.

Geoffrey soon disillusioned

Satan in his element

Geoffrey returns to Mavis Claire.

CRITICISM

The Sorrows of Satan was Griffith's last feature for Paramount, and, despite the director's dislike for the subject and the executive interference in its production, the film must rank as the best of Griffith's Paramount trio.

Marie Corelli's novel *The Sorrows of Satan* was first published in 1895, and was a great success with the public, if not with the critics. Paramount purchased the film rights with Cecil B. DeMille in mind to direct. However, when DeMille left to form his own independent producing organization, Griffith was asked to film what he himself described as a "dreadful" novel.

Before shooting began, a number of changes were made in the plot. The heroine, Mavis Claire, became an impoverished would-be writer rather than the phenomenally successful novelist of the book, who is scorned by the critics, representing the corrupted viewpoint of a corrupted society, but worshiped by the public who buy her books in vast quantities. Mavis Claire does not appear until the novel is almost half over, and at the end, after his wife has killed herself, it is suggested that Geoffrey Tempest will marry her. It is obvious that Mavis Claire is a self-portrait of Marie Corelli, who is presented as an almost saintly, spiritually minded woman. Also in the novel

there is no Princess Olga, played so admirably in the film by Lya de Putti. Tempest marries an English girl, Lady Sybil, daughter of an impoverished father, who virtually puts her up for sale. She is beautiful, but thoroughly corrupt, unable to feel or believe in anything, and, like Princess Olga, she commits suicide in the end.

There is much to admire in Griffith's production, in particular the lighting and the camerawork (especially in the sequence where Satan, revealed as the eerie shadow of a batlike creature, pursues Tempest), and the superb sets of art director Charles Kirk. The prologue showing Satan's ejection from heaven is breathtaking; it was conceived and shot by stage designer Norman Bel Geddes, and then reshot by Griffith. Prints surviving today hint that this sequence was once longer and possibly even more stunning.

Adolphe Menjou is a suave and elegant Satan, making of him a man-about-town, and one feels far greater sympathy for him than for the hero and heroine. As Epes W. Sargent noted in *The Moving Picture World* (October 23, 1926): "He is such an urbane and agreeable devil [that] he gains greater interest than the nominal protagonist, who is pretty poor stuff to make a hero out of."

Carol Dempster as Mavis Claire gives the performance of her career. It was easy enough in *Isn't Life Wonderful* to have her made up to look dowdy so that audiences might believe she was actually acting the role, but here, with no such aid, she really gives a performance. "Carol Dempster's acting is something exceptional," wrote Mordaunt Hall in the New York *Times* (October 13, 1926). *The Sorrows of Satan* marked Miss Dempster's farewell not only to the screen but also to the director who had devoted all his cinematic greatness to making her a star. With *The Sorrows of Satan*, Griffith made of Dempster something more than a star; he taught her to act.

The Sorrows of Satan opened in New York simultaneously with two other Paramount productions, *Beau Geste* and *Old Ironsides*, and fared badly against such competition. Both *Beau Geste* and *Old Ironsides* were set in the past, but they had a timeless appeal. *The Sorrows of Satan* was based on a thirty-year-old novel, which had once been daring, but which, in the age of the flapper, was merely, as one critic noted, tiresome and preachy. The critics at the time saw only a dated melodrama, not the intelligent direction. When they mentioned the director it was in comments such as Laurence Reid's in *Motion Picture News* (October 23, 1926): "If *The Sorrows of Satan* had been made by an unknown director it would have created little reputation for him."

A. S.

Princess Emanuella (Mary Philbin), Duke Cathos de Alvia (Lionel Barrymore), and (Count Leonardo) Don Alvarado

30

DRUMS OF LOVE

SCENARIO AND TITLES: Gerrit J. Lloyd

PHOTOGRAPHY: Karl Struss

ASSISTANT CAMERAMEN: Harry Jackson and Billy Bitzer

SET DESIGNER: William Cameron Menzies

FILM EDITOR: James Smith

MUSIC: Charles Wakefield Cadman, Sol Cohen, and
Wells Hively

COSTUMES: Alice O'Neill

LENGTH: 8,350 feet

PRODUCTION: Art Cinema Corporation

DISTRIBUTION: United Artists

NEW YORK PREMIÈRE: January 24, 1928

RELEASED: March 31, 1928

MARY PHILBIN (*Princess Emanuella*)

LIONEL BARRYMORE (*Duke Cathos de Alvia*)

DON ALVARADO (*Count Leonardo de Alvia*)

TULLY MARSHALL (*Bopi, the court jester*)

EUGENIE BESSERER (*Duchess de Alvia*)

CHARLES HILL MAILES (*Duke of Granada*)

WILLIAM AUSTIN (*Raymond of Boston*)

ROSEMARY COOPER (*the maid*)

JOYCE COAD (*the little sister*)

THE STORY

Princess Emanuella, daughter of the Duke of Granada, agrees to marry Duke Cathos de Alvia in the interest of peace in their domains. She is attracted by Cathos's brother, Leonardo, when he comes to escort her to her husband, but shocked when she finds her husband an ugly and, to her, a repulsive hunchback.

Without the knowledge of Cathos, Emanuella and Leonardo drift into a clandestine love affair, which is unfortunately observed by the malevolent court jester, Bopi. Bopi alerts Cathos and advises him to return from a military campaign. He does so, discovers the lovers together, and kills them both.

An alternative ending, filmed later, had Cathos and Bopi stab each other to death and Cathos forgive the lovers.

CRITICISM

The tale of Francesca da Rimini and her blighted love for Paolo Malatesta has fascinated writers, artists, and musicians for centuries. Immortalized by Dante in his "Inferno," it has been the subject of dramas by Silvio Pellico, Paul Heyse, D'Annunzio, and Stephen Phillips; paintings by Ingres and Alexandre Cabanel; operas by Hermann Goetz and Ambroise Thomas; a symphonic poem by Tchaikovsky, etc. One of the most important early American plays was George Henry Boker's five-act tragedy *Francesca da Rimini*. First produced in 1855, it was revised and revived in 1882 with Lawrence Barrett, Marie Wainwright, and Otis Skinner.

No wonder Griffith set about filming such a famous story with a glad heart. He had been invited to return to Hollywood, where he had not made a film since 1919, by Joseph M. Schenck, who promised him considerable artistic freedom and complete financial backing. Griffith's next three features were to be produced by Schenck's Art Cinema Corporation, for release through United Artists.

Drastic changes were made in the traditional story before a script was ready for Griffith to direct, but these

were nothing compared to the change made after the film's première.

The script, first titled *Dance of Life* and then *Scarlet Apple*, was prepared by Gerrit J. Lloyd, who had previously been Griffith's publicity man. Lloyd transferred the story from Italy to the South American empire of the king of Portugal, with a background of power struggles between the Duke of Granada and the Duke de Alvia, substituting for the Rimini and Malatesta families, and called his work, *Drums of Love*.

Drums of Love is both a curiosity and a well-produced spectacle. It features Mary Philbin, as Princess Emanuella, giving one of the best performances of her career. From the opening scene with her, in which she appears chasing and cradling a cat, onward, one realizes that Griffith has taken this Universal contract player and molded her into a typical Griffith heroine. As the Duke Cathos de Alvia, whom Emanuella is forced to marry, Lionel Barrymore turns in a fine performance, giving a sympathy and a warmth to his role. Aside from Barrymore, *Drums of Love* reunited Griffith with another of his old company, Tully Marshall, who had been with the director at Triangle. Marshall seems strangely miscast in the role of Bopi, the court jester who is to be the catalyst in this tragic love triangle.

Although set in South America, and not Ruritania, *Drums of Love* is very much in the tradition of *The Prisoner of Zenda*. One can almost believe that it is Rex Ingram and not D. W. Griffith who is directing the drama, and that the leading lady is Alice Terry, not Mary Philbin. Indeed, it is a curious coincidence that Mary Philbin should be wearing a blond wig in this production, just as Alice Terry did in the bulk of her features. And, just as Alice Terry added a great dignity to her films, so does Mary Philbin add a dignity to *Drums of Love*, with her beautifully serene and tranquil face and her complete composure, whatever the situation.

As in the novels of Anthony Hope, honor plays an important part in this film. It is honor that insists Emanuella must marry Cathos, despite her growing love for his brother, Leonardo. When Cathos says to her, "If you wish now to withdraw from the marriage, you may return home, and none shall be the worse," honor dictates that Emanuella's reply must be, "It is willingly, my Lord." Ultimately, honor will demand the final sacrifice. Told by Bopi of the affair between his wife and his brother, Cathos will kill them! Thus will honor reign supreme, the final sacrifice having been made.

Drums of Love has some curious aspects. One is a lavishly produced and well-directed battle scene, which occupies a few seconds of screen time at the beginning of the film, and must have been the most expensive portion to produce. Why so much money obviously spent for so little screen time? One historian has suggested that Griffith, aiming, as always, for perfection when he began shooting, overspent his entire budget on the battle scenes, and that this is the reason for the lack of spectacle elsewhere in the production.

The other curiosity is the use of a vast number of glass shots. Eileen Bowser notes that "from time to time expensively produced glass shots are inserted—for no apparent reason other than to break up the lengthy indoor scenes." Actually there was a more valid reason for them. According to publicity material on the production, Griffith was aiming at a three-dimensional effect in pictures, and *Drums of Love* gave him an opportunity to experiment. The director's problem was that he wanted glass shots that would not look flat on the screen.

As a publicist explained:

D. W. . . . felt that there must be some solution. To substantiate his hypothesis he happened to be looking at some illustrations one day. Among the volumes whose pages he turned was Gazo's *History of France*, illustrated by De Neuville. He noted a peculiar quality of the black-and-white sketches of this noted Frenchman. Although they were shaded and more or less traditionally executed, the figures stood out. There was something that lent to them an almost three-dimensional quality.

Starting out on the assumption that the camera must be able to produce the same effects, Griffith went to work with his cameraman, Karl Struss. They experimented for weeks. Oil paintings, etchings, tapestries, were photographed with varying results.

And then human beings. A set was taken. Then a background. Later an entire scene. The result was amazing. The characters walked about on the silver sheet as if they were real people. Rather, they seemed to be walking in front of the screen.

Drums of Love was previewed at the Regent Theatre, Riverside, California, on December 9, 1927, and was well received. It followed another lavish production, Douglas Fairbanks's *The Gaucho*, into New York's Liberty Theatre, for its première on January 24, 1928. Critical reception was favorable. Laurence Reid, in *Motion Picture News* (January 28, 1928), commented: "Who said Griffith was through? The master of shadings and shadows, the builder of climaxes, demonstrates again that he has a firm hold on the treatment of a screen story."

However, one part of the film plot proved unpopular at the box office, and a pretty major part at that—the tragic ending. Nineteen twenty-eight was no year for tragedy. Griffith shot a new ending, drastically altering the plot, so that Bopi and Cathos stab each other, leaving the lovers free to marry, with Cathos's forgiveness and blessing. The new ending was shot and edited into the picture by February 28, 1928, as a letter in the D. W. Griffith Collection at the Museum of Modern Art informs us. History does not record Griffith's feelings on the matter. Somehow one suspects he was not too happy with the change.

Undoubtedly Griffith was pleased to receive a letter from David Belasco, in which the great stage producer wrote:

Whoever loves good acting, whoever loves beauty, whoever loves the artistic, whoever loves love should see this picture —and all true enthusiasts of the screen and lovers of the artistic should assemble to crown you with the laurel to which the conqueror is entitled. You have earned it, dear, wonderful David Wark Griffith. I salute you!

Despite its new ending, *Drums of Love* did make it seem that D. W. Griffith was once again back in his stride. The success of his first feature for a new company must have given him high hopes for the future. As fate would have it, those hopes were not to be realized.

A. S.

31

THE BATTLE OF THE SEXES (1928)

SCENARIO: Gerrit Lloyd, based on *The Single Standard* by Daniel Carson Goodman

PHOTOGRAPHY: Karl Struss and G. W. Bitzer

FILM EDITOR: James Smith

MUSIC AND SOUND EFFECTS: Nathaniel Shilkret and his Orchestra

LENGTH: 8,180 feet/10 reels

PRODUCTION: Art Cinema Corporation

DISTRIBUTION: United Artists

NEW YORK PREMIÈRE: Rialto Theatre, October 12, 1928

RELEASED: October 12, 1928

JEAN HERSHOLT (*Judson*)

PHYLLIS HAVER (*Marie Skinner*)

BELLE BENNETT (*Mrs. Judson*)

DON ALVARADO (*"Babe" Winsor*)

SALLY O'NEIL (*Ruth Judson*)

WILLIAM BAKEWELL (*Billy Judson*)

JOHN BATTEN (*a friend of the Judsons*)

THE STORY

The Judsons are a happy family, and newly rich—father, mother, daughter, and son—but the father falls into the clutches of Marie Skinner, a pretty blonde gold digger, who takes an apartment next door and proceeds to scrape an acquaintance with him, that she may fleece him both in her own interest and in that of her lover, "Babe" Winsor.

When Mrs. Judson comes upon her husband and Marie dancing, "in sensuous embrace," in a nightclub, she is so shocked and distressed that she very nearly goes out of her mind. The mother's condition has an almost equally upsetting effect upon her daughter, who seizes a revolver and confronts Marie in her apartment. Chance draws both Judson and Marie's caddish lover into the situation. Shocked to find his daughter in what seems like a compromising position, Judson starts to rebuke her, but she denounces him mercilessly and causes him to see himself as he is. His daughter's tongue-lashing and the disillusionment he has now experienced concerning Marie combine to bring Judson to his senses. Some months later the good offices of the children achieve a reconciliation between husband and wife.

Mrs. Judson (Belle Bennett) is horrified to find her husband (Jean Hersholt) with Marie Skinner (Phyllis Haver) in a night club.

232

Judson disciplines his daughter (Sally O'Neil).

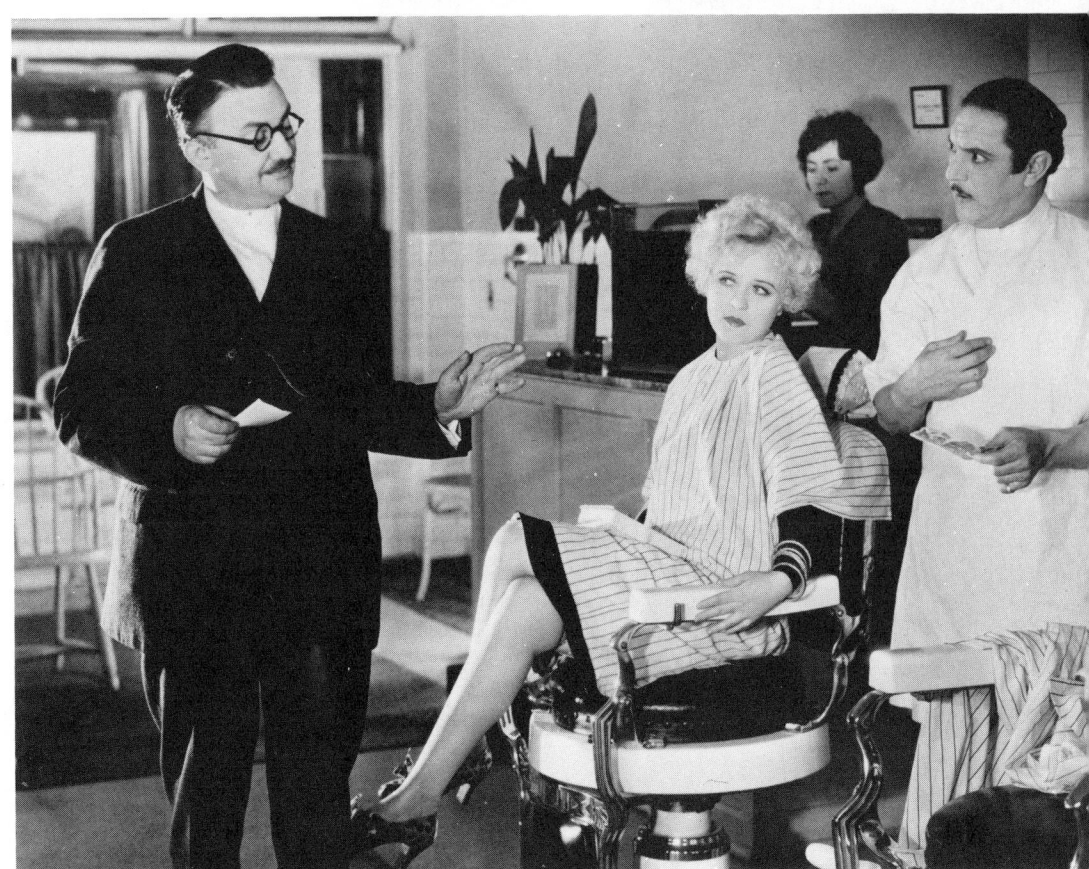

Marie with "Babe" Winsor (Don Alvarado)

CRITICISM

"Here I promise one picture with real entertainment," said D. W. Griffith of *The Battle of the Sexes*. Entertainment the film possibly was—it was certainly nothing more.

The feature opened with a ridiculously pompous caption: "This battle rages always and shall always for the struggle of desire pursued and desire running away with or against its will struggling, convoluting and out of this convolution emerges life always going on. Even in death still is life and out of this death and life ever is reproduced more life and more death."

The Battle of the Sexes then gets underway, with its director manifesting a curiously out-of-character view of life, denigrating the family, and exalting the behavior of the gold digger, portrayed by the popular blonde comedienne Phyllis Haver. As the couple on whose marriage Haver wreaks havoc, Jean Hersholt and Belle Bennett were particularly well cast. Hersholt could always be relied upon to appear somewhat ludicrous, intentionally or not, and Belle Bennett, after her performance in *Stella Dallas*, had become the screen's most famous mother.

The production survives today only in a silent version, although it was originally released with a synchronized musical score, including a theme song by Phyllis Haver. The score was not to the director's liking; he considered that it hurt the picture considerably.

It is all too obvious that Joseph Schenck had forced Griffith into making what Schenck hoped would be a commercial success, although it is hard to understand the producer's belief that a remake of a 1914 melodrama, even if played partly for laughs, could make money.

Griffith's brother, Albert L. Grey, explained to a United Artists executive that "one of Mr. Griffith's failings is to make pictures for the critics and the highbrows. He has tried to remedy this picture so it will make money in the picture houses." At the same time, the director himself was busy explaining to the same executive that *The Battle of the Sexes* might be compared to the short stories of Chekhov. "It struck me," he wrote, "that something out of this idea might be gotten to the critics, particularly the highbrows, in some casual, offhand manner, because we certainly cannot advertise it as a great production or as one of Griffith's greatest."

The director was undoubtedly correct. Louella Parsons might hail *The Battle of the Sexes* as "a popular success" in the Los Angeles *Examiner*, and *Film Daily* might consider that "Griffith's reputation as a box-office director can stand more like this one," but most critics were inclined to compare it to the 1914 production and to judge the former a far better picture in its day. It is significant that when Griffith tried to display an ultrasophisticated view of life, he failed, and his critics then remembered with pleasure the Victorian attitudes of his earlier productions, for which they had previously berated him.

Shooting on *The Battle of the Sexes* was completed by December, 1927, and I suspect Griffith did not look forward too happily to Christmas and the New Year. One Christmas cable from fellow director Herbert Brenon possibly brightened his holiday, JOE [SCHENCK] TOLD ME LAST NIGHT ABOUT THE GREAT PICTURE YOU HAVE JUST MADE. NO ONE IS LESS SURPRISED NOR HAPPIER THAN I. MY DEAR TEACHER A MERRY CHRISTMAS WISH FROM YOUR PUPIL.

A.S.

32

LADY OF THE PAVEMENTS

SCENARIO: Sam Taylor, based on a story, "La Paiva," by Karl Vollmoeller

TITLES: Gerrit Lloyd

DIALOGUE: George Scarborough

PHOTOGRAPHY: Karl Struss

FILM EDITOR: James Smith

SET DESIGNER: William Cameron Menzies

THEME SONG: "Where Is the Song of Songs for Me," composed by Irving Berlin

MUSICAL ARRANGER: Hugo Riesenfeld

COSTUMES: Alice O'Neill

LENGTH: 7,495 feet (Silent Version) and 8,329 feet (Sound Version with music and dialogue sequences)

PRODUCTION: Art Cinema Corporation

DISTRIBUTION: United Artists

LOS ANGELES PREMIÈRE: United Artists Theatre, January 22, 1929

RELEASED: February 16, 1929

LUPE VELEZ (Nanon del Rayon)

WILLIAM BOYD (Count Karl von Arnim)

JETTA GOUDAL (Countess Diane des Granges)

ALBERT CONTI (Baron Finot)

GEORGE FAWCETT (Baron Hausemann)

HENRY ARMETTA (Papa Pierre)

FRANKLIN PANGBORN (M'sieu Dubrey, the dancing master)

WILLIAM BAKEWELL (a pianist)

THE STORY

Karl von Arnim, an attaché of the Prussian legation at Paris, discovers that his fiancée, Countess Diane des Granges, is unfaithful to him. Breaking with her angrily, he infuriates her by declaring that he would rather marry a woman of the streets.

The revengeful Diane makes up her mind that he shall do just that. Enlisting the reluctant offices of Napoleon III's chamberlain, Baron Finot, she arranges to enlist the services of Nanon del Rayon, a Spanish girl who sings and dances at The Smoking Dog cabaret. Having been groomed in all the social graces and fashionably attired, Nanon is introduced into court society as a convent-bred singer, La Piave. Here she meets Karl, who falls in love with her and finally asks her to be his wife.

By this time, however, the girl is sincerely in love with him and therefore unwilling to marry him under false pretenses. Rather than give up her cherished revenge,

Diane hypocritically pledges friendship to Nanon and promises never to tell Karl about The Smoking Dog, only stipulating that she must be allowed to give the couple their wedding banquet. This condition having been accepted, Diane betrays Nanon and revenges herself upon Karl by employing the orchestra of The Smoking Dog to furnish the entertainment at the banquet, and Nanon's background is unveiled. "You wanted to marry a woman of the streets," Diane tells Karl. "Well, you have." Diane is disgraced when Nanon tells the assembled guests of Diane's treachery, but Nanon considers Karl lost and runs despairingly from the room.

She returns to The Smoking Dog and the kindly Papa Pierre, who conducts the orchestra there, and resumes her old life as a singer. But Karl, who has now had time to understand the true situation and his own feelings as well, seeks her out and claims her as his wife.

Jetta Goudal as Countess Diane de Granges

Nanon (Lupe Velez) at the Smoking Dog café

Nanon with Baron Pinot (Albert Conti)

Count Karl (William Boyd) breaks with Diane

Karl weds Nanon.

Griffith directing the banquet scene. Henry Armetta as the
conductor of the orchestra, Papa Pierre

CRITICISM

Griffith's last silent film, *Lady of the Pavements*, was a stylish and sophisticated production, with little in it to suggest either his personality or his methods. Though the scene is Paris in 1868, the atmosphere is more suggestive of the Balkans of such writers as Anthony Hope and George Barr McCutcheon. There is nothing of much cinematic interest except for the image of the Smoking Dog, which identifies and typifies the café where Nanon sings (its recurrent appearances are used to stress the contrast between present and past circumstances) and the brilliantly photographic scene toward the end in which the brokenhearted girl, trying to sing again after the disaster at the wedding feast, sees the features of her (as she now supposes) lost lover in all the men who are listening to her.

Neither Lupe Velez nor Jetta Goudal is exactly a Griffith kind of heroine, nor is William Boyd (not yet Hopalong Cassidy) quite a Griffith hero. Indeed the only player who suggests anything that had appeared in earlier Griffith films is George Fawcett, who performs valiantly in what he has to do, which is not enough notably to affect one's final impression. If one asks, then, why Griffith chose this story, the answer is simply that he did not. *Lady of the Pavements* was assigned to him by Joseph M. Schenck; it had previously been intended for Sam Taylor, who had even prepared a shooting script.

There is of course nothing wrong in an artist trying something new, but when that something has been arbitrarily assigned to him and is without roots in his own tastes, convictions, and life experience, the results are not likely to be impressive. Jetta Goudal is not called upon to do much but wear beautiful clothes, designed by herself, and appear as hateful as possible, and though Lupe Velez is not without her moments of pathos, she seems curiously passive and subdued in Griffith's hands. Except that he does not remotely suggest a European army officer, young William Boyd is pleasing enough, in a conventional sort of way. Quite the best performance is that of Henry Armetta as the hyperactive, kindly orchestra leader at the café, which, in view of this actor's work elsewhere, can hardly have owed much to Griffith's direction. Armetta does, however, achieve an almost stylized, ballet-type of movement; if Lupe Velez had been able to do something like this in the scenes in which she is being groomed for her appearances in society, her performance would have been more interesting than it is.

The most unpardonable thing about *Lady of the Pavements*, however, is the way in which it leaves the audience uncertain about the character of the heroine and consequently of the attitude they are supposed to take up toward her. If "lady of the pavements" means anything, it certainly indicates a prostitute. Clearly this is what the Countess believes Nanon to be (otherwise there could be no point to her plot), and through most of the film the audience does also. Yet toward the end we are blithely informed that the head and front of the girl's offending was merely her appearing at a disreputable café (and we see nothing very shocking even there); actually she had been a good girl all along. Was this a last-minute inspiration prompted by censorship considerations or merely an attempt to make Nanon more "sympathetic"? Perhaps the producers should have remembered *Thaïs*, *Camille*, Edward Sheldon's *Romance*, and a hundred other works in which a "bad" girl becomes "sympathetic" precisely because she has been redeemed by a true, unselfish love. Either way, however, the confusion does not help *Lady of the Pavements*.

E. W.

33

ABRAHAM LINCOLN

STORY AND PRODUCTION ADVISER: John W. Considine, Jr.

CONTINUITY AND DIALOGUE: Stephen Vincent Benét and Gerrit J. Lloyd

PHOTOGRAPHY: Karl Struss

ART DIRECTOR: William Cameron Menzies

SETS EXECUTED BY: Park French

FILM EDITORS: James Smith and Hal C. Kern

ASSOCIATE DIALOGUE DIRECTOR: Harry Stubbs

MUSIC ARRANGER: Hugo Riesenfeld

SOUND RECORDED BY: Harold Witt

COSTUMES: Walter Israel

PRODUCTION MANAGER: Orville O. Dull

PRODUCTION STAFF: Raymond A. Klune and Herbert Sutch

LENGTH: 8,704 feet

PRODUCTION: Feature Productions

DISTRIBUTION: United Artists

NEW YORK PREMIÈRE: October 25, 1930

RELEASED: November 8, 1930

WALTER HUSTON (Abraham Lincoln)

UNA MERKEL (Ann Rutledge)

KAY HAMMOND (Mary Todd Lincoln)

E. ALYN WARREN (Stephen A. Douglas)

HOBART BOSWORTH (General Lee)

FRED WARREN (General Grant)

HENRY B. WALTHALL (Colonel Marshall)

FRANK CAMPEAU (General Sheridan)

FRANCIS FORD (Sheridan's aide)

LUCILLE LA VERNE (midwife)

W. L. THORNE (Tom Lincoln)

HELEN FREEMAN (Nancy Hanks Lincoln)

IAN KEITH (John Wilkes Booth)

OSCAR APFEL (Secretary of War Stanton)

OTTO HOFFMAN (Offut)

EDGAR DEERING (Armstrong)

RUSSELL SIMPSON (Lincoln's employer)

CHARLES CROCKETT (sheriff)

HELEN WARE (Mrs. Edwards)

JASON ROBARDS (William Herndon)

GORDON THORPE (Tad Lincoln)

CAMERON PRUDHOMME (John Hay)

JAMES BRADBURY, SR. (General Winfield Scott)

JAMES EAGLE (young soldier)

HANK BELL, CARL STOCKDALE, RALPH LEWIS, GEORGE MAC QUARRIE, ROBERT BROWER

THE STORY

Abraham Lincoln, a biographical film, has no organized plot. It begins with Lincoln's birth during a storm, which is imaginatively presented with sound effects. We see him clerking at New Salem, Illinois, and later functioning as a young lawyer, with William Herndon as his partner. A marked individualist with standards of his own, he still shows himself easily capable of holding his own against his contemporaries on the midwestern frontier. A highly emotional sequence is devoted to what historians now regard as the legendary love affair with Ann Rutledge, whose death brings Lincoln bitter grief.

He meets Mary Todd at a ball given by Governor Ninian Edwards. The bridegroom fails to appear on the first occasion chosen for their wedding, but later Lincoln and Mary are reconciled and married. Lincoln's debates with Stephen A. Douglas win him a national reputation, and in 1860, with civil war threatening, the Republicans choose him as their presidential candidate.

The only military episode presented directly is Sheridan's ride, which turns the tide of a battle. For the most part we are in the White House with Lincoln: placing Grant in charge of the Union forces; conferring with Stanton, General Winfield Scott, and others; signing the Emancipation Proclamation; resisting those who, in Lincoln's view, are willing to sacrifice the Union to an early peace; etc. The almost stock episode of Lincoln's saving the life of a Union soldier who had fled from his regiment during a battle is included.

The film ends with Lincoln's assassination at Ford's Theater, after having delivered an address from his box, drawn largely from the Second Inaugural. After Booth has fired his shot, "a woman screams out: 'Mr. Lincoln has been shot.' The uproar in the theater gives way to the tremendous sobbing of an unseen multitude. Then a grave voice calls out: 'Now he belongs to the ages.' "

Young Lincoln (Walter Huston)

Lincoln and Herndon (Jason Robards)

Lincoln with Ann Rutledge (Una Merkel)

244

Lincoln at the grave of Ann Rutledge

Lincoln with Mary Todd (Kay Hammond)
and Stephen A. Douglas (E. Alyn Warren)

![The Lincoln-Douglas debates](top image)

The Lincoln-Douglas debates

President Lincoln

Lincoln with General Grant (Fred Warren)

Lincoln with General Winfield Scott (James Broadbury, Sr.)

247

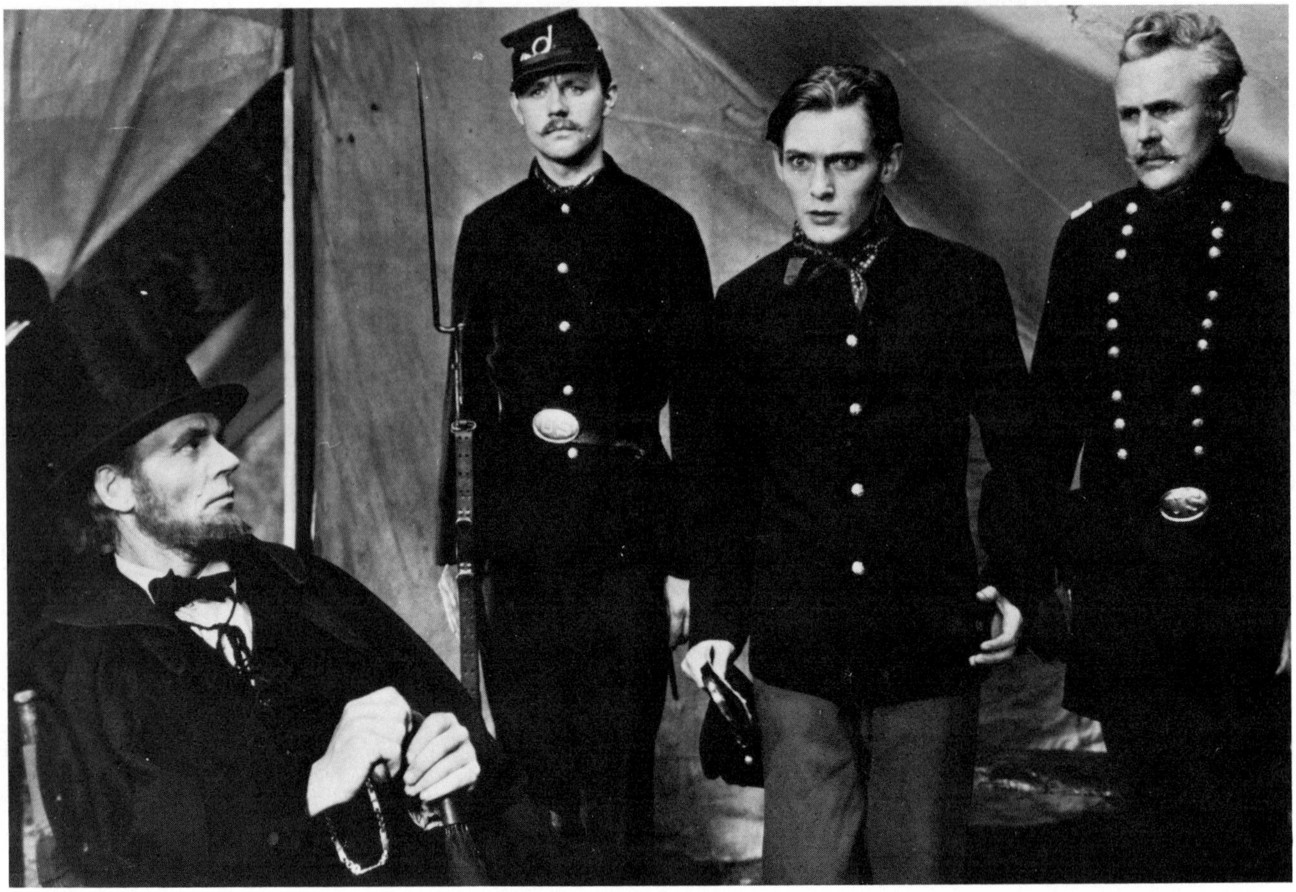

Lincoln pardons the young soldier (James Eagle)

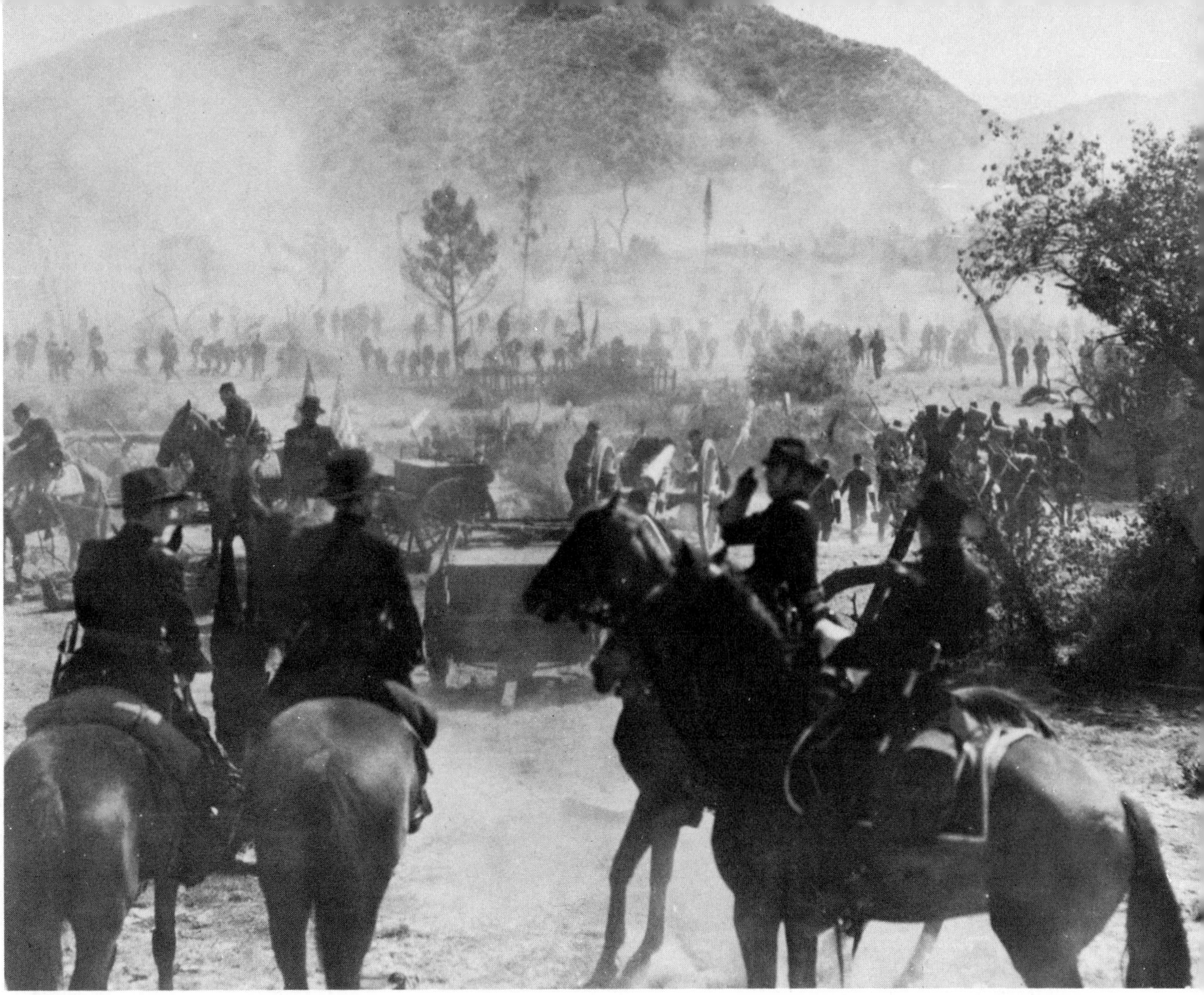

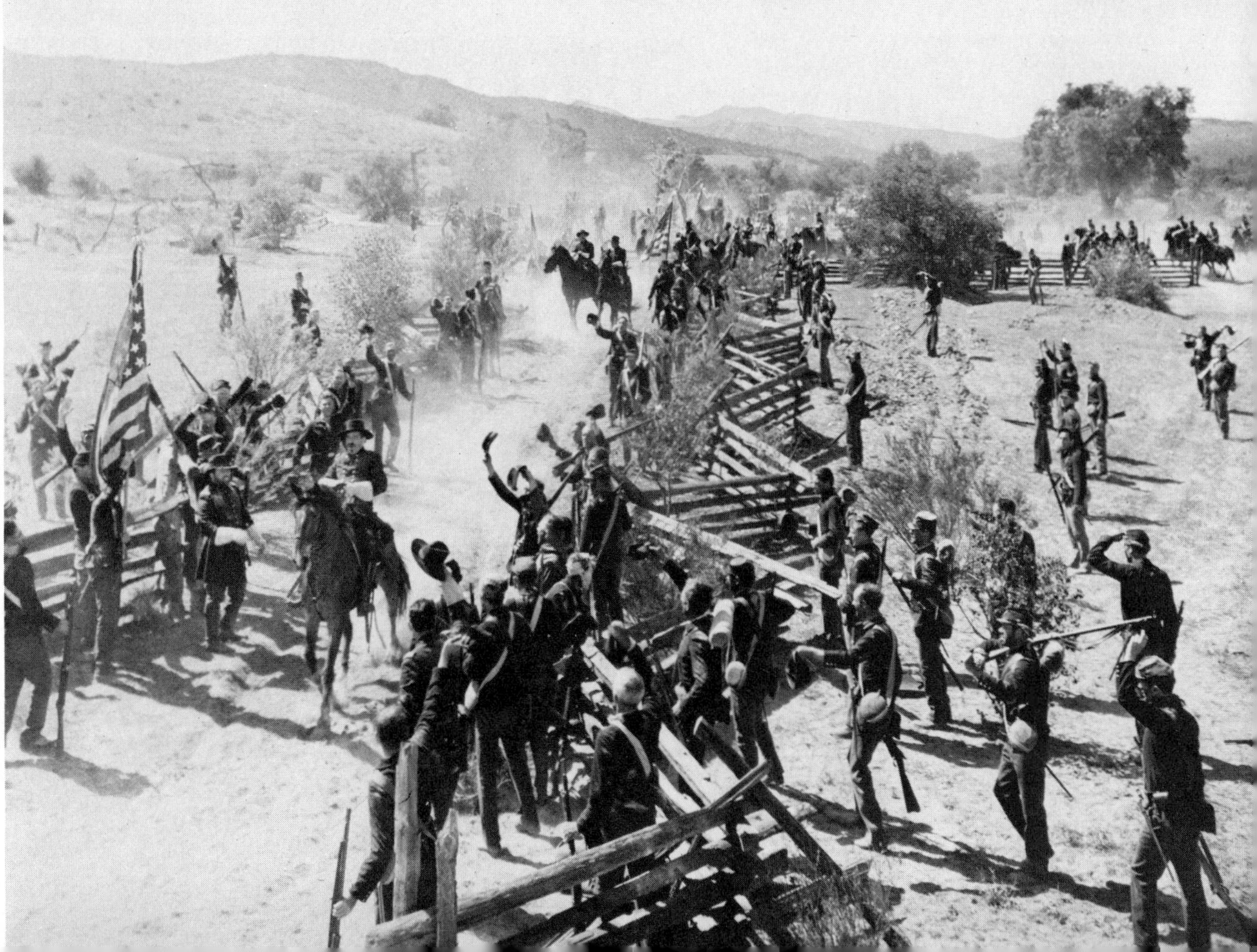

Henry B. Walthall as Colonel Marshall

Hobart Bosworth as General Robert E. Lee

Booth (Ian Keith) shoots Lincoln.

CRITICISM

For his fourth film for producer Joseph Schenck, Griffith considered a biography of John Brown, based on Stephen Vincent Benét's *John Brown's Body*. Schenck turned down the idea, apparently because he had never heard of either Benét or John Brown. The director then suggested a film on the life of Abraham Lincoln, which met with Schenck's approval.

Griffith began happily researching his subject. He read Carl Sandburg's two-volume history, and then telephoned the author to suggest a collaboration. On October 30, 1928, Sandburg telegraphed Griffith that he would be willing to come to Hollywood and work on the film for a fee of $30,000. The historian's fee was a little more than Schenck was willing to pay, and so, instead, Griffith turned to Stephen Vincent Benét, who was signed to write the script. Benét and Griffith worked well together; the writer wrote his wife, "I like Griffith. He's a human being."

However, much of Benét's original script, written in collaboration with Griffith, was discarded. There was constant interference in the production by Schenck, whom Benét called "Old Black Joe," and, eventually, after Griffith had completed shooting, the production was edited by John Considine, Jr., a Schenck-appointed supervisor, without the director's cooperation. Griffith did not see the final cut until after the film had been previewed, and then it was too late to make changes.

Viewing *Abraham Lincoln* today, it would be gratifying to place most of the blame for the film's failings upon Considine. Certainly, it is difficult to understand why contemporary critics were so impressed by this dull, episodic, overlong production.

Not that *Abraham Lincoln* does not have its share of great scenes. There is one true Griffith moment during the courtship of Lincoln and Ann Rutledge, when the director slowly pans the camera to and from the couple, seated under a tree, against a pastoral background, complete with cow and cowgirl. It is a scene reminiscent of the best of *True Heart Susie* and *A Romance of Happy Valley*. Yet this sequence is spoiled by inferior dialogue, in which Lincoln compares his longing for Ann Rutledge's love to a child's craving for gingerbread. This would have been acceptable had not the response been, "Yes, Abe. You've got your gingerbread." Nor does Una Merkel help; her portrayal of Ann Rutledge must qualify as the worst example of miscasting in the history of the cinema.

One of the most exciting uses of sound and movement in the film, and one which may be compared favorably to a scene from any other sound production of this era, is the sequence in which General Sheridan rallies his soldiers. This episode is possibly even more impressive because it follows an unbelievably slow dialogue sequence between Lincoln and Secretary of War Stanton (a jolly-looking

fellow, as portrayed by veteran Edison director-actor Oscar Apfel).

A particularly moving scene in the production occurs between Hobart Bosworth and Henry B. Walthall as General Lee and Colonel Marshall. Lee countermands an order of Marshall's, sentencing a Northern spy to death, reminding him that the defeat of the South is imminent, and that there is no reason for more killings. Lee returns to his tent, and sinks, sadly and wearily to his knees in prayer. Griffith could not have asked for, nor expected, better performances from two such noble actors as Bosworth and Walthall. It really is extraordinary the presence so many old-timers bring to *Abraham Lincoln*. Another Griffith stalwart, Lucille La Verne, appears only in one scene, that of Lincoln's birth, and yet her image remains with one throughout the film, and hers is one of the few performances that are rememberd long after the film is over.

Of course, chief acting honors must go to Walter Huston in the title role. As Charles F. Hynes wrote in *Motion Picture News* (August 23, 1930): "He gives the role all the Lincoln resolution, all of the humor of the part. He is a human Lincoln, who will appeal to all classes." Huston is tenderly moving as in his reaction to the news of Ann Rutledge's imminent death and amusing as in many of his scenes with Kay Hammond as Mrs. Lincoln. (Griffith appears to use Mrs. Lincoln as a substitute for the Negro comic relief of many of his other productions.)

Huston should have been given the opportunity to read more of Lincoln's great speeches, such as the Gettysburg Address. It is almost as if Griffith chose to ignore some of the traditional aspects of a Lincoln biography, or, at least, to gloss over them. Lincoln's debate with Stephen A. Douglas is hardly a debate at all. Instead of an exciting cross-fire of dialogue, the two participants deliver one line of dialogue each, while slow editing makes the whole sequence totally dull.

The assassination has none of the sparkle or emotion of the same scene in *The Birth of a Nation*. Indeed, it cannot even compare favorably to John Ford's reconstruction of the incident for his 1936 production, *The Prisoner of Shark Island*. Interestingly, as critic John Dorr has pointed out before me, Ford ends his *Young Mr. Lincoln* (1939) in a similar fashion to Griffith's production, with a shot of the Lincoln Memorial, accompanied by "The Battle Hymn of the Republic."

It is more than unfortunate that most critics and historians, in the past, have praised *Abraham Lincoln* as Griffith's last great film, and ignored *The Struggle*, for it is the latter production that today must be reckoned the true Griffith masterpiece. *Abraham Lincoln* was best forgotten.

A. S.

34

THE STRUGGLE

SCENARIO AND DIALOGUE: Anita Loos, John Emerson, and D. W. Griffith, based on an original screenplay by Loos and Emerson

PHOTOGRAPHY: Joseph Ruttenberg

EDITOR: Barney Rogan

MUSIC COMPOSED AND ARRANGED BY: Philip A. Schieb and D. W. Griffith

UNIT MANAGER: Raymond Klune

FIRST ASSISTANT DIRECTOR: Richard Bladen

SECOND ASSISTANT DIRECTOR: Jack Aichele

LENGTH: 9 reels (1 hour and 27 minutes)

PRODUCTION: D. W. Griffith, Inc.

DISTRIBUTION: United Artists

NEW YORK PREMIÈRE: Rivoli Theatre, December 10, 1931. No general release

HAL SKELLY (*Jimmie Wilson*)

ZITA JOHANN (*Florrie, his wife*)

CHARLOTTE WYNTERS (*Nina, a cabaret girl*)

EVELYN BALDWIN (*Nan Wilson*)

JACKSON HALLIDAY (*Johnnie Marshall*)

EDNA HAGAN (*Mary, Jimmie's daughter*)

CLAUDE COOPER (*Sam, Jimmie's friend*)

ARTHUR LIPSON (*Cohen, the insurance collector*)

HELEN MACK (*a catty girl*)

CHARLES RICHMAN (*Mr. Craig, Johnnie's employer*)

SCOTT MOORE (*Al, a gigolo*)

DAVE MANLEY (*Tony, a millworker*)

KATE BRUCE (*a grandmother*)

Griffith's idealized version of a pre-Prohibition beer garden

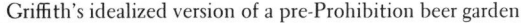

Florrie and Mary (Edna Hagan)

255

Jimmie breaks up the party.

STORY AND CRITICISM

In the spring of 1931 Griffith came to Lillian Gish's apartment and "with his usual secretiveness spoke guardedly of a film that he was planning," a film that turned out to be *The Struggle*. Griffith had long held a grudge against reformers, and prohibitionists in particular. In *Intolerance* he had accurately predicted the consequences of making alcohol illegal by showing home stills and police interference with the private affairs of citizens. His antiprohibition stance had not helped *Intolerance*, and some newspapers accused him of being a tool of the liquor interests. In 1926 he was still annoyed enough to send a number of letters to various civic and church leaders concerning the Prohibition laws. He claimed that the law was "making a criminal of their God, their God being Jesus Christ." The first of Christ's miracles was the turning of water into wine (which Griffith had shown in *Intolerance*) and throughout the Bible wine was seen "as a blessing not as a curse." Conditions are such, he said, that "if Christ came to the United States today . . . we

would call Him a bootlegger and put Him in jail." Indignantly, he added that America is the "only nation so egotistical and so brazen that they pretend to be better than their God."

These thoughts stayed in Griffith's mind throughout the twenties, and up to the time of The Struggle he collected various clippings and articles about Prohibition. Originally he had thought about intercutting a number of stories, as in *Intolerance*, to show the evils of Prohibition. By the time the script was completed, however, there was only one story, that of an alcoholic. Ignoring the fact that audiences in the midst of the Depression wanted laughter, romance, and excitement, Griffith almost perversely chose a tale already hackneyed, something uncomfortably close to *Drink*, a drama by Charles Reade that had been based on Zola's *L'Assommoir*. Griffith saw *The Struggle* as an argument for tolerance and sanity in terms of alcohol; but unfortunately, to most of the public the film seemed more like an argument against drink than against Prohibition. Some of its arguments and narrative logic were ruined when the film was hurriedly recut after its première in an attempt to make the film more palatable. Griffith was unhappy with the reedited version because it had lost much of its emotional power, but the film was out of his hands.

The Struggle begins on an idyllic day in 1911, and shows couples strolling in the park in a typical Griffith bucolic scene. People sit in an outdoor beer garden and talk about "the Biograph Girl." The conversation then shifts to alcohol, and it is agreed that although beer and wine are all right, hard stuff is not.

The time changes to 1923, as the pleasant music of 1911 is supplanted by raucous jazz. Beauty has gone, Griffith implies, the gentility of a Sunday afternoon vanished, the harmonious strains of music silenced, and the time now sadly out of joint. The countryside and even the concept of drinking at an outdoor table have disappeared, replaced by the urban environment and the dim-lit speakeasy.

Griffith then proceeds to create the working-class milieu of New York City, its cluttered streets, shabby stores, and poverty-stricken faces. It is the same kind of city world that Griffith had depicted in such Biograph films as *The Musketeers of Pig Alley* and later in *The Mother and the Law*. To Griffith's realistic eye, the city was not Fifth Avenue or Madison Avenue, but a sordid cross street with a grocery store, a pawnshop, and a saloon. Griffith did not forget how he had lived in a walk-up apartment when he was a struggling actor in New York.

Besides the accurate settings, he also included some of the city's ethnic types. There are an old Irish lady (brogue and all), a Jewish insurance salesman anxious to collect a few pennies on a policy and worrying about savings, an Italian with a pregnant wife ("Santa Maria, what am I-a gonna tell-a my wife?"), and a Negro maid hired for an occasion ("Can't you say anything but 'Y's'um?' 'Y's'um.' ").

The central character in *The Struggle*, Jimmie, is first seen swigging from a pocket flask and making a fool of himself. When his fiancée-to-be (Zita Johann) tells him she doesn't like to see him like this because she loves him, he is surprised and pleased at her affection, and promises that he will never touch the stuff again.

Jimmie marries the girl and for a while their life goes well. On the night of his daughter's birth, Jimmie goes into their bedroom to see the new mother and smiles down on her face, vowing that she never looked more beautiful. One day, as a surprise, he brings back a table lamp that she wanted. This lamp will appear in many scenes, a subtle reminder of how much their relationship deteriorates.

One day Jimmie's child (this episode is unfortunately now missing from extant prints of *The Struggle*) gets sick, and while her life hangs in the balance, his friends ask him to go for a drink, call him a "pansy" when he demurs, and finally inveigle him into the saloon. The child recovers. Later, when an Italian loses his job, Jimmie goes to a bar to console him. The wife gets nervous and calls the watchman and only later does Jimmie show up, drunk.

Jimmie's complete return to alcoholism starts because of his sister's engagement party. The cause seems minor enough, but so indeed are many of the things that shape our lives. Jimmie's wife wants him to wear a lavender tie she has bought. Disliking it (in the original version of the film he says that it is "effeminate"), Jimmie sneaks out to get fortified. The wife goes back into the bedroom, sees that he is missing, then returns to her guests, and rather desperately says, "Let's have some music." The radio is turned on and organ music starts to peal forth until someone complains that it sounds like a church. Soon after, Jimmie returns and starts to be obnoxious. In particular he annoys Johnnie's boss, Mr. Craig. Johnnie had been an orphan and Mr. Craig had treated him well (Griffith's obsession with orphans never left him). When Jimmie is rude to him, the party is ruined. The sister reluctantly breaks off the engagement because she feels that, with her brother as he is, she can only hurt Johnnie's chances with Mr. Craig. Furthermore, she feels she is needed to support the family, for Jimmie finally loses his job at the factory.

The one piece of security the family still has is an insurance policy. Griffith makes some effective crosscuts as he contrasts the wife and the sister talking about cashing in the policy and Jimmie as he discusses the same subject with a B-girl from a dance hall. Telling him she has a friend who makes a fortune importing liquor from Canada, she convinces Jimmie to cash in the policy, but of course he is bilked out of the money.

After the wife has been evicted from her apartment, Jimmie, in a scene, melodramatic as it may be, but with all the primal emotion at Griffith's command, wanders sadly to the now empty apartment and laments his loneliness as he leans drunkenly against the wall. Across the airshaft some children (who in the original script were also drinking beer) turn on a radio and out comes the sound of a woman's unctuously reassuring voice:

And again, dear radio audience, remember, if you only look for it, the world is—

The dial is switched and an authoritative, preacherlike voice intones:

I am the Way and the Truth and the Light. No one cometh unto the Father but by me.

Then comes the sound of "Abide with Me" played on an organ. This is Griffith's only attempt to make some contrapuntal use of sound in the film.

Repentant, Jimmie tries to get a job, but collapses. He no longer has the strength, and ends up staggering around the streets and asking for money. Some neighborhood children see him and tauntingly tell his daughter that her father is a "beggin' bum." The girl runs down the street after her missing father and follows him up some rickety stairs to an abandoned room. Then she hurries back to her house to get her mother, but she isn't there. The girl leaves a note giving the address and runs back to her father. But Jimmie, now almost entirely disintegrated— his face a study of ruination—goes into delirium tremens, and abuses the girl. The mother, who meantime has come back home, finds the note and runs down the street. A thunderstorm begins as the father begins to beat the girl. (The storm and the sound of thunder are cut from existing prints; only occasional lightning flashes remain.) Finally the mother arrives, the door is broken in, and the girl saved. Griffith obviously reverted to the chase and to an attack on a young vulnerable girl as his one sure-fire method of arousing an audience. But times had changed, and what was once dramatic now appeared hackneyed and even comical.

The wife nurses Jimmie, and, in a scene now cut, a doctor tells her that of the eight cases he had that week, six died. If Jimmie's foot doesn't stop jiggling, he is through. In the scene that remains, Johnnie tells the wife, who has been up for three days and nights with Jimmie, to get some sleep. She answers with Christ's remark, "Couldst thou not watch one hour with me?" (Matthew 26:40). Finally he awakens, but thinks he has killed his daughter. In the last scene, they are in a better apartment and Jimmie comes back from his job to tell them that the factory has closed. When the wife laments this, he adds that they are closing in order to install the new invention he designed, and so all ends happily.

When *The Struggle* opened at New York's Rivoli Theatre on December 10, 1931, Griffith anxiously watched the audience. He hoped for the spontaneous applause that often punctuated his previous films. Instead, he heard snickering. People were laughing at some of the serious scenes. Some patrons walked out. The audience had wanted excitement and fun, not a slow-moving drama of someone sinking into degradation. They wanted beautiful photography, full of pearly highlights, not dull and flat shots. One critic called *The Struggle* the worst photographed film of the year. But what appeared ineptness then, in these days of documentary effects seems realistic.

Of course the opening night's production cannot be seen, since only the trimmed version exists, but, even so, the remaining one is by no means a terrible film. In fact, it holds up better than *Abraham Lincoln*, has a point of view and, despite its weaknesses, better dramatic construction. The film was honest and sincere, and, except for the almost obligatory happy ending, was very un-Hollywoodish; it had no false glamour, no "beautiful" people, and no consciously artistic lighting and photography. It observed instead the decline of a human being and the effects on his family, but this kind of subject matter is dangerously close to what people like to term "soap opera." The point is that soap opera, with all its clichés, twists of fate, coincidences, and dramatic moments and confrontations, is actually closer to what life really is than many a more sophisticated form. Certainly *The Struggle*, to those people who are familiar with the director's silent films and are not carried away by fashion, is one of the best of Griffith's later pictures. Although many films of 1931 now seem far more absurd and dated than *The Struggle* and are indeed laughable at moments not supposed to be humorous, this fact was of no consolation to Griffith whose creative life hung on its success.

Arthur Lennig

35
OTHER GRIFFITH PROJECTS

Besides the features covered in this volume, Griffith became involved in a considerable number of other film projects. Some of these never left the planning stage; some were turned over to others; some Griffith completed on behalf of others. There are also three shorts, dating from the teens, which are both lost and forgotten.

In the autumn of 1916, the director took himself and his "personal artistic staff" to Albany for several days, to produce a one-reel short titled *A Day with Governor Whitman*. The New York State governor, the previous spring, had vetoed a severe film censorship bill, and Griffith, to show his appreciation, and that of his fellow producers, directed the short as a testimonial to Whitman, and, incidentally, to help the governor's campaign for reelection. According to *Motography* (November 4, 1916): "Many of the big motion picture producing and distributing companies have united to take care of the making of one hundred prints and their distribution throughout the State."

On August 31, 1971, *Variety* reported that Griffith had shot a propaganda film for the United States government to aid the Czarist Russian recruiting program: "Guy Croswell Smith, general manager for *Intolerance*, has gone to Petrograd in the interests of the recently completed David Wark Griffith recruiting film, the picture being taken in the United States with the different Russian characters enacted here, and it is expected to stimulate Russian army recruiting." No information as to even the title of this film appears to exist, and Miss Gish doubts that it was ever made.

In memory of his mother, the director agreed, in June of 1919, to produce a short film record of the Centenary Celebration of the Methodist Minute Men at Columbus, Ohio. The finished film, titled *The World at Columbus*, was used as part of a drive to raise $120 million for the extension of Methodist work throughout the world.

According to Blanche Sweet, one of the earliest of Griffith's unrealized film projects was a contemplated adaptation of Flaubert's *Salammbô*, which the director wished to shoot after completing *Judith of Bethulia*. Recalls Miss Sweet: "I got the book, and read and read and read. It was Hannibal crossing the Alps with his elephants; I was going to be one of the elephants. It would have been the size of *Intolerance*—a tremendous produc-

tion. Goodness knows where he'd ever have got the money for it. It never got beyond the talking stage."

It would appear that for a while the director had the notion that one big spectacle had to follow another. Miriam Cooper, in her autobiography, writes that, after completing *Intolerance*, Griffith planned to make a film suggested by *The Rubáiyát of Omar Khayyám*. This project has not been authenticated, but there is considerable evidence that Griffith did consider making a film on *The Quest of the Holy Grail*, sometime during the shooting of *Intolerance*, and possibly even before.

While attending the Boston première of *The Birth of a Nation*, he spent some time at the Boston Public Library, studying the paintings of Edwin Austin Abbey, which deal with the Holy Grail. The director told *The Moving Picture World* (May 1, 1915):

For the past two years, I have been desirous of producing *The Quest of the Holy Grail* for the screen. I have been studying those wonderful paintings in the Boston Public Library on the subject. The rights of reproduction are controlled by Mrs. Edwin Austin Abbey, the artist's widow. I have written to Charles Scribner, the New York publisher, who is Mrs. Abbey's brother-in-law, and who manages her affairs opening negotiations for the motion production [sic].

Nothing ever came of this idea, despite a news item in *Variety* of May 28, 1915, stating that Griffith was "to make a big production out of the Holy Grail."

In 1920 the director secured an option to film Joseph Hergesheimer's novel *Java Head*, published the previous year. The book was eventually brought to the screen by Paramount, in 1923, with George Melford directing, and Leatrice Joy and Jacqueline Logan starring.

According to Lillian Gish, Griffith planned to produce *Faust*, after the completion of *Dream Street*, with Miss Gish as Marguerite, but she dissuaded him, fearing it would be a financial disaster.

Among Griffith's unrealized films were a number dealing with the West. In the late twenties, he considered the fall of the Alamo; a history of Texas, titled *Into the West*; a screenplay by Harry Carr on *The Pioneer Women*; and a parody on Westerns, *The Medicine Man*, to star W. C. Fields. (A film with this last title was, in fact, produced by Tiffany in 1930, featuring Jack Benny and Betty Bronson.)

Other ideas that Griffith considered during the mid-twenties included a life of Florence Nightingale; a screen

259

D. W. Griffith in later years

version of Sardou's *Cleopatra*, to star Norma Talmadge; and a film adaptation of Dreiser's *An American Tragedy*, which was eventually to be screened by Josef von Sternberg in 1931. There was even talk, in 1927, of Griffith's directing a film to be titled *War*, and scripted by H. G. Wells.

Aside from the films for which he received directorial credit, Griffith assisted on a number of other productions. In 1916, under the pseudonym of Granville Warwick, Griffith wrote the screenplay for *Hoodoo Ann*, which marked Mae Marsh's debut as a star for the Triangle Company. This delightful tale of an orphan girl who believes herself doomed to a life of bad luck was credited to contract director Lloyd Ingraham, but as *The Moving Picture World* (March 25, 1916) noted: "Active as he is in the supervision of Fine Arts pictures for the Triangle program, David W. Griffith has surprised his associates on the Coast by the active direction he has given to the forthcoming Mae Marsh release, *Hoodoo Ann*."

Just how much direction Griffith actually contributed to the film is open to speculation. Despite the above report in *The Moving Picture World* and the general feeling that a viewer of *Hoodoo Ann* has that he is watching a Griffith production, there is doubt as to whether Griffith contributed anything to this and the other Triangle releases. While in Chicago on October 1, 1916, the director told Louella Parsons, then with the Chicago *Herald:* "I haven't seen a Triangle picture in four months. I have never produced a Fine Arts production, and the words 'supervised by David W. Griffith' were put on the screen without my knowledge. My time has been spent making *Intolerance* which has occupied all my working hours." Miss Gish, however, says that Griffith carefully supervised all Fine Arts Triangle pictures.

Two features that Griffith was involved in during the twenties both had as their subject matter blackface comedy. The first, *His Darker Self*, released on March 16, 1924, has an interesting history.

It was based on an original story, "Mammy's Boy," by Arthur Caesar, and was to have starred Al Jolson under Griffith's direction. For reasons unknown, Jolson suddenly walked out on his contract with Griffith, and departed for Europe. There was some talk of replacing him with Eddie Cantor, but, eventually, Griffith decided to hire Lloyd Hamilton, who was starring in Educational Comedies, and to hand over the direction to John W. Noble.

His Darker Self was finally released as a five-reel feature, distributed by W. W. Hodkinson, and presented by Griffith's brother, Albert L. Grey. Besides Hamilton, it featured three Griffith players—Tom Wilson, Kate Bruce, and Lucille La Verne (in another blackface role after her success in *The White Rose*). The film, which appears

only to have survived in a two-reel version, had Hamilton as a writer of detective stories don blackface to enter the Black Cat Café, "for culled folks 'sclusively," and capture a gang of Negro bootleggers. As *The Moving Picture World* (April 5, 1924) noted: "It is all good fun, plus good melodrama with fights and thrills, and while as a whole it cannot be taken seriously it will provide smiles and laughs for the most hardened."

When Griffith returned to Hollywood in 1927 to work for Joseph Schenck, he did not begin directing *Drums of Love* immediately, but instead was asked by Schenck to do some work on the Duncan Sisters' vehicle, *Topsy and Eva*, showing them as the characters with which they were triumphantly successful over many years in musical comedy and vaudeville. The film had been going through some difficulties. Its first director, Lois Weber, had left the production, protesting what she considered its racist overtones, and had been replaced by Del Lord. Then, as Griffith's assistant, Raymond Klune, explained in a letter, dated June 17, 1927, to Albert Banzhaf:

Del Lord who directed *Topsy and Eva* with the Duncan Sisters made a mess of it evidently, because Schenck in disgust turned it over to Mr. G. shortly after his arrival here and asked him to do something with it. He shot quite a few additional scenes and recut the greater part of it, and from the comments I have heard he improved it a rare degree. As a matter of fact J. S. made the remark that the picture is now worth $300,000 more. (It must have been worth about 40 cents before.) I saw the opening of it last night at the Egyptian and thought it quite good, however, not exceptional. Of course I did not see it before Mr. G. took it in hand therefore I cannot vouch for the improvement.... He did not supervise *Topsy and Eva*—he remade it.

Griffith embarked on one final, abortive project toward the end of his life. In the summer of 1939 he came to the Hal Roach Studios to direct *One Million B.C.* for release through the company that he had helped found, United Artists. He never made the film; it was eventually released with Hal Roach taking the directorial credit, and with Victor Mature and Carole Landis as its stars.

Mae Marsh recalled:

I had gone to see him because he wanted me to play the mother in *One Million B.C.* He said, "They refused that. They refused to have other people I wanted in it. They're not taking any advice of mine. First I was asked to direct it; then I was asked to advise. They're not letting me do either, and I think I will not be able to stand it." He quit. We had lunch, and he said he was very sad. That was the last time he was in any studio that I know of.

D. W. Griffith died in Hollywood on July 23, 1948, at the age of 73. I somehow suspect that he vainly considered many projects in those final, lonely years. Such projects with those that we know of undoubtedly far outnumber the great man's completed works. Many as his films are, the greatest tragedy is that he was allowed to direct so little.

A. S.

D. W. Griffith receives an honorary award from the Academy of Motion Picture Arts and Sciences in 1935. *Left to right:* Frank Capra, Griffith, Jean Hersholt, Henry B. Walthall, Frank Lloyd, Cecil B. DeMille, Donald Crisp.

D. W. Griffith postage stamp, designed by Fred Otnes, and issued by the U. S. Postal Service at Beverly Hills, California, May 27, 1975.

Mae Marsh and Robert Harron in *Hoodoo Ann*

Lloyd Hamilton and Irma Harrison in *His Darker Self*

263

The Duncan Sisters (Rosetta and Vivian) as Topsy and Eva

Rosetta Duncan as Topsy

APPENDIX

A List of Biograph Films Known or Believed to Have Been Directed by D. W. Griffith, with Their Dates of Release

1908

July

14   The Adventures of Dollie
17   The Fight for Freedom
28   The Redman and the Child
31   Deceived Slumming Party

August

4   The Bandit's Waterloo
7   A Calamitous Elopement
11   The Greaser's Gauntlet
18   The Fatal Hour
21   The Love of Gold
25   Balked at the Altar
28   For a Wife's Honor

September

1   Betrayed by a Handprint
4   Monday Morning in a Coney Island Police Court
8   The Girl and the Outlaw
11   Behind the Scenes
15   The Red Girl
18   The Heart of O Yama
22   Where the Breakers Roar
25   A Smoked Husband
29   The Stolen Jewels

October

2   The Devil
6   The Zulu's Heart
9   Father Gets in the Game
15   The Barbarian Ingomar
16   The Vaquero's Vow
20   The Planter's Wife
26   The Heart of a Jewess
27   The Call of the Wild
30   Concealing a Burglar

November

3   After Many Years
6   The Pirate's Gold
10   The Taming of the Shrew
15   The Guerrilla
17   The Song of the Shirt
20   The Ingrate
24   A Woman's Way
27   The Clubman and the Tramp

December

1   The Valet's Wife
4   Money Mad
8   The Feud and the Turkey
11   The Reckoning
15   The Test of Friendship
18   An Awful Moment
22   The Christmas Burglars
24   Mr. Jones at the Ball
29   The Helping Hand

1909

January

1   One Touch of Nature
4   The Maniac Cook
7   Mrs. Jones Entertains
11   The Honor of Thieves *and* Love Finds a Way
14   A Rural Elopement *and* The Sacrifice
18   The Criminal Hypnotist *and* Those Boys!
21   Mr. Jones Has a Card Party *and* The Fascinating Mrs. Francis
25   The Welcome Burglar *and* Those Awful Hats
28   The Cord of Life

February

1   The Girls and Daddy
4   The Brahma Diamond
8   A Wreath in Time *and* Edgar Allen [sic] Poe
11   Tragic Love
15   The Curtain Pole *and* His Ward's Love
18   The Hindoo Dagger *and* The Joneses Have Amateur
     Theatricals
22   Politician's Love Story *and* The Golden Louis
25   At the Altar

March

1   His Wife's Mother *and* The Prussian Spy
4   A Fool's Revenge
8   The Roué's Heart *and* The Wooden Leg
11   The Salvation Army Lass
15   The Lure of the Gown *and* I Did It, Mamma
18   The Voice of the Violin
22   The Deception *and* "And a Little Child Shall Lead
     Them"
25   A Burglar's Mistake
29   The Medicine Bottle *and* Jones and His New
     Neighbors

April

1   A Drunkard's Reformation
5   The Road to the Heart *and* Trying To Get Arrested
8   A Rude Hostess *and* Schneider's Anti-Noise
     Crusade
12   The Winning Coat *and* A Sound Sleeper
15   Confidence
19   Lady Helen's Escapade *and* A Troublesome Satchel
22   The Drive for a Life
26   Lucky Jim *and* Twin Brothers
29   'Tis An Ill Wind That Blows No Good

May

3   The Eavesdropper *and* The Suicide Club
6   The Note in the Shoe *and* One Busy Hour
10   Jones and The Lady Book Agent *and* The French
     Duel
13   A Baby's Shoe
17   The Jilt
20   Resurrection
24   Eloping with Aunty *and* Two Memories
27   The Cricket on the Hearth
31   Eradicating Aunty *and* His Duty

June

3   What Drink Did
7   The Violin Maker of Cremona

10   The Lonely Villa *and* A New Trick
14   The Son's Return
17   Her First Biscuits *and* The Faded Lilies
21   Was Justice Served?
24   The Peachbasket Hat *and* The Mexican Sweet-
     hearts
28   The Way of Man

July

1   The Necklace
5   The Message
8   The Country Doctor
12   The Cardinal's Conspiracy
15   The Friend of the Family *and* Tender Hearts
19   The Renunciation
22   Sweet and Twenty *and* Jealousy and the Man
26   A Convict's Sacrifice
29   The Slave

August

2   A Strange Meeting
5   The Mended Lute
9   They Would Elope *and* Jones's Burglar
12   The Better Way
16   With Her Card
19   His Wife's Visitor *and* Mrs. Jones's Lover; or "I
     Want My Hat"
23   The Indian Runner's Romance
26   The Seventh Day *and* "Oh, Uncle"
30   The Mills of the Gods

September

2   The Sealed Room *and* The Little Darling
6   "1776" or, The Hessian Renegades
9   Comata, the Sioux
13   Getting Even *and* The Children's Friend
16   The Broken Locket
20   In Old Kentucky
23   A Fair Exchange
27   Leather Stocking
30   The Awakening *and* Wanted, A Child

October

4   Pippa Passes
7   Fools of Fate
11   The Little Teacher
14   A Change of Heart
18   His Lost Love
21   The Expiation
25   In the Watches of the Night
28   Lines of White on a Sullen Sea

November

 1 The Gibson Goddess *and* What's Your Hurry?
 4 Nursing a Viper
 8 The Restoration
11 The Light That Came
15 Two Women and a Man
18 A Midnight Adventure *and* Sweet Revenge
22 The Open Gate
25 The Mountaineer's Honor
29 The Trick That Failed *and* In the Window Recess

December

 2 The Death Disc
 6 Through the Breakers
 9 The Redman's View
13 A Corner in Wheat
16 In a Hempen Bag *and* The Test
20 A Trap for Santa Claus
22 In Little Italy
27 To Save Her Soul
30 The Day After *and* Choosing a Husband

1910

January

 3 The Rocky Road
 6 The Dancing Girl of Butte
10 Her Terrible Ordeal
17 On the Reef
20 The Call
24 The Honor of His Family
27 The Last Deal
31 The Cloister's Touch

February

 3 The Woman from Mellon's
10 The Duke's Plan
14 One Night, and Then———
17 The Englishman and the Girl
21 His Last Burglary
24 Taming a Husband
28 The Final Settlement

March

 3 The Newlyweds
 7 The Thread of Destiny
10 In Old California
14 The Converts

17 The Love of Lady Irma
    The Man[1]
21 Faithful
24 The Twisted Trail
28 Gold Is Not All

April

 4 As It Is in Life
 7 A Rich Revenge
11 A Romance of the Western Hills
18 Thou Shalt Not
25 The Way of the World

May

 2 The Gold-Seekers
 5 The Unchanging Sea
 9 Love Among the Roses
16 Over Silent Paths
23 Ramona
30 The Impalement

June

 2 In the Season of Buds
 6 A Child of the Ghetto
 9 A Victim of Jealousy
13 In the Border States
16 The Face at the Window
23 The Marked Time-Table
27 A Child's Impulse
30 Muggsy's First Sweetheart

July

 4 The Purgation
 7 A Midnight Cupid
11 What the Daisy Said
14 A Child's Faith
18 A Flash of Light
21 As the Bells Rang Out *and* Serious Sixteen
25 The Call to Arms
28 Unexpected Help

August

 1 An Arcadian Maid
 4 Her Father's Pride
 8 The House with Closed Shutters
11 A Salutary Lesson

[1] A Bulletin on this film appears at this point in Bowser, *Biograph Bulletins, 1908–1912,* but the release date is cut off. Contemporary trade journal sources do not indicate the release of *The Man* at this point, nor have we been able to locate it elsewhere.

15   The Usurer
22   The Sorrows of the Unfaithful
25   Wilful Peggy
29   The Modern Prodigal

September

 5   A Summer Idyll
 8   Little Angels of Luck
12   A Mohawk's Way
15   In Life's Cycle
22   The Oath and the Man
26   Rose O' Salem-Town
29   Examination Day at School

October

 3   The Iconoclast
 6   A Gold Necklace
10   That Chink at Golden Gulch
17   The Broken Doll
20   The Banker's Daughter
24   The Message of the Violin
31   Two Little Waifs

November

 3   Waiter No. 5
 7   The Fugitive
10   Simple Charity
14   Sunshine Sue
21   The Song of the Wildwood Flute
28   A Plain Song

December

 1   Effecting a Cure
 5   A Child's Stratagem
12   The Golden Supper
15   His Sister-in-Law
19   The Lesson
26   Winning Back His Love

1911

January

 2   The Two Paths
 6   When a Man Loves
 9   The Italian Barber
16   His Trust
19   His Trust Fulfilled
23   Fate's Turning
30   A Wreath of Orange Blossoms

February

 2   Three Sisters
 6   Heart Beats of Long Ago
13   What Shall We Do with Our Old
16   Fisher Folks
20   The Diamond Star
23   His Daughter
27   The Lily of the Tenements

March

 2   The Heart of a Savage
 6   A Decree of Destiny
 9   Conscience
16   Was He a Coward?
20   Teaching Dad to Like Her
23   The Lonedale Operator
30   The Spanish Gypsy

April

 6   The Broken Cross
10   The Chief's Daughter
17   Madame Rex
20   A Knight of the Road
24   His Mother's Scarf
27   How She Triumphed

May

 1   The Two Sides
 8   In the Days of '49
18   The New Dress
22   The Crooked Road
25   The White Rose of the Wilds
29   A Romany Tragedy

June

 5   A Smile of a Child
12   Enoch Arden, Part I
15   Enoch Arden, Part II
22   The Primal Call
26   Her Sacrifice
29   Fighting Blood

July

 6   The Thief and the Girl
10   The Jealous Husband
13   Bobby the Coward
17   The Indian Brothers
24   A Country Cupid
27   The Last Drop of Water

August

  3 Out from the Shadow
  7 The Ruling Passion
 14 The Sorrowful Example
 17 The Blind Princess and the Poet
 24 The Rose of Kentucky
 28 Swords and Hearts

September

  4 The Stuff Heroes Are Made Of
  7 The Old Confectioner's Mistake
 14 The Squaw's Love
 18 Dan, the Dandy
 25 The Revenue Man and the Girl
 28 Her Awakening

October

  5 The Making of a Man
  9 Italian Blood
 16 The Unveiling
 19 The Adventures of Billy
 26 The Long Road
 30 Love in the Hills

November

  6 The Battle
  9 The Trail of Books
 16 Through Darkened Vales
 20 The Miser's Heart
 27 Sunshine Through the Dark
 30 A Woman Scorned

December

  7 The Failure
 11 Saved from Himself
 18 As in a Looking Glass
 21 A Terrible Discovery
 28 The Voice of the Child

1912

January

  1 The Baby and the Stork
  8 A Tale of the Wilderness
 11 The Eternal Mother
 18 The Old Bookkeeper
 22 For His Son
 29 A Blot in the 'Scutcheon

February

  1 The Transformation of Mike
  8 A Sister's Love
 12 Billy's Stratagem
 15 The Mender of Nets
 22 Under Burning Skies
 26 The Sunbeam

March

  4 A Siren of Impulse
  7 A String of Pearls
 14 Iola's Promise
 18 The Root of Evil
 25 The Goddess of Sagebrush Gulch
 28 The Girl and Her Trust

April

  4 The Punishment
  8 Fate's Interception
 15 The Female of the Species
 18 Just Like a Woman
 25 One Is Business; The Other Crime
 29 The Lesser Evil

May

  6 The Old Actor
  9 A Lodging for the Night
 16 His Lesson
 20 When Kings Were the Law
 27 A Beast at Bay
 30 An Outcast Among the Outcasts

June

  6 Home Folks
 10 A Temporary Truce (2 reels)
 17 Lena and the Geese
 20 The Spirit Awakened
 27 The School Teacher and the Waif

July

  1 Man's Lust for Gold
  8 An Indian Summer
 11 Man's Genesis
 18 Heaven Avenges
 22 The Sands of Dee
 29 Black Sheep

August

1 The Narrow Road
8 A Child's Remorse
12 The Inner Circle
22 A Change of Spirit
29 A Pueblo Legend (2 reels)

September

9 An Unseen Enemy [1]
19 Two Daughters of Eve
23 Friends
30 So Near, Yet So Far

October

3 A Feud in the Kentucky Hills
14 In the Aisles of the Wild
21 The One She Loved
24 The Painted Lady
31 The Musketeers of Pig Alley

November

4 Heredity
11 Gold and Glitter
14 My Baby
21 The Informer

December

2 Brutality
5 The New York Hat
16 The Burglar's Dilemma
23 A Cry for Help
26 The God Within

1913

January

2 Three Friends
6 The Telephone Girl and the Lady
16 An Adventure in the Autumn Woods
23 The Tender-Hearted Boy

February

3 Brothers
6 Oil and Water
24 A Chance Deception
27 Love in an Apartment Hotel

[1] It is possible that *Blind Love* (September 12) should be added. Mrs. Bowser does not give this to Griffith, but Blanche Sweet, who offers one of her finest performances in it, believes that he directed it.

March

8 Broken Ways
15 The Unwelcome Guest
20 Near to Earth
22 Fate
29 The Sheriff's Baby

April

5 The Perfidy of Mary
12 The Little Tease (2 reels)
19 A Misunderstood Boy
26 The Lady and the Mouse

May

3 The Wanderer
10 The House of Darkness
17 The Yaqui Cur (2 reels)
19 Olaf—An Atom
24 Just Gold
31 His Mother's Son

June

7 A Timely Interception
14 Death's Marathon
21 The Mothering Heart (2 reels)
28 Her Mother's Oath

July

5 The Sorrowful Shore
12 The Mistake
26 The Coming of Angelo

August

9 The Reformers, or The Lost Art of Minding One's Business (2 reels)
23 Two Men of the Desert

1914

February

26 The Massacre (2 reels)

March

8 Judith of Bethulia (4 reels)
28 The Battle at Elderbush Gulch (2 reels)

April

25 Brute Force (2 reels)

BIBLIOGRAPHY

Aitken, Roy E. (with Al P. Nelson). *The Birth of a Nation Story* (Denlinger, 1965).

Barry, Iris. *D. W. Griffith: American Film Master*, with an Annotated List of Films by Eileen Bowser (The Museum of Modern Art–Doubleday, 1965).

Bitzer, G. W. *Billy Bitzer, His Life* (Farrar, Straus and Giroux, 1973).

Bowser, Eileen. *Biograph Bulletins, 1908–1912* (Farrar, Straus and Giroux, 1973).

Brown, Karl. *Adventures with D. W. Griffith* (Farrar, Straus and Giroux, 1973).

Cooper, Miriam (with Bonnie Herndon). *Dark Lady of the Silents* (Bobbs-Merrill, 1973).

Croy, Homer. *Star Maker: The Story of D. W. Griffith* (Duell, Sloan and Pearce, 1959).

Everson, William K. *The American Movie* (Atheneum, 1963).

Fulton, A. R. *Motion Pictures: The Development of an Art from Silent Films to the Age of Television* (University of Oklahoma Press, 1960).

Geduld, Harry M., editor. *Focus on D. W. Griffith* (Prentice-Hall, 1971).

Gish, Lillian (with James Frasher). *Dorothy and Lillian Gish* (Scribners, 1973).

Gish, Lillian (with Ann Pinchot). *Lillian Gish: The Movies, Mr. Griffith and Me* (Prentice-Hall, 1969).

Griffith, Mrs. D. W. (Linda Arvidson). *When the Movies Were Young* (Dutton, 1925; Dover Books, 1969).

Hart, James, editor. *The Man Who Invented Hollywood: The Autobiography of D. W. Griffith: A Memoir and Some Notes*, edited and annotated by James Hart, including the Unfinished Autobiography of the Film Master (Touchstone Publishing Company, 1972).

Henderson, Robert M. *D. W. Griffith: His Life and Work* (Oxford University Press, 1972).

——. *D. W. Griffith: The Years at Biograph* (Farrar, Straus and Giroux, 1970).

Jacobs, Lewis. *The Rise of the American Film: A Critical History* (Harcourt, Brace, 1939).

Lennig, Arthur. *The Silent Voice: A Text* (The Lane Press, 1969).

Lindsay, Vachel. *The Art of the Moving Picture* (Macmillan, 1915).

Loos, Anita. *A Girl Like I* (The Viking Press, 1966).

Munden, Kenneth W., editor. *The American Film Institute Catalog: Feature Films 1921–1930* (R. R. Bowker Company, 1971).

Niver, Kemp R. (with Bebe Bergsten). *Biograph Bulletins, 1896–1908* (Historical Films, 1971).

——. *D. W. Griffith: His Biograph Films in Perspective* (Historical Films, 1974).

——. *D. W. Griffith's The Battle at Elderbush Gulch* (Historical Films, 1972).

——. *The First Twenty Years: A Segment of Film History* (Historical Films, 1968).

——. *Mary Pickford, Comedienne* (Historical Films, 1969).

——. *Motion Pictures from the Library of Congress Paper Print Collection, 1894–1912* (University of California Press, 1967).

O'Dell, Paul. *Griffith and the Rise of Hollywood* (A. S. Barnes, 1970).

Paine, Albert Bigelow. *Life and Lillian Gish* (Macmillan, 1932).

Pickford, Mary. *Sunshine and Shadow* (Doubleday, 1955).

Pratt, George C. *Spellbound in Darkness: A History of the Silent Film* (New York Graphic Society, 1973).

Ramsaye, Terry. *A Million and One Nights: A History of the Motion Picture*, two volumes (Simon and Schuster, 1926).

Slide, Anthony. *Early American Cinema* (A. S. Barnes, 1970).

——. *The Griffith Actresses* (A. S. Barnes, 1973).

Stern, Seymour. "The Birth of a Nation: A Monograph," *Sight and Sound*, Index Series, No. 4 (1945).

——. "An Index to the Creative Work of D. W. Griffith," *Sight and Sound*, Index Series, No. 8, II (Sept. 1946).

——. "Griffith: I, The Birth of a Nation, Part I," *Film Culture*, No. 36 (Spring-Summer, 1965).

Vardac, A. Nicholas. *Stage to Screen: Theatrical Method from Garrick to Griffith* (Harvard University Press, 1949).

Wagenknecht, Edward. *The Movies in the Age of Innocence* (University of Oklahoma Press, 1962).

INDEX